GASCONY
AND
ARMAGNAC
ON A BUDGET

ROSTERS LTD. LONDON

About the Author

Patrick Delaforce was educated at Winchester, served as a troop Commander from Normandy to the Baltic in the 1939/1945 War. Became a Port Wine Shipper in Portugal, and also worked in New York and the City of London.

He recently returned to Brighton after seven years as a vineyard owner in France and is now fully occupied as an author. Among his recent writing are books on historical research, French regional wines and Lady Frances 'Fanny' Nelson.

Other Rosters books by Patrick Delaforce:–
- Burgundy and Beaujolais on a Budget
- French Riviera on a Budget
- Champagne on a Budget

GASCONY
AND
ARMAGNAC
ON A BUDGET

PATRICK DELAFORCE

ROSTERS LTD. LONDON

Published by ROSTERS LTD.
60 Welbeck Street, London W1
© Rosters Ltd.
ISBN 0 948032 33 2

First Edition 1989

Designed and published by ROSTERS
Typeset by Lovell Baines Print Ltd, Newbury, Berkshire.
Printed and bound in Great Britain by Cox & Wyman Ltd, Reading, Berkshire.

Every care has been taken to ensure that all the information in this book is accurate. The author and publishers cannot accept responsibility for any errors that appear or their consequences.

CONTENTS

CHAPTER ONE:
LAND OF MUSKETEERS

Gascony meant to me, for many years, a far-off romantic place – situated somewhere between Bordeaux and the Pyrenees – reminiscent of swashbuckling Musketeers, drinking uproarious toasts in their favourite, fiery Armagnac plotting perhaps a 'coup d'état' in distant Paris, and of course boasting of their conquests on the battlefield and in the boudoir and of fine feats still to come!

Although the last twenty years of ownership of a stone-built farmhouse on the Gascon borders has done little to change the boyhood image quoted above, it has added a very considerable dimension and knowledge of the two Gascon 'départements' which form the basis of this book.

The English connection

It is curious to realise that Queen Eleanor's dowry of 1152, which presented Aquitaine to the English throne, produced the longest-lived colony of all time! For three centuries London ruled a huge area with Bordeaux as its capital, which at one stage extended east to the Auvergne and north into Limousin. The 'Roles Gascons' in the Public Record Office and the Calendar Letter Books of London have documented this interesting period.

This book is concerned with two large 'départements'. The Landes (de Gascogne) which the English controlled lock, stock and barrel for the entire three hundred years, and the Gers (immediately to the east) which was known as Gascony until all the départemental names were changed in 1790. Gers was not always English-dominated despite the scores of bastide towns built there by orders from London. To some extent it was No Man's Land depending on the whim of the Counts of Armagnac and the distance away of the Black Prince's armies!

Family roots

As a family historian living in the area with access to all the archives of Aquitaine it was fascinating to discover that my ancestors had been petty princes in Gascony. They ruled for two centuries an area between Auch (the capital of Gers/ Gascony) and Montauban (to the east) with titles of Prince de Verdun, and de Saves (the latter taken from the river of that name). The first positive sighting of the family was about AD 980, as younger sons of the Dukes of Gascony with marriage alliances into the powerful Armagnac family. I followed their careers and adventures. This included a thirty year stint in London as Gascon wine traders in the period at the end of the thirteenth century. Then in the mid fifteenth century the French armies eventually swept back into the region, absorbing Gascony and the Landes. My family moved north as traders leaving their lands behind (the town of la Force near Bergerac, Forces/Fources in Gascony and several more villages and châteaux of la Force in the Auvergne). Eventually as Huguenots they arrived in London – initially in 1550 and finally in 1690.

As a member of a wine growing family which owned vineyards in the Gironde around La Réole in the twelfth and thirteenth centuries and more recently in Portugal in the nineteenth and twentieth centuries, I have always been interested in the wines of the region. In this book you will be introduced to all of the local wines of the Gers/Gascony and the Landes (Madiran, St. Mont and Tursan) as well, of course, to the famous Armagnac brandies. It is pleasant to record that the Vins de Pays des Côteaux de Gascoigne are now enjoying such a success. These delicate, pale white wines have been upgraded in quality by the new generation of wine makers in the region and are widely available throughout the UK at modest prices.

Rural contrasts

In modern Gascony you will find an astonishing mélange – some very interesting architectural sites (often with an English historical context), castles, châteaux, cathedrals, abbeys and bastides. You will find a countryside mainly agricultural in the Gers, bisected by small rivers sourced in the south by the Pyrenees and flowing into the mighty Garonne. A patchwork of vineyards, cattle pastures, corn and wheat crops, sunflower and rapeseed, geese farms for 'confits d'oie' production. To the west the Landes present a greater contrast. In the north and centre, the huge pine forests growing in sandy soil often harbour flocks of sheep and heron colonies. The prosperity of the region depends largely on the pinewood resin. The western border is the Bay of Biscay and the Atlantic rollers come pounding in on a hundred miles or more of glorious sandy beaches. Instead of ribbon development the French have created a dozen plage-towns which are ideal for young families 'en vacance'.

The two 'départements' together have a population of 500,000 and a landmass of 15,500 km, with the Landes being half as large again as the Gers. The Landes is about 100 km in a square shape, and Gers about 80 km in a squarish-rectangle shape. The towns of consequence are Mont de Marsan (30,000), Dax and its suburb St. Paul-lès-Dax (27,000) and Auch, capital of Gers (23,000). There are a thousand villages or small towns in the two 'départements', all connected by excellent major and minor roads.

Native swagger

My 1890 edition of Nuttalls Standard Dictionary has various amusing definitions. A Gascon was predictably 'a native of Gascony in France', but he was also simply 'a boaster'. A Gasconade was 'boasting; bravado; bragging'. A Gasconader was 'a great boaster'. Certainly the natives have had to live with this description of their character for a considerable time. Alexandre Dumas invested the swashbuckling Musketeers with braggadocio!

Jean Froissart, writing towards the end of the Hundred

Years War as a well-travelled Anglo-French journalist and historian, said 'Such are the Gascons, they are very unsteady, but they love the English in preference to the French.' In an age of unusual alliances, the Anglo-Burgundian armies fighting savagely against the French-Scottish armies, it is not altogether strange to find the fidelity of the Gascons to their English over-lords rather than to the equally distant French based in Paris.

Old Gascony was the focal point of four major pilgrim routes converging on St. James de Compostella in north west Spain. One erudite pilgrim wrote these comments in the 'Codex de Compostella' in the thirteenth century:

'Les Gascons sont rieurs, parleurs, moqueurs, prompts aux plaisirs, enclins à boire, prodigues en nourriture, mal peignés et mal habillés, mais courageux, guerriers et surtout très hospitaliers pour les pauvres.'

These very apt comments are worth translating:

'The Gascons are humorous and jolly (literally laughers), garrulous, scoffers, pleasure-loving, like their drink, like their food, unkempt, not well-dressed, but brave, war-like (you ought to see them playing Le Rugby in the twentieth century) and above all very hospitable towards the poor, i.e. generous.'

Dumas' heroes

In his famous book 'The Three Musketeers', published in 1844, which described the troublemaking Gascons at the court of Louis XIII, Alexandre Dumas depicted his heroes, the musketeers of 1622, in various ways. D'Artagnan (in real life Charles de Batz de Castelmore) was described as a Don Quixote clothed in a blue woollen doublet, face long and brown, high cheekbones and the maxillary muscles enormously developed. This latter feature is an infallible sign by which a Gascon may always be detected even without his cap set off by a feather. D'Artagnan's father gave him this advice: 'You ought to be brave: you are a Gascon – never fear quarrels but seek adventures. Fight on all occasions. Fight the more for duels being forbidden.' As a consequence every smile was taken as an insult, every look as a provocation. A fund of audacity, shrewdness and intelligence made the Gascon gentleman. Tenacity, familiarity, and a lack of patience were other characteristics. Gascons were usually considered to be poor, as proud as the Scots – and able to see, like cats, in the dark. Their motto in the Gascon musketeers was 'All for one, and one for all'.

The other three Gascon Musketeers were Armand Athos d'Auterielle, Henri d'Aramitz (Aramis) and Isaac de Portau (Porthos).

Gascons today

Many of the pilgrim's shrewd comments apply today. The Gascons do talk a lot, are generous, do have *all* the appetites as well as a great sense of humour. There is a Gascon language, quite different from the strange Basque language, quite different from the 'patois' of the Gironde or the Lot and quite different from everyday French. One wine farmer in the Madiran wanted his children to have a minimum of one hour's tuition a week at school learning the Gascon language. His own vocabulary was rather over 200 words. However, unlike the Basques, there is no vociferous demand for an independent Gascony!

Julien Samson of Cayron-Beaumarchés wrote the following verses in the Gascon dialect about 1940:

Enloc mès coum aci n'auri biscut urous!
(*This is the only place where I could die happy!*)
Enloc mès .. De petit enlà, tout ço de nousto
(*Nowhere else .. since childhood, everything is here at home*)
Que m'estouc luts e gay de cado jour: la brousto
(*that makes the light and joy of everyday: the branch*)
Burguerento au printemps de barbauts e d'ausèts
(*quivering in spring with the insects and birds*)
Lou diguens amistous, la cansoun dous husèts
(*the friendly interior, the song of the weaving spindles*)
La hournèro touto aulourento de hario
(*the kitchen stove smelling fragrantly of flour*)
Lou casau, l'auranleto e lou bolo-mario
(*the garden, the swallows swooping and the ladybirds*)
E lous trabalhs, toustem, p'ou tour de la maysoun

11

(*and always the daily work around the house*)
Jumplan bras e pensado au briu de la sasoun ...
(*soothing arms and thoughts of the coming season*).

There are four styles of Gascon dialect – from Bearn and Bigorre in the deep south, and from the Landes and Armagnac in the north. There were two famous Gascon troubadors about 1150 AD called Cercamon and Marcabro. Dastros, the Gascon vicar of St. Clar, wrote in the seventeenth century:

Crey-me, gascoun, n'ajes Gergougno
De nosto lengo de Gascougno
Ni de l'auji ni d'en parla.
(*Believe me, gascon, have no shame of our language of Gascony, neither to listen to it, nor to speak in it ..*)

Learning the basics

In a companion book on the wine regions of France, 'Burgundy and Beaujolais on a Budget', I gave some basic advice to first-time travellers to the region. About the necessity for a green card for car insurance, about hotel room selection (bringing soap and perhaps a small portable electric lamp) and other suggestions based on thirty years of travelling across France. But this time, if my reader-traveller has reached Bordeaux en route for Gascony, he or she will have surmounted three or four hundred miles of, I hope, pleasurable and leisurely travel on the way south. No longer perplexed by signs such as 'Toutes Directions' or 'Autres Directions'. No longer disquieted by Madame the hotel-owner 'forgetting' to proffer a 'Prix Fixe' menu at Francs 45 and hoping for a Tourist Menu Gastronomique to be selected – faute de mieux – at Francs 90! Looking for the good value local wines 'en pichet' at the very back of the wine list. Turning up for lunch from mid-day, and not appearing for dinner after 8.30 pm. Apart from a few of the smarter 'plage' towns in the Landes the traveller will need to have *some* knowledge of French.

Money matters

A major purpose of this book is to show the reader how to see all the splendid sights of Gascony 'Old' and 'New' on a very practical budget of not more than Francs 400 per couple per day, travelling across the region by car. The budget is broken down as follows:

		Francs
1.	Double bedroom in modest hotel	100
2.	Continental breakfast for two	30
3.	Picnic lunch of bread, butter, paté, cheese, fruit, and supermarket-purchased bottle of local wine	50
4.	Petrol – short daily distances for a small car	30
5.	Château, museum, other entry fees	25
6.	Prix fixe dinner	100
7.	One bottle or pichet of local wine at hotel price	30
8.	Coffee, aperitifs or soft drinks	35
		400

As I wrote in my previous book 'Burgundy and Beaujolais on a Budget', it is a matter of luck and taste whether this budget is exceeded or not. Recently my wife and I have toured the whole of Gascony on a budget of about Francs 350 per day. However in the high summer season the resort towns in the south of the Landes are very popular and it is therefore more difficult to secure low-priced hotel rooms.

Warm welcome

As will be seen later on, the two départements have a wide variety of attractive sights. I have listed on page 14 the annual monthly centigrade temperature guide to the two areas, which shows that they can be visited by the tourist at *any* time of the year – except perhaps February.

You will need the following Michelin Maps: No. 78 for the Landes, No. 82 for the Gers, and No. 79 for the northern boundaries of the Gers, and the eastern borders of the Landes.

Bricks and mortar

Gascony is unique in one way. It has a hundred bastide towns mostly built by the English government (or rather funded by

	Aquitaine	**Midi-Pyrenées**
Jan	10.0	10.0
Feb	9.4	9.0
Mar	12.2	12.3
Apr	19.5	18.3
May	18.0	19.1
Jun	23.7	26.4
Jul	27.2	27.6
Aug	25.7	27.2
Sep	24.2	25.0
Oct	19.7	19.3
Nov	15.4	15.5
Dec	11.0	9.8

Note: annual monthly centigrade temperature.

them) in the period 1280–1300. They were built on a grid basis, sometimes with a fortified external wall. There would have been four main fortified town gates, perhaps with towers at each quarter. Most of the streets would centre on the main square which was fortified by galleried arcades, making defence relatively easy! The principal church would probably be part of the main square and also be fortified with thick walls and crenellated towers.

There are a couple of hundred gascon-style châteaux scattered over the Gers and the southern half of the Landes de Gascogne. They do not of course compare with the sophisticated elegant châteaux of the Loire or Burgundy. In Gascony they were built to withstand siege, and can be described more accurately as agricultural strongholds – small country houses with towers and very strong walls. Sometimes they might have as many as six 'étages', but more usually two or three levels and a tower at each corner, probably on the crest of a hill. (See Valence, Fleurance, Cologne, Gimont and Mauvezin).

The churches and abbeys do not stand comparison with the greatest in France (Paris, Rheims, Chartres, Vezelay etc.) Having said that, the Abbey of Flaran (Cistercian), the romanesque churches of Sabazan, Vopillon, Mouchan and Lialores, the gothic churches of Lectoure, Condom, Mirande,

Eauze, la Romieu and Fleurance and the red-brick Toulousain style of Lombez and Simorre are definitely worth a visit and it would be a great pity if you missed the great cathedral of Auch.

There are many intact windmills, clocktowers (Barran), isolated dovecots (pigeonniers gascons) with crenellated towers standing on massive pillars, many medieval private mansions and 'hotels' (Condom and Lectoure). There is one curious classic nineteenth century style of architecture – the 'minero-thermal' spa bath facades (Castera-Verduzan, Aurensan and Barbotan-les-Thermes) with white stone arcades and pseudo-Roman pillars.

Memories of Gascony

Let me recall several fascinating vignettes in Gascony.

- A warm Saturday evening in Aire sur Adour waiting for the Courses Landaises and bullfight to commence. The bands are playing in the streets, the market traders are making their very final 'closing down' sales, the crowds are bustling around the 'arena' on the banks of the river – shades of Ernest Hemingway.

- A visit to the beautiful, tiny walled and fortified 'cité' of Larresingle – across the drawbridge into the peaceful resort of the old prelates, the Bishops of Condom.

- A warm summer morning halfway up the 360 steps of the wide stone staircase up the hillside at Auch – perched between the sleepy river Gers and the noble cathedral of Sainte Marie at the top. A few minutes spent looking at the giant stone statue of the most famous Gascon of all, the Captain of the King's Musketeers.

- An afternoon stroll on the golden sandy beaches of Mimizan watching a beautiful medieval sandcastle being eroded by the tide as its twentieth century builder hastily reinforces his crumbling walls.

15

- A picnic in the evergeen pine forests of the Landes. Listening to the birds and looking at the resin-taps on the trees that help provide the prosperity of the region.

So without more ado 'Bon voyage, bonnes vacances et courage!'

CHAPTER TWO:
FROM THE STONE AGE TO THE
TWENTIETH CENTURY

The southwest of France has always been a treasure trove of archeological finds which have identified the local tribes and inhabitants of the past. There are scores of sites in Gascony where troglodyte caves, mammoth teeth and flints used by Neanderthal man have been found as well as arrow heads, tumuli, barrows and necropoli of the Stone, Bronze and Iron Ages. From a later period a hundred or more Gallo-Roman villas and mosaics can still be seen, as well as many other traces of the 'Pax Romana'.

The little 'country' of the Chalosse, east of Dax (Landes), along the river Luy de France is particularly rich in prehistoric discoveries. Sorde-L'Abbaye, Brassempouy and Saint Sever are centres of archeological finds of distinction. Roquelaure in the Gers is one of several prehistoric sites.

A dozen or more fine museums display these troves to the visitor to Gascony. All the main archeological sites and museums are listed later in this book.

About the sixth century BC the Celtic tribes from the north, and the Ligures in the south were conquered by the Iberes, who came north over the Pyrénées. The Spanish influence in southwest France started at this point. Soon the Vascons, who were related to the Basques, settled, and 'Vasconia' became 'Gascony'.

Roman rule

When Julius Caesar sent his legions under Crassus into southwest France in 56 BC he found there the local tribes of Tarbelli (around the Tarbes – Dax area), the Elusates (around Eauze

17

and the Armagnac area), the Lactorates (around modern Lectoure) and the Ausci (around Auch). The Tarusates lived around Aire sur l'Adour and Tartas. They and the Sotiates, whose capital was Sos, fought the Roman legions fiercely but to no avail. A tribe of Basques lived in the Biscay ports including Cap Breton before the Romans dispossessed them. The Sotiates and the Elusates coined their own money, which has been found at Manciet and Laujuzan.

In 25 BC the Emperor Augustus renamed the area 'Novempopulanie' i.e. the new peoples, and Crassus received their official submission on the hill of Ario at Lannepax. Elusa (modern Eauze) was made the capital, and Dax together with Augusta Auscorum (modern Auch) knew unparalleled prosperity during the Roman rule. The Roman garrisons spent about three centuries in almost total control of Gascony – the same length of time as the English at a later stage, in the thirteenth to the fifteenth centuries.

The Romans built their straight roads, the Roman Ways. The two most well-known were the Bordeaux – Dax – Bayonne route, north to south, and from Toulouse to Bordeaux via Auch. Part of a Roman aquaduct can be seen at modern Pavie, then called Spartacus.

There are Roman military encampments all over Gascony and dozens of villas, some with intricate mosaics (Seviac and Sarbazan being two lovely examples). In Geaune there is a massive Roman 'donjon' or keep to be seen. Flavius Vegelius mentioned the thermal baths of Dax and Castera Verduzan in his third century writings.

The Romans introduced the vines to Gascony. The young vines arrived in rustic amphora from Tuscany. Remains of these amphora have been found in St. Jean de Castets and in Lectoure. Many of the Roman mosaics still show bunches of grapes in their design. In Sanguinet (Landes) the Romans had an extensive distillery of resinous products.

The Romans were energetic industrialists. In Bastennes (Landes) they worked bitumen mines, and ironworking mines at Sorten-Chalosse. Coins with Caesar Augustus' face on them have been found at Lugion, Moustey, Le Levy, Castelnau-Chalosse, Laluque and Brassempouy.

The pagan gods were worshipped. Lectoure (Gers) has a 'taurobolia' bull-worship altar, set up by the pagan cult of Cybele, the great earth-mother. At Roquebrune (Gers) is the remains of a temple 'La Monjoie' dedicated not only to Cybele but also to Mithras, the Persian god of light! Escorneboeuf and St. Michel-Escalus have statues to the god Jupiter. Blaziert (Gers) has a temple to Apollo.

There were many early Christian saints in Gascony. The Celtic saint Gemme was martyred for his faith in AD 138. Saint Luper de Loissan lived and was martyred in Eauze in the third century. Saint Taurin evangelised Auch in the fourth century and was martyred in Aubiet. St. Girons of the fourth century (his Roman crypt near Hagetmau (Landes) is one of the classic religious sights); St. Sever in the fifth century; St. Germier, Bishop of Toulouse, who had his own cult or sect named after him; St. Creatus, who was martyred but founded the town of Saint Créac in the sixth century. The female Sainte Quittérie, a Visigoth princess, was martyred at Le Mas d'Aire in AD 476. Her relics in the church of her name have been a centre of pilgrimage since AD 629 and she has become the patron saint of Gascony.

About 300 AD, with troubles back in Rome, taxes were sharply raised by the tax collectors in Gascony. Emperor Constantine granted freedom to the new religions, including Christianity, in 313 AD. But the Pax Romana began to wane. As the legions left Britain from AD 383 the same thing began in southwest France.

Wave of invaders

The writing had been on the wall for some time, as Roman power slackened. In AD 276 an invasion of Germaines had sacked Dax and most of Armagnac. The march of the northern wave of Barbarians started in the middle of the fourth century. In AD 409 the Vandals invaded Gascony and sacked Eauze. Their stables, and mosaics adorning their tombs, can be seen at Seviac. The Visigoths (the West Goths) and Franks from Germany followed in AD 507. They buried their dead in Gascony and left behind many traces of their occupation (in

19

Beaucaire and Gelleneuve in particular). Towns and villages whose name ends in 'ans' or 'ens' were built or renamed by these invaders. For instance Escalans, Cassen, Noulens, Brenens, Carlens etc.

The Iberian invaders left their town names behind. 'os' in the Iberian language of the time meant 'health and security'; to be found in Sos, Narrosse, Onesse, Peyrusse etc. The Visigoths were finally beaten by the Christian King Clovis in 507 AD at Vouille, and locally the Bishop of Lescar led a small army of Christian warriors to fight them at Mimizan. He had the unusual name of St. Galactoire. The Vascons, towards the end of the sixth century, left their influence behind with towns or villages such as Bascous (Gers) and Bascons (Landes).

Later on the Moors in the seventh century left their more obvious trace-names behind, such as Maurens (Gers), Marambat, Mauries, Maurrin (Landes). A later saint was St. Fris, a nephew of Charles Martel, who died fighting the Saracens and was buried at Bassoues. The Saracens had settled by 719 AD in Amou (Landes) and Castelsarrazin (Landes) and devastated Eauze and Aire sur l'Adour.

In this terrible time it seems as though every marauding tribe was determined to settle in the relatively prosperous south-west of France. A Greek colony settled in Sore and, believe it or not, a Scots tribe called the Malvins settled in Mauvezin d'Armagnac!

The Merovingian Kings (486–751 AD) gave little protection to Gascony but when Charles Martel, a Frankish King, defeated the Arab hordes at Poitiers in AD 732 there was a brief breathing space in the south west.

Charlemagne's influence in Gascony was noticeable. In AD 778 he founded the abbey of St. Girons at Hagetmau and donated many other religious offerings during the year of Roncevalles where Roland, Comte of the Marches of Bretagne, died. He also had built in AD 788 the town of Mont de Marsan (Landes), mainly to keep his Gascon subjects in order. The bastide here was started in 1133, the earliest of the region, decades before the area became British owned.

After Charlemagne's death in 814 AD the dark ages descended again. The Norman fleets sailed down the Garonne towards Toulouse sacking, pillaging and raping as they went. In the Landes they took Cère in 840 AD, Arjuzanx in 850 AD, Aire sur l'Adour in 854 AD and occupied, often temporarily, Bostens, Cagnotte, Labouheyre, Faget-Abbatial and scores of other communities.

Pilgrims' progress

In 840 AD began the extraordinary phenomenon of the European pilgrimage to the shrine of St. Jacques in Compostella in northwest Spain. Five routes converged on Bayonne and most of the pilgrims crossed the Pyrenees at Roncevalles. Tens of thousands of weary grey-cloaked figures carrying the traditional pilgrim's staff plodded through France and then Spain on their way to pay homage to St. James. He was the missionary who brought Christianity to Spain, was martyred in the Holy Land where his body was placed in a boat, set adrift and eventually arrived in the Campus Stellae (modern Compostella). The pilgrims travelled in groups and often paid for their lodgings and food at the many hospices along the route which were built and maintained by the three great religious orders of Cluny, Citeaux (both in Burgundy), and St. Jean-de-Jerusalem. They had a vested interest not only in the physical welfare of their flocks – that they survived in reasonable shape the thousand or so miles they might have travelled on mule or horseback or on foot, with staff and scallopshell badge – but above all their spiritual health. So the hospices had two purposes: to provide physical and spiritual comforts for the weary pilgrims. The Codex de Compostella dates from 1140 AD i.e. nearly three centuries after the first pilgrimage. Most of it warned the pilgrims against the dangers en route from the wickedness of the local populations they would meet!

The pilgrimages lasted until the sixteenth century – well over seven hundred years – an astonishing length of time. Eventually the pilgrims needed permission from the King, backed by authorisation from their local priest, which apparently acted as a deterrent.

There were two main pilgrim routes through the Gers. One

was Lectoure, Condom, Eauze and Nogaro, and the other from the east was L'Isle Jourdain, Gimont, Auch, Barran and Marciac. Both channelled into the other routes in the Landes coming from Bordeaux. Mimizan was one of the few shelters on the coast road. Another route went through the many small villages of the modern Parc Naturel des Landes and yet another route through Agen and Aire sur l'Adour.

Ducal leadership

The Norman invaders controlled most of Aquitaine in 923 AD and the Gascon lords implored the Kingdom of Navarre to send their armies across the Pyrenees to protect them from the Viking fleets. The younger Royal son, Garcia-Sanche, became the first of the Dukes of Gascony. In 963 AD the Duke gave the church of Bostens to the monastery of St. Sever. In 982 AD the Duke Guillaume de Sanche gave the church of Mimizan to the same abbey of St. Sever. In the same year he beat the Normans back at Taller in the Landes. By and large the rule, which lasted for two centuries, of the Dukes of Gascony was beneficial to the province. They fiercely defended their subject tribes as best they could, but each spring the formidable sailing ships oared by the northern warriors came down the tributaries of the Garonne as far as Toulouse, sacking and pillaging every village on their way.

It was towards the end of the tenth century that the local Gascon lords, subject to the Dukes of Gascony, enhanced their own fiefs by building their own châteaux-forts. In the next three centuries the 'Châteaux Gascons' were built roughly to the same design, on a hill overlooking the surrounding countryside. They had no moat or even defensive ditch (which is strange). The primitive stone keep was square, sometimes oblong, with two smaller towers at one end. The ground floor was used as an armoury, food store and kitchen and had no windows. Access to the two floors above were by wooden ladders which could in emergency be drawn up. The second floor would have windows and on top was the castellated flat roof with battlements and watchtowers. These were very strongly fortified houses doubling as strongpoints. They should not be confused with the 'bastides' which had no fortified château.

In this same period marvellous churches, monasteries, abbeys, even cathedrals were being built. Many were financed by the Dukes of Gascony, Charlemagne and other distant Kings. Dax had been a bishopric from the fifth century. The Benedictine Abbey of St. Sever was built in the tenth century above the martyred fifth century saint.

Rule from London

During the eleventh century the Duchy of Aquitaine was linked by marriage to the Duchy of Gascony (and Poitou) however everything was back in the melting pot when in April of 1137 William VIII, the Duke of Aquitaine, died on a pilgrimage to Compostella and left as his heiress a daughter, Eleanor, a girl of sixteen. She was married the next year to King Louis of France and fifteen years later, incompatible in temperament and mother of daughters, was divorced by the Archbishop of Sens. To everyone's surprise, two months later she married Henry Plantaganet who had inherited Maine, Touraine and Anjou, and, on his father's death, Normandy and Brittany. When in 1154 Henry was recognised as King Stephen's rightful heir and was crowned King Henry II of England, France was effectively cut in two. The new Angevin (Anjou) empire was to last through many vicissitudes for another three centuries. The French King Louis VII was unable to shift the balance of power, but when Philip Augustus came to the French throne in 1180 he encouraged rebellion by Richard and John, Henry and Eleanor's sons.

The Gascons initially struggled against the rule from London and called the English 'Godons' from Goddam (Dieu me damne). Richard Coeur de Lion as a young man was very popular in his native land of Anjou, but his absence on crusades and captivity in Germany made him an ineffectual ruler of Gascony after his father's death in 1189. His death ten years later meant John's accession, but Eleanor, indomitable to the last, maintained her position as Duchess of Aquitaine until her death at Fontevrault in 1204. John was no match for the wily French King, and English control of one third of France was rapidly diminished. By 1205 Philippe Auguste had pushed the English out of all their French lands except for Gascony. When King John died in 1216, the new King Henry III did not visit the Duchy until 1230, fourteen years after coming to the throne. The Crusade of the Albigensiens further to the east in 1209–1213, brutally put down by Simon de Montfort, had little effect on Gascony. The export of Gascon wines to England brought prosperity to the region.

Direct rule from London continued with close administrative and financial control even though the overland route from London, to Bordeaux took three weeks! The sea route could take as little as two weeks or as much as two months if the master was waiting for favourable winds! The Black Prince was held up in Plymouth for six weeks in 1335 waiting for a favourable wind, although the sea voyage was 'only' eleven days.

The King of England was also Duke of Guyenne (Aquitaine) which was ruled by the seneschals of Guyenne, Landes, Bigorre and the Agenais. Assizes were held at Bordeaux, Bazas (in the Gironde), Dax and St. Sever (both in the Landes). The Armagnac fiefs in the east were then Labarthe, Aure, Rivière-Basse, Pardiac, Brulhois, L'Isle Jourdain and Magnoac. Their barons were unreliable and often changed sides! In the south Lescun, Sarvance, Beost and Audoins all supported the English. The ports of Bayonne and Biarritz were very strong supporters of the English, possibly because of the importance of the maritime trade with England.

De Montfort takes charge

In 1225 Richard of Cornwall led a Gascon military expedition which warned Louis VII in Paris and the Kingdoms of Aragon and Navarre that England was determined to hold Aquitaine and therefore Gascony. King Henry III even spent a year in his Duchy and a daughter was born to the Queen in Bordeaux. In 1248 Henry appointed his brother-in-law, Simon de Montfort as his lieutenant in Gascony.

Simon de Montfort was the third son of the leader of the crusade against the wretched Albigensians who were hounded

24

to their deaths. His mother had been the sister of the Earl of Leicester who had died without male heirs. Simon, the young son, went to England, married the King's widowed sister, and was made Earl of Leicester. He had a reputation as a crusading fighting man and was given a seven year patent by the King to rule Gascony. He skilfully made a truce with Queen Blanche in Paris, who was Regent during Louis' crusade in the Holy Land, and also a diplomatic agreement with King Thibault of Navarre, securing his southern flank. He still had many problems of near revolt with his subject lords, particularly with Gaston de Bearn, cousin to the Queen of England. King Henry III arrived in Bordeaux in September 1253 to find the Duchy in ferment, partly because of Simon de Montfort's tough, aggressive rule, and partly because the local barons 'rob the earth, and burn and pillage and ride by night in the manner of thieves'.

Charter of 'pariage'

The King and Simon de Montfort encouraged the building of new bastide towns, and over a hundred were authorised in the period 1250–1350. The charter of 'pariage' was a division of lordship between two or more powers i.e. the holders of the land and the King or local Lord who made himself responsible for the laying out of the town, and, just as important, for its administration and protection. A charter of liberties and responsibilities was an attractive feature of a new bastide. The charter was good for the new inhabitants, for the church, who kept their flocks under their eye and control, for the merchants who traded in the 'Halle' in the centre square, and for the Seigneur, who not only dispensed justice, but also raised revenues by the impots or taxes on the 'marches'. One of my ancestors' villages was Fources/Forces, which was converted into a circular bastide in 1255 and later received from King Edward I its 'charte de coutumes' (charter) in 1289.

The new towns were laid out in a gridiron pattern, often 440 metres × 240 metres, with rectangular building sites. The four parallel main streets, each 8 metres wide, ran from gates to the central square. The narrow lateral paved paths (ruelles)

25

were only 2 metres wide and thus easy to defend. Frequently there were 12 towers around the walls with 4 main gates, often with a 'Pont-Levis' or drawbridge. Deep ditches were dug around the town wall perimeter. The walls were often 15 metres high and usually 1.4 metres wide. Architecturally the central square is usually very interesting. The arcaded overhangs are called 'cornières'. The merchants' 'Halle' would be a large covered building open at the sides, and occasionally the old weights to ensure fair trading have been preserved and are displayed there. Dominating the scene is the fortified church with massive thick walls with slits for the archers, and castellated roofs for the defenders to throw down hot pitch and other deterrents on the invaders' heads. Outside the walls each citizen was allowed and encouraged to farm a 'jardin potager', a market garden, of ¼ arpent (6–7 acres).

Peace treaty

The Treaty of Paris was signed on 4th December 1259 between the Kings of France and England. The latter agreed not to pursue his claim to French lands which had been confiscated from King John. Louis IX wanted peace so that he could pursue his crusades to rescue the Holy Land.

Even before Henry III's death in 1272 his son Edward had lived much of his life in Gascony since his marriage to Eleanor of Castille in 1254 as a fifteen year old youth. Edward I signed the Treaty of Amiens in 1279 with his cousin, the new King of France, Philip III, who was subsequently killed in an abortive campaign in Aragon in 1285. Meanwhile Edward I, who had been successful in bringing peace and relative harmony to Gascony, was faced by a rebellion in Wales – also in 1285. His loyal Gascons were the most effective soldiers in the Welsh campaign. Their contingent of 210 horsemen and 1313 foot-soldiers armed with crossbows helped their King to restore peace.

During this period of peace and prosperity Quercy came under the control of the British, and from 1259 an additional fief eastwards to the Auvergne opened up for commerce along the river Dordogne. Three Delaforce families settled there and there are La Force hamlets or château remains to this day around Aurillac and Mauriac. Records exist of their activities spread over two centuries.

War years

Almost by mistake war broke out between France and England and lasted from 1294–1303. Edward still had problems in Scotland and Wales and the French King Philip uncharacteristically provoked the English and ordered his agents to occupy Bordeaux, the Agenais and the English lands in Perigord.

Various expeditions were sent to Gascony under Edmund of Lancaster and the Earl of Lincoln. Bordeaux and Bayonne held out against the French but Dax was taken and the small English army suffered a major defeat in 1297 at Bonnegarde, southeast of Dax. Pope Boniface VIII endeavoured to arbitrate but the war only came to an end after Philip suffered a major defeat at Courtrai by the Flemings in 1302 and a peace treaty was signed in 1303. Philip handed back all his occupied territory to the English but for some reason tried to hold Mauleon d'Armagnac. Perhaps the 'eau-de-vie' was to his liking?

In the year after the Scots defeat of the English at Bannockburn (1314) the rural population of English Aquitaine (Guyenne) was two thirds of a million. Bordeaux had a population of 30,000, as large as London! Bayonne, the second town, had 8000 population, and the smaller towns such as La Réole, Libourne, Bazas and Dax about 2,500 each.

Wine trade

The greatest commercial commodity was the export of wine, and my ancestors in the Gironde, Auvergne and London played their part as successful merchants. Bayonne was a very important port served by the river Adour, and ships carried trade to Spain as well as England and Flanders. In the year 1308/9 103,000 tuns of wine were exported. The Gascon tun was 750–900 litres, a rather large cask. The

English tun was equal to two casks or pipes totalling 252 gallons/900 litres. Between 1305–1330 the level of exports averaged 85,000 tuns bringing considerable revenue to the Crown. Originally the royal right was to take two tuns from each ship at a fixed price, but in 1302 a new tax of 2 shillings a tun was imposed.

The medieval sums of money were all based on the 'livre' or pound, made up of twenty 'sous' or shillings, each worth twelve 'deniers' or pennies. The pound sterling in England, the 'livre tournois' or 'livre parisis' and the 'livre bordelais' in Gascony fluctuated in exchange values just as they do today. The 'livre bordelais' ranged in value from four to five shillings sterling and the 'livres tournois' and 'parisis' ranged from five to six shillings sterling.

Peace and prosperity reigned now until Philip VI came to the throne in 1328 and campaigning began again in 1337–40.

Turbulent times

The most important problem between French and English Kings since Eleanor of Aquitaine's wedding dowry was the differing interpretation of the precise status of the Duchy of Aquitaine. The view from Paris was that a mere peer of France (i.e. the Duke of Aquitaine) must pay homage to the crowned King on his Parisian throne. The view from London was that submission of fealty by Aquitaine to Paris was impossible if the King of England was also Duke of Aquitaine.

In 1320, when Philip V was crowned at Amiens, homage was performed with the usual English 'reservations', and when Charles IV succeeded his brother in 1322 the question of homage was inevitably raised again. The War of Saint Sardos in the Agenais was a storm in a teacup but the French army captured La Réole and the Agenais and Saintonge defected to the French King. English Gascony had now shrunk to a narrow coastal strip between Bordeaux and Bayonne 50 miles wide and the hinterland around Saint Sever (Landes).

However Gascony changed hands twice in two years. In 1326 the Duchy of Guyenne/Aquitaine was restored to its new Duke, Prince Edward, on payment of 60,000 livres parisis, but the French held on to the Agenais and La Réole. In the same year the unfortunate King Edward II was dispossessed of his throne by Queen Isabella and Roger Mortimer, Earl of March. King Charles immediately re-occupied the Duchy!

The wretched young 14 year old King Edward III was forced to agree to a one-sided treaty on 31 March 1327 which gave him back his much diminished Gascon lands with another indemnity of 50,000 marks. Charles IV died in February 1328 and Philip VI, his cousin, acceded to the throne. But Edward III was the son of Philip IV's daughter! Nevertheless in June 1329 Edward crossed to France to meet Philip to pay homage for Aquitaine (with reservations on both sides) and sign the Treaty of Amiens. An uneasy peace followed with Philip bribing the Count of Armagnac and Gaston, Count of Foix and Bearn to take his side. On 24 May 1337 Philip VI again confiscated the Duchy and, in exasperation, King Edward now claimed as his legal right the Kingdom of France, and both sides promptly went to war! The town of La Réole changed hands no less than eight times in a hundred year period!

The French armies captured or recaptured most of the towns in the Gironde and camped outside Bordeaux. They also seized Tartas in the Landes. King Edward in 1339 bribed the powerful de l'Isle family (eastern Gers) to stay faithful to the English. The truce of Espléchin in 1340 suspended hostilities but the French garrisons stayed in place.

Henry of Grosmont, Earl of Derby, was selected by Edward to lead a new army of invasion which landed in Bordeaux on 9 August 1345 and quickly liberated Bergerac; Angouleme and La Réole voluntarily surrendered. But 1346 was the 'annus mirabilis'. King Edward landed in Normandy and the battle of Crécy (26 August) split the French kingdom in two. After the fall of Calais in 1347 a truce was arranged. The Anglo-Saxon forces, helped by the powerful Albret, regained some towns and by the end of the year the English had control of the Duchy again. Ralph, Baron of Stafford, who was the Earl of Derby's son-in-law, was one of England's successful generals in this campaign. On his father's death Ralph became Earl of Lancaster and King Edward made him a Duke in 1351. When he died in 1361 his title passed to Edward's third son,

John of Gaunt.

Unfortunately disaster struck again with the advent of the Black Death which arrived in July 1348 brought by Genoese sailors from Marseilles. The plague decimated the countryside; the vineyards were left untended and both Kings' revenues suffered accordingly in a land of desolation.

Rule of the Black Prince

In July 1355 the King appointed his eldest son as his lieutenant in Gascony. For the next fifteen years the Black Prince and his military advisers, Sir John Chandos and James Audley, dominated the Gascon scene. The so-called 'chevauchées' were in effect cavalry raids of destruction which ranged as far afield as Carcassone and Narbonne. Villages were captured, pillaged and burnt. There were no pitched battles with the French troops. By 1st December the Anglo-Gascons were back in the Gironde loaded down with booty. Of the Prince's army of 8000 no less than 5000 were Gascons under the Captal de Buch.

The Gascon footsoldiers formed a major part of the English Army under the Black Prince and Sir John Chandos. It destroyed the French knights under King John at the battle of Poitiers in September 1356. The triumphant Anglo-Gascon army with its royal prisoner was back in Bordeaux in the following month.

The French countryside after the cessation of official hositili-ties was now at the mercy of the mercenary soldiers banded together as 'Free Companies'. A large number of rootless, unemployed English and Gascon commanders and soldiers made their fortunes.

Two treaties of London in 1358 and 1359 were mainly concerned with King John's ransom terms. Edward III mean-time launched an ignominious campaign in northern France in the autumn of 1359 and failed to capture Rheims. The follow-ing year the Treaty of Brétigny (near Chartres) was signed. Edward agreed to renounce his claim to the French throne but Aquitaine was retained, even extended from the Loire to the Pyrénées. A huge ransom was eventually paid and King John returned to France for a while. He died in London in April 1364. Louis of Anjou, the King's son, broke his parole and the laws of chivalry forced his father to return in person to London as a hostage!

The Black Prince now settled down to rule the huge Duchy of Aquitaine but was often sidetracked by military adventures in Spain. The only advantage was that the mercenary 'Free Companies' with Anglo-Gascon troops were used in the Iberian ventures. In 1366 Capbreton (Landes) was the meeting place between King Pedro the Cruel and the Black Prince. Najera was the third of the Black Prince's victories, but was less relevant than Crécy or Poitiers. One of the prisoners taken by the Anglo-Gascon army was a French commander called Bertrand Du Guesclin.

France fights back

The young French King Charles bided his time, stabilised his government, taxed his subjects, and built up his armies again. He had money to spare to foment trouble in Gascony. The Count of Armagnac fell out with the Black Prince over pay-ment of the 'fouage' tax of 1364 and again in 1368. His nephew Albret, an erstwhile loyal subject to the English, became a vassal of Charles V who provided him with a huge pension. By March 1369 nearly a thousand castles, towns and strongholds in the Duchy had recognised King Charles' sovereignty. Charles in May 1370 confiscated Guyenne/ Aquitaine and fighting broke out again. The Black Prince was very ill with dropsy and dysentery.

With an aging King and ailing Prince the war became less popular in England although the overall budget through increased taxation was considerable. The holding operation in the north of France took 63% of the budget and Aquitaine received only 14%. There were no more opportunities for profitable raids and 'chevauchées'.

Du Guesclin, now Charles V's senior general had a masterly policy of harassment and minor skirmishes and never could be manoeuvered into a pitched battle. In April 1372 the Earl of Pembroke was named lieutenant of Aquitaine, but his naval squadron was attacked off La Rochelle and defeated by a Franco-Castilian fleet. The Earl and his army's wages were seized. La Rochelle came under siege, Poitiers was taken and the famous Gascon commander, Captal de Buch, was captured at Soubise. This gallant soldier refused to turn French despite many inducements and died in captivity in Paris in 1376. King Edward made one more effort to save the Duchy and in the summer his large expedition was ready to sail for Bordeaux. It seems incredible, but the 200 ships never sailed because the autumn gales were deemed too strong.

John of Gaunt, in the following summer, attempted a great 'chevauchée' from Calais, but harried by Du Guesclin he had lost half his troops by the time he reached Bordeaux and could not mount a military campaign. By the summer of 1374 La Réole had surrendered to the French and a truce was proclaimed which lasted until 1377. When fighting resumed Bergerac was taken and the Dordogne-Gironde towns surrendered. Altogether the French regained 134 towns and castles that year. The Black Prince had died in 1376, King Edward in 1377 and Charles V in 1380.

Years of truce

Nevertheless the English did not give up. In the 1380s they still held Calais, Brest and Cherbourg in the north, and Bordeaux and Bayonne in the south. Both sides were exhausted by the constant wars: moreover the wine trade had been reduced to a miserable 12,500 tuns. The new King Richard II made John of Gaunt, now Duke of Lancaster, the legal owner of Aquitaine. He remained sovereign, an unpopular decision with the jurats of Bordeaux and the remaining Gascon lords loyal to England. In 1396 King Richard married the six year old Princess Isabel of France and concluded a 28 year truce with France. Three years later Richard was deposed by Henry of Derby, heir to the Duchy of Lancaster, who became Henry IV. War broke out again in 1407 with attacks near Bordeaux by the Duke of Orléans. King Charles VI was insane and the French Dukes fought each other for power, with the English taking the side of the

Burgundians. Henry V inherited the English throne in 1413, and the young hothead first invaded France in 1415. The battle of Agincourt encouraged the Gascons: so too did the Treaty of Troyes, which named Henry as heir and regent of France in 1420.

The population of English Guyenne in 1414 was calculated at about 150,000, a quarter the size of the Duchy a century before. The countryside was denuded of farm workers who fled into the towns and bastides.

During the 1420s some local military successes were achieved, including the recapture of Marmande and Bergerac. In March 1433 the Bishop of Dax visited London for financial help, and Bayonne was granted permission to mint their own coinage. The Congress of Arras in 1435 was yet another inconclusive peace treaty. Joan of Arc, the national heroine of France, was sold by the Burgundian troops to the English, who burnt her at the stake for witchcraft and heresy in 1431. Two of her loyal companions were Gascons called La Hire from Laurede and Poton de Xaintrailles. In 1442 the French army, commanded by King Charles VII, crossed Armagnac and the valley of the Adour and captured Saint Sever. Soon La Réole, Marmande and Langon were recaptured by the French.

British sovereignty ends

In May 1444 a marriage was finally arranged between King Henry VI and Margaret of Anjou, which heralded a two year truce. Charles VII denounced the Treaty of Tours in 1449 and launched an offensive in Normandy. In the south he encouraged his vassal, the count of Foix, to menace Bayonne. Another French force occupied Bergerac and in the spring of 1451, under the command of Dunois, the Bastard of Orléans, blockaded the Gironde against help from England. Charles offered Bordeaux such generous terms for surrender that once Bourg and Fronsac were taken, the end of British sovereignty was imminent. Bayonne as well as Bordeaux surrendered without a fight.

The Gascons were concerned about their market for wines

under their new French rulers, and a delegation left Bordeaux for London in August 1453 saying they would welcome the English back provided a substantial fleet and army were to be forthcoming. King Henry sent John Talbot, Earl of Shrewsbury, an elderly general, with a force of 4000 men which arrived outside Bordeaux on 22 October. Bordeaux and many towns in the Gironde changed sides again. The French army could not possibly garrison more than a few towns at a time. The impatient and inept old general sallied forth and was killed at the battle of Castillon on the 17th July together with most of the Anglo-Gascon army of 6000. King Charles arrived in August and, despite some resistance, Bordeaux surrendered (again). This time the conditions were more severe but the English troops were allowed to return to England and 20 Gascon nobles were exiled. The Wars of the Roses followed and the loss of Aquitaine and Gascony was soon forgotten.

Louis XI in 1461 removed the new taxes in Bordeaux and reduced the wine duties. The town was to have two trade fairs a year, and soon it was back to its old prosperous self. The Treaty of Picquigny was signed between King Louis and Edward IV in 1475 after yet another abortive invasion. The seven year truce finally ending the fighting. Measures to increase trade reciprocity were included, as well as an annual pension to the English King of 25,000 gold crowns each year.

Many of the Gascon émigrés, including the Delaforce family, left the area. Lord Bernard Delaforce fought and died at the battle of Barnet in 1471 and was buried in London. His son John was a merchant trader with a licence from King Henry VI, trading between Paris and London. Later, as Huguenot refugees, they finally settled in England.

Civil war

But peace did not come to Gascony. During the early part of the sixteenth century the wars of religion started. Nérac, just north of Fources and Montreal, was the royal residence of Jeanne d'Albret, whose son was to become King Henri IV. The Reform movement in France started here and the Huguenots (as the new religious movement was called) were soon dominant in the southwest of France – particularly in Gascony. Bitter civil war followed as the Protestant armies fought the Catholic armies, burning and ransacking towns and churches of the other faith. Montgomery ravaged the country-side on behalf of the Huguenots and Monluc did exactly the same thing on behalf of the Catholics. For fifty awful years the battles continued until Henri became King in 1589. For the sake of peace Henri turned Catholic – 'Paris is worth a mass'. In 1607 the Landes and the rest of Gascony were formally attached to the Royal Crown by Henri IV, who had scores of Gascon friends at court.

King Louis XIII occupied Gascony in 1620 for the crown, but when Cardinal Richelieu commenced his campaign to pacify France he caused scores of towns and bastides in Gascony to have their ramparts and defensive towers torn down. In Condom in 1635 there was a popular rising against the misery caused by the State in the name of unity. The taxes were raised drastically. Plague and pestilence were frequent, beggars were everywhere. The fields were left untouched and the crops not harvested. Other revolts followed in Eauze and Manciet at the senseless destruction ordered by Paris.

At this sad time Charles de Batz known as d'Artagnan, captain of the King's musketeers, was born at the Château of Castelmore. His true adventures were chronicled by Courtilz de Sandras, then by Auguste Maquet and finally by Alexandre Dumas.

Building prosperity

But slowly and painfully peace and prosperity came to Gascony. The spa towns caused the fashionable gentry to come to seek a cure and spend liberally in the process. The Intendant of Etigny in 1752 developed the road network and helped the commercialisation of the local wine industry. In the eighteenth century the Revolution brought inevitable confusion and terror once again. In 1790 the département of the Landes was created by the reunion of Chalosse, Marsan, Tursan, Gabardan, Marensin, Lande, Born and Othe.

Wellington's troops surged through the Pyrénées in 1813

and in the following year forced Marechal Soult's armies to surrender after fighting along the southern boundaries of Gascony.

The war of American Independence, and the needs of the revolutionary armies caused an upsurge in demand for Armagnac brandy, and the Marquis de Bonas invented the double distillation process. Shortly afterwards the engineer M. Brémontier started the schemes in the Landes where the sand encroachment was arrested, pine forest grown and wood and resin industries developed.

In a century the population increased by 150%, agriculture prospered, china and porcelain industries were established, and the Empress Eugénie encouraged the spa water towns development.

World War I took its toll of young Gascon soldiers fighting pointlessly on the Somme and the plains of Picardy. In World War II resistance to the Germans was relatively low-key since the German garrisons were few and far between, mainly in the coastal towns and harbours, Mont de Marsan and Dax.

Post war developments

The three most encouraging features post war for Gascony have been the discovery of oil and gas fields at Lacq and Parentis and St. Marcet. Parentis produces practically 100% of French oil but only 6.5% of the national requirements. Secondly, the resurgence of wine and Armagnac exports and finally, the relatively new tourist industry (plus EEC subsidies on many agricultural crops) are bringing prosperity to the region. Perhaps you may agree with me that after the ravages of Visigoths, Viking, Saracens, the English and their own religious wars, the Gascons deserve some peace and tranquillity!

CHAPTER THREE:
GASCON HIGHLIGHTS

The majority of visitors to Gascony will arrive from the north –
perhaps from Bordeaux, Agen or Moissac. Some will come
from Montauban in the northeast or Toulouse in the east –
many heading for Bayonne and Biarritz towards northwest
Spain or south to Pau, Tarbes and Lourdes.

I have devised a Grand Tour for visitors who plan to spend a
week in the region. I did this by identifying twelve of the most
attractive towns and cities, five of the most beautiful châteaux
and castles, five of the most interesting 'ecclesiastical' sites of
cathedrals and abbeys, and of course the most famous wine-
growing areas including Armagnac, Madiran, St. Mont and
Tursan. A more complete summary of each town and sight is
to be found later in the text of this book with suggestions for
hotels and restaurants.

From Agen to Auch

Assuming that the visitor starts from Agen (Michelin Map 79),
the major town just north of the river Garonne and the
Autoroute A 6 Bordeaux to Toulouse, then take the N 21 (via
the D 305 and D 17) appropriately parallel to the river Gers,
signed due south towards Auch (the préfecture capital of the
département). After 17 km one comes to Astaffort, then 8 km
south to **Sainte-Mère** where there is a classic gascon château
on a hill. There take a minor road east to Miradoux and
Flamarens (pop. 160) where there is an outstanding fifteenth
century château in the small village with some of the best
views in the département.

Then southwest on the D 40/D 7 (now on Michelin Map 82)

37

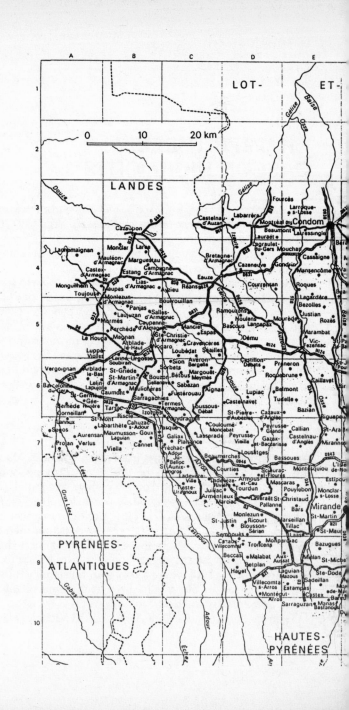

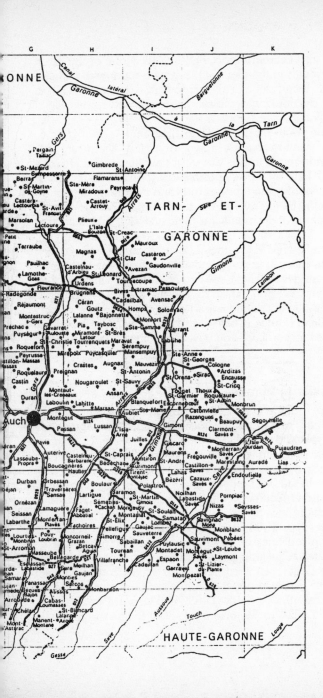

and west into **Lectoure** (pop. 3800). This is one of the most attractive towns in the Gers with a superb fourteenth century cathedral, picturesque streets, towers, ramparts, classic museum, overlooking a valley. There are several excellent low-cost hotels – well worth a stay.

Continue south on the N 21 to **Fleurance** (pop. 6000), a thirteenth century bastide town occupied alternately by English and French troops with a noteworthy gothic church, and then 24 km on the N 71 into **Auch** (pop. 23,000). This is the large, sophisticated, prosperous and interesting capital of Gers bisected by the river of the same name. There is a great deal to see in and around the medieval city, including the Armagnac Tower, statue of D'Artagnan, the fifteenth century Cathedral of Sainte Marie, the old quarter on the slopes overlooking the valley, and several notable châteaux (St. Cricq and Marin). Consider staying a day or two in Auch, which makes an excellent base from which to visit the east (Mauvezin and Gimont, bastide towns and important markets), and the northwest, St. Jean Poutge (Château of Herrebouc), Vic-Fezensac (Armagnac and corridas), and Lavardens (château with unique features).

From Boular to Mirande

The next part of the Grand Tour is towards the southeast and south via the D 626 through Pessan, Castelnau-Barbarens and **Boular** (a splendid abbey), Saramon, to Lombez and Samatan – a distance of 40 km. Wellington's troops marched along the valley which contains the river Save, and his skirmishes are still remembered in Lombez and Samatan! Six centuries before that the pilgrims wended their slow weary way along the same route towards St. James of Compostella.

Lombez (pop. 1300) has an unusual fourteenth century cathedral in red brick and **Samatan** (pop. 2000) has half a dozen châteaux including the seventeenth century Latour. The writer Belleforest lived here, who almost certainly gave our William Shakespeare half a dozen 'ideas' for his early plays! Next southwest on the D 632 and west at Bernadas on the D 566/D 234 to **Simorre** (pop. 800) to see the unusual fortified brick church of the thirteenth century. The famous Viollet-le-Duc chose to restore the church to its current excellent state of repair.

Then west on the D 27 to Meilan, Masseube and D 127 to **Mielan** (a thirteenth century bastide) and northeast on the N 21 14 km to **Mirande** (pop. 4800) where a stay is recommended. It is a pretty bastide town dominated by a large handsome fortified gothic church with a huge flying buttress. The well-known Museum of the Beaux-Arts is next to the church and pedestrian precinct.

From Montesquiou to Eauze

Northwest 15 km on the D 137 is **Montesquiou** (pop. 600), a pretty hill village famous for its D'Artagnan family connections. There are half a dozen châteaux nearby including De la Motte. Due west on the D 943 5½ km is 'Bassoues** (pop. 500), a classic bastide village with a splendid Château des Archevêques with a huge crenellated fourteenth century donjon-tower. This is the best example of military architecture in the Gers, well worth a visit! And due south is the old Cistercian abbey in **Berdoues-Ponsampere** (pop. 500).

Now we are heading towards the wine country of Gascony, which is covered in some detail later on – so west on the D 946 18 km to **Plaisance** (pop. 1600), a fourteenth century bastide which is the centre of the Madiran and St. Mont vineyards, watered by several river tributaries of the Adour which flows eventually into the Atlantic. Follow the river Arros northwest on the D 935 for 14 km looking out for the six-floored Tower of the **Baron de Termes**, rising like a medieval silo on the hillside on the right of the road 9 km from Plaisance. Turn right on the D 25 due north 12 km to **Nogaro** (pop. 2000), the centre of Courses Landaises and corridas (bullfights) for the region. There is a major wine and Armagnac co-operative here.

Keep on the D 931 18 km northeast via **Manciet** (pop. 1000) to **Eauze** (pop. 4400), which is one of the main centres of the Armagnac distillers. Consider staying a day and a night here to visit some of the many attractions. Eauze was a prosperous city in the third century: it is still a picturesque small town with many local châteaux and the gothic fifteenth century cathedral of St. Luperc, as well as a classic archaeological museum displaying many of the mosaics, coins and sarcophagi of two thousand years ago!

From Gondrin to Condom

Follow the N 124, which was a major pilgrim route to Compostella, via **Gondrin** (pop. 1000) which has a wine cave co-operative to **Mouchan** (pop. 400) to see the romanesque church of St. Austrésegile and on to **Condom** (pop. 8000), a total of 29 km via **Cassaigne** (pop. 200), a gascon village with two châteaux to see.

Condom, despite its unfortunately topical name, is a very interesting town. Besides being the centre of the Armagnac production area and having a score of typical gascon châteaux in the region, the Cathedral and cloisters of St. Pierre are famous. It is recommended that the visitor spends a day and a night in Condom, because there are a dozen essential sites to visit. To the southeast **St. Puy** (sparkling wine of Gascony), **Terraube** (fortified village with thirteenth century château) and **Caussens** (château of Maréchal Lannes); to the northeast **La Romieu** (fourteenth century collegiate church of St. Pierre and cloisters – a classic site); to the northwest look at **Fources** (the only round bastide town in France – very pretty and one of the Delaforce fiefs in the tenth–thirteenth century!); to the west and southwest **Larressingle** (the most attractive fortified medieval village in the whole of Gascony) and **Valence-sur-Baise** (the splendid Cistercian abbey of Flaran nearby).

It can be seen that this region of Bas-Armagnac, of which Condom is the capital, is the centre of some marvellous attractive sights set in the midst of Armagnac and Côteaux de Gascogne white wine vineyards – not forgetting the gastronomic delights of 'confits d'oie' and 'foies gras'.

From Montreal to Barbotan-lès Thermes

From Condom due west (Michelin Map 79 again) on the D 15 via Larressingle (a detour of 1 km to the southwest) to

Montreal (pop. 1500), another fortified bastide town (due south of Fources, both on the river Auzoue), which has half a dozen gascon type châteaux nearby, notably Balarin, a gothic church, a twelfth century romanesque church of St. Pierre of Genens, the mosaics of Seviac, and a museum with gallo-roman remains, westwards through Castelnau-d'Auzan (pop. 1200) to **Barbotan-lès-Thermes**, the flourishing spa town twinned with neighbouring Cazaubon (pop. 1800). Barbotan is a curious place – many elderly disabled people seeking a cure from the remedial waters (a highly organised sophisticated business) and as many young, active people having a good time (excellent restaurants, visiting Courses Landaises and Chais d'Armagnac).

That is the end of the Grand Tour that takes place in the Gers. I have selected only a score of places out of the 500 towns and villages in the département. The tour takes you through delightful countryside interspersed with archaeological sites, abbeys, cathedrals, bastides and châteaux. Along the way you can enjoy culinary and vinous delights. So on to the Landes de Gascogne!

Entering Landes

The Landes has three different faces to it. The northern half consists mainly of pine forest but also contains the interesting Parc Naturel Regional des Landes de Gascogne. The western sector bordering the Atlantic Ocean/Bay of Biscay has no less than 17 plage-resorts. The south and eastern section is a continuation of the Gers. An undulating green countryside full of small rivers, hills, bastide villages and a few wine growing areas. The 'Grand Tour of Gascony' covers this region.

From Labastide d'Armagnac to Mont de Marsan

Entering the département from the east from Barbotan-lès-Thermes one drives through a cluster of villages with the sobriquet d'Armagnac towards **Labastide d'Armagnac** (pop. 800) still on the D 626. On the way is one of the three notable pilgrimage sites and this one is worth a detour. The other two are Notre Dame de la Course Landaise at Bascous and Notre Dame du Rugby at Larrivière St. Savin. Notre Dame des Cyclistes is set back from the road by a few hundred yards on the north side. It is an eleventh century Chapelle de Geou devoted to the many hundreds of thousands of cyclist fans in France who make pilgrimages to this spot. Next to it is a small museum of 'cyclisme'. Remember the Tour de France in July is a national – now international – race covering neighbouring countries and attracting English, Irish, Scots and American riders. It lasts several weeks and brings the countryside to a halt. Labastide d'Armagnac is an absolute gem. Around the main arcaded bastide square (the 'place royale') are old thirteenth century houses, a romanesque church, museum and remains of a gallo-roman villa. This is Armagnac producing country, with a small co-operative and marvellous food. Do not miss!

Continue on the D 626 for 4 km and turn left and southwest at St. Justin on the major road the D 933 towards **Mont de Marsan** (pop. 30,000) 18 km away. This is the Prefecture town of some substance straddling the rivers Douze and Midou, which logically then become the Midouze! Plan to spend a day or two in this attractive, bustling town which boasts many towers, ramparts, châteaux, 'hotels' (i.e. substantial town houses owned once by the nobility), parks, bullfighting arenas, several churches and no less than four unusual museums. There are plenty of good low-cost hotels and restaurants.

The next six sites to be visited on the Grand Tour are within a 30 km radius southeast, south and southwest of Mont de Marsan.

Excursions from Mont de Marsan

Take the N 124 due south for 15 km to **Grenade sur l'Adour** (pop. 2000) which was an English bastide of 1322. Wellington's army marched through it in 1814 so it has several historical links. The southern suburb village across the river Adour is **Larrivière**, the national 'sanctuaire des jouers de rugby' with many donations of jerseys, footballs etc.

The N 124 continues east and south for 18 km via Cazères to **Aire sur l'Adour** (pop. 7000). If you have time spend a day and night here. It is the centre of the VDQS Tursan wine-growing area and of 'foie gras' and 'confits d'oie'. From November to February major markets of these delicacies are held here. The town has a Spanish flavour to it, particularly in summer, with its corridas, courses Landaises, fairs and fêtes. The river Adour flows through the town which has narrow bustling streets, market places, parks, plus one architectural gem. A short walk out of town up a hill is the romanesque Eglise Sainte Quittérie du Mas d'Aire which has an outstanding crypt. The patron saint of Gascony, a Meringovian young princess, was decapitated in 476 AD outside the church for refusing to marry a pagan prince. There are several low-cost hotels and restaurants in Aire sur L'Adour, which, like Cazères, was an English bastide for over three centuries, and was an important battlefield in 1814 when Wellington's troops beat those of Marshal Soult.

Due southwest on the N 134 for 3 km and then west on the D 2 takes one to **Geaune** (pop. 700) where the major wine co-operative in the Landes is based. The town has a notable church and several classic towers to look at. Seven kilometres to the north (i.e. due west of Aire) is the pretty little spa village of **Eugénie-les-Bains.**

From Saint Sever to Hagetmau

Via the D 2 and D 944 28 km northwest (Map 78) to **Saint Sever** (pop. 4800) an English stronghold and the archaeological centre of the Landes. The eleventh century romanesque abbey is in the centre of one of the prettiest of all the Gascon towns. On the top of a hill, it overlooks the valley of the Adour and the prospering countryside, and was named 'Cap-de-Gascogne', the chief (town) of Gascony. Well worth a visit and perhaps a stayover from which to see half a dozen nearby sites on the morrow. The gascon festival is held here on the first Sunday in July.

Due west of St. Sever 7 km on the D 32 is **Montaut**

45

(pop. 700) which has the Château d'Arcet and two distinctly notable churches. The fortified clocktower on the romanesque church of Brocas is an example of fourteenth century English military architecture. The course Landaise arenas hold 2000 places – in addition there are two fountains where miracles have taken place. Ten km west on the same road is **Mugron** (pop. 1500) known for its excellent wine co-operative of Haute Chalosse.

Due south of Mugron there is a cluster of three villages best reached by the D 18 southeast to **Hagetmau** (pop. 4400), where Charlemagne founded the Abbey of St. Girons in 778 AD. The romanesque twelfth century crypt is worth a visit; it is on the D 18 west of Hagetmau. Consider an overnight stay here.

From Brassempouy to Dax

Then look at **Brassempouy** (pop. 300) famous for its extra-ordinary prehistoric grottos and 'fishspine' bastide shape constructed by the English overlords in the thirteenth century. The 'Dame à la Capuche' which figures amongst the thousand architectural treasures of France, now in the museum of St. Germain, was discovered here. Three km to the west is **Gaujacq** (pop. 500) where the Château de Sourdis, and **Amou** (pop. 1500) 9 km due south has a classic château and romanesque church and chapelle royale displaying the arms of the Plantaganet Kings. From these villages one can see the Pyrenées mountains to the south.

Now a cross-country route southwest to the valley of the river Gave de Pau to link up with the N 117 westwards towards **Sorde L'Abbaye** (pop. 600) which is just south of the Bayonne-Pau autoroute. Sorde was the prehistoric capital of the Landes, still encircled by ramparts. The twelfth century abbey overlooks the meeting of the rivers Pau and Oloron. Cross country due west for 5 km is the equally famous twelfth century **Abbey of Arthous**, and 3 km still west is the old English bastide of **Hastingues** (pop. 400) created by Jean de Hastings about 1300. A few kilometres due north across the river is **Peyrehorade** (pop. 3000) which has several notable châteaux including Montreal and Aspremont. This is the southernmost part of the Landes.

Now due north via the N 117, D 33 and D 6 to **Dax** (pop. 19,000) via a minor wine area (Pouillon, Labatut, Belus and Orthieville). Dax is now a large sprawling town across the river Adour. Richard Coeur de Lion regarded Dax as one of his royal towns when he was not crusading in the east. On the western outskirts of the town is the suburb of **St. Paul lès Dax** (pop. 8200). Tucked away in the centre is the eleventh century romanesque church of that name – one of the leading monuments of the Landes. Dax itself has been famous for its hot springs since Julius Caesar took the town in 17 BC. Its thermal waters are known throughout France and many of its hotels cater exclusively to cure-takers. It was an English stronghold until 1451. It has many Spanish characteristics including corridas and pelota and a nonstop series of markets, fairs, fêtes and 'concours'. Consider spending a couple of days and nights in Dax, from which sightseeing tours can be made easily to the southwest to Bayonne and Biarritz, to the seaside plage-resorts of Cap-Breton, Hossegor, Vieux-Boucau, and north into Castets or Morcenx and the National Park of the Landes.

All the towns in the south of the Gers are 'stations climatique d'hiver', i.e. have a gentle climate for winter visits.

CHAPTER FOUR:
THE SECRET CHARM
OF ARMAGNAC

Armagnac is the 'eau de vie' of Gascony. The 'water of life' in the fifteenth century was a pharmaceutical product. As 'l'aqua ardente', the burnt water (distilled grape juice), it revived the dying, served as an antidote during the plague and pestilence and so helped the living as well!

My family firm of winegrowers in Portugal have produced a Portuguese brandy for many years. I remember well in Oporto smelling the colourless young distilled brandies: at that stage the 'nose' was more important than the taste. Years of maturing in oak casks lay ahead before being bottled for market. The Iberian brandies are poor cousins in relation to the rich splendours to be discovered in Cognac and Armagnac – the only two Appellation Controlée spirits of France.

France's oldest brandy

Armagnac was known and charted as early as 1411, thus making it much older than its grand neighbour northwest in the Gironde. Originally Armagnac was 'burned' or distilled in the area of Auch and Saint-Sever. In the seventeenth century the Dutch, who have a long history as distillers, purchased huge quantities of *wine* from the French Atlantic coast (except that of Bordeaux which was naturally the English preserve). Bypassing the Gironde they made purchasing contracts of *wine* from Gascony, but the shipments by the river Garonne were blocked by the canny Bordelais. The Dutch encouraged the Gascons to distill on their own account for shipment to the Low Countries, since by law the Bordelais could not embargo spirits! Originally the casks were concentrated at Mont de

Marsan and shipped down the river Adour to the Bay of Bayonne for overseas markets. The young white alcohol was blended with other wines in Holland for onward sale to the thirsty Germans and Scandinavians.

There seems little doubt that the Gascons at the Parisian courts of Henri IV and Louis XIII encouraged the drinking and popularity of Armagnac. However, it never rivalled in quantity the beautiful Cognacs nourished by the Anglo-Scots-Irish firms of Martell and Hennessey.

Connoisseurs choice

Armagnac is now marketed outside France as 'L'Autre Brandy', as 'Pas le plus connu mais connu des meilleurs' (not the best known but known by the best (people)), and also 'Le secret le mieux gardé de France' (France's best kept secret). What is the secret charm of Armagnac? Not an easy question. The Armagnac industry is heavily segmented and each distiller guards its secrets closely. 'Le Dégustateur professionnel', 'Le Maître de la Maison', the boss of the great caves where hundreds of oak casks quietly mature their contents, 'Le Tonnelier', boss of the cooperage making the oak casks, 'Le Maître de Chai', 'Le Distillateur' and of course at the start of the cycle 'Le Vigneron', all play their part. So the end result is that there are many styles of Armagnac. They have a full taste of the grape and tend to be more sturdy, more robust, and have a more earthy 'goût de terroir' than their northern neighbour. They are usually darker in colour than Cognac, due to the greater amount of tannin derived from the oak barrels.

Three regions

Since 1909 the Armagnac producing area has been clearly defined. Distilled only from white wines (of which more anon) spread over nearly 50,000 acres of vineyards, these are the three areas:

(1) **Le Bas-Armagnac** also known as Armagnac Noir because

49

of the dense dark forests of pines and black oaks is the flat northwestern area with 11,000 hectares (27,000 acres) of vineyards (but only 7548 hectares are allowed to produce Armagnac). Eauze is the centre of the Bas-Armagnac area, which has 60 communes in the Gers and 24 in the Landes. Other main towns include Nogaro, Cazaubon and Gabarret in the Gers; Villeneuve de Marsan, Labastide d'Armagnac, Lagrange and others in the Landes. The Cave des Producteurs Reunis is in Nogaro and the Co-operative Producteurs de Bas Armagnac is sited in Villeneuve de Marsan. The Landes has 1462 hectares (3500 acres) of vineyards producing Armagnac, less than a seventh of the Gers. The characteristics of this region on the hills and in the valleys of the rivers Midour and La Douze, are based on the sandy acid soils known as 'sables fauves' (the tawny coloured sands). This produces an eau-de-vie of 'finesse' and perfume and taste of 'pruneaux' (plums).

(2) **Le Ténareze** is an area with 9000 hectares (22,500 acres) of vineyards but only 5127 hectares (12,500 acres) are allowed to produce Armagnac. The soil is 'argilo-calcaire', clay and limestone, producing the characteristics described as 'chaleureuses et caressantes' – warm, vigorous, tannic and fiery with a plum-like flavour and sometimes a perfume of violets. Condom is the centre of the region which possesses a remarkable Armagnac museum. The area is to the east of Bas-Armagnac and includes some parishes in the Lot and Garonne to the north (Nérac, Mezin and Francescas). The other main towns in the Gers to the south are Montreal, Valence, Vic-Fezensac and Aignan. The little rivers called La Gelise, L'Azoue and La Baise trisect this area – parallel tributaries flowing northwards into the Garonne.

(3) **Le Haut-Armagnac** is the third and smallest area. Geographically it is the largest with Auch as its capital, but the winegrowing area is confined to 500 hectares (1250 acres) of which only 157 (375 acres) may produce Armagnac. This area is also called 'White Armagnac' for its chalky soils.

Summary: Although there are 20,000 hectares (50,000 acres) of vines producing 1,500,000 hectolitres of wine of 8.5° to 9° Gay Lussac strength, only rather less than 13,000 hectares produce Armagnac. An annual total of between 50,000 and 60,000 hectolitres of pure alcohol which should produce 21 millions of bottles of Armagnac (70 centilitre bottles with an alcoholic strength of 40° Gay Lussac).

Distillation

The cépages or wine varieties are quite unusual. The three white grapes are Folle Blanche (known as Piquepoul de Pays), Ugni Blanche of Cognac (known as the St Emilion), and Colombard. The Ugni Blanche dominates in quantity, followed by Colombard, and can be blended with the older regional varieties of Jurancon, Blanquette, Plante de Graisse, Baccozza, Mauzac, Meslier, Clairette and Plant de Grèce.

The harvest is usually made a little early to ensure a slightly acid wine from not too ripe grapes so that the aromatic substances are not impaired. It is a little like Vinho Verde in Northern Portugal which has a petillant taste. The sun does not ripen the grapes to produce the more usual sugar content giving 10° or more in alcoholic strength. The result is a delicate, fragrant, very light coloured wine, which is left on its lees and sediment in the vat until distillation to ensure a maximum grapy flavour.

In the mid-nineteenth century no less than 100,000 hectolitres of distilled eau-de-vie was produced, compared to an average of a third of that in the last few years. The dreaded disease of Phylloxera devastated the area towards the end of the nineteenth century and replanting was inevitably a slow and laborious process using American stock on which the local varieties were grafted.

By law the distillation process must take place before the 30th of April after the vintage, and is usually done in mid-winter when the young wine is about four months old. Distillation and distillers have a long tradition and reputation in Gascony. The ubiquitous Cistercian monks first learned the art. In the nineteenth century and indeed until quite recently

51

up to a hundred ambulating Heath Robinson style mobile stills roamed the countryside from one Gascon farmer to another during the winter months, staying for a week or two at each until the farmer's wine had been distilled. There was a certain amount of low-key tax evasion as well since much of the Armagnac distilled was for private consumption amongst families and friends. These mobile stills can still be seen in good working order. The large Co-op at Villeneuve de Marsan and the Museum at Condom, together with several of the largest Armagnac producers such as Janneau, have kept one as a practical souvenir of bygone days. They look like a cross between a vintage locomotive and a steam engine.

For a time the pot still was prohibited in Gascony but was reintroduced in 1972. Until the mid nineteenth century only pot stills needing two distillations similar to those used for Cognac production were used in Armagnac. In 1801 a Montpellier chemist, Edouard Adam, invented the continuous distillation process called 'Alembic Armagnacais' or 'Coffey' still, which is unique to the region. By 1850 it had been perfected by a Monsieur Verdier. Wine flows from the vat through the pure, rolled-copper still, vaporises over the heated baffles, is again condensed by the inflowing coil, and comes out in a gigantic double percolator. The wine acts as a cooling agent allowing the alcohol vapours to condense. At one point the wine and vapour flow in opposite directions allowing the vapour to absorb some of the qualities of the incoming wine. The largest producer – Janneau – use both methods of distillation and say the pot stills in which the wine is distilled twice in two separate operations tend to have more finesse and are able to mature more evenly. Janneau blend brandies from both styles of distillation to give the final advantage of character and balance.

The Armagnac continuous still produces raw spirit at 52°–55° of alcohol against 70° to 72° from the double distillation of the pot still. The quality of the flame, the fire that produces the heat to 'burn' the wine is all important. Too hot and it produces 'le coup de feu' which leaves the young spirit hard and raw. Lacking the correct heat it renders the eau-de-vie neither strong nor consistent. The wood for the fire should be a mixture of oak and alder. It should not be green or resinous.

Le vieillissement

The end result of the distillation is a pure clear alcohol and it is the next process of aging, 'le vieillissement', which adds so much more character. The spirit is filled into the casks, 'pièces' of 400 litres. These are made by hand from oak staves deriving from the forest de Monlezun in Bas-Armagnac. The Maître de Chai takes over command from the alchemist, the wizard who has distilled the very young brandy. The black oaks of the forest are felled in winter when the sap is low and the split staves dried in the open air, one year for each centimetre of thickness. The staves are then limbered over an oak flame into an arc shaved a little at each end before being linked together with a dozen steel bands of the correct diameter.

The dissolving wood tannins impart amber colour and powerful aroma to the young brandy to produce a subtle, earthy, rustic flavour. The annual loss of 3% due to evaporation is traditionally called the 'angel's share' (la part des anges). The walls of the caves or ware-houses where the full casks are stored are covered with a grey mildew which produces a special mushroom, called 'le Torula', nourished by the alcohol vapours! The caves are 'ombreux' i.e. quite dark, since bright light and sunshine is inimical at this stage, and the temperature is kept cool and constant at 12°.

The next stage of aging is for the young Armagnac to be removed to casks described as 'épuises', completely dried out, without tannin in the wood. Gradually the high alcohol content is reduced every two months by the addition of 'petites eaux', a mixture of distilled water and Armagnac, until the legal shipping strength of 40° has been reached. By now several blending processes will have been enacted to produce the company's 'style'. This is called 'La Coupe'. If an older Armagnac even of 30 years of age is added to one of four years of age for blending purposes, the end result legally and commercialy is still that of one only four years old.

Each 'Maître de Chai' has his own traditional secrets of

blending, his 'tour de main' it is called. He has to achieve his 'pied de cuve' to ensure the high standards of blending are maintained and *never* differ! He has to balance not only the taste and the colour but especially the aroma. A sensitive nose is needed.

Once the fateful decision to bottle the Armagnac is made, the aging process finishes. The ideal Armagnac is one that has recently been bottled, since the 'bottle' flavour adds nothing to the intrinsic character of the old eau-de-vie. Bottles are usually of 70 centilitres, often in a Gascon 'pot' style, a squat flagon, sometimes called a 'basquaise'. Until 1918 all Armagnac shipments were in casks, now over 90% is shipped in bottles.

Language of labels

Now we get into the language of labels. As in the Burgundy region there are many titles which are meaningless! For instance disregard 'Monopole', 'Selection de Luxe', 'Couronne', 'Etoile', 'Lettre' etc. 'Trois Etoiles' i.e. Three Stars, indicates a minimum of one year spent in cask and is the lowest priced. 'V.O.' (Very Old) and 'V.S.O.P.' (Very Superior Old Pale) and 'Reserve' mean a minimum of four years spent in cask. The Cognac definitions are roughly the same. It is curious how the English descriptions have been accepted for the definition of these standards. 'Extra', 'Napoleon', 'X.O.' (Yes that's right, Extra Ordinary), 'Hors d'Age' and 'Vieille Reserve' are for Armagnac with over five years in cask.

Some producers offer a single vintage year, 'Le Millésime', which has had no blending during its life. As will be seen later on, each Armagnac producer has his own speciality. Janneau's VSOP is a blend of fine Armagnacs not less than 12 years aged in wood! Every hyper-market in France stocks a range of Armagnacs.

A recent survey of 30 such stores in the Paris region showed these results:

- Three Stars/Trois Etoiles – the most popular brand was Cles des Ducs with an average price of Francs 73, followed by Janneau at Francs 70, Saint Vivant, De la Mazière, Sempé, Montesquiou and Samalens. De la Mazière was the cheapest at Francs 56.

- In the VSOP category – Cles des Ducs was the most popular at Francs 87 followed by Janneau at Francs 93, Samalens and De Maillac.

Statistical background

Each year the distillation figures for the industry are published. If for any reason the wine vintage is disastrous the distillation figure for that year suffers proportionally. 1979 was a bumper year and 87,154 hectolitres were distilled compared to 12,521 in 1977. The average is about 36,000 hectolitres. The production formula is as follows: 100 litres of wine at 10° produce 20 litres of eau de vie at 50°.

Consumption in France has been reducing each year and, once at 20,000 hectolitres, is down to a shade under 15,000 hectolitres. Exports remain steady at about 17,500 hectolitres, although there have been bumper years as high as 25,000 hectolitres. But exports in bottle rise each year, with the leading markets being West Germany, the UK and Japan with USA and Benelux following. The total annual value of exports is now 180 million Francs (£18 million/30 million US$). The UK has tripled its requirements in a few years to £2 million at producers' prices or about 20,000 cases a year.

An eagle-eyed mathematician may have noticed that the production figures for the Armagnac 'vendage' do not quite tally. There are several reasons. Apart from the angel's share of litres each year lost by evaporation, remember that there are many small farmers distilling Armagnac for themselves and their friends, who just may not have got themselves included in the statistics!

Flower of Gascony

Floc de Gascoigne (Flower of Gascony) is an aperitif of 17°, a blend of Armagnac and grape juice, officially called 'vin de liqueur à l'Armagnac'. It is made either of red or white grapes. The Armagnac has to be at least 52° in strength before it is blended with the grape juice. The recipe was originally introduced in the sixteenth century, but Floc has only been seriously introduced since 1977. The proportion of the blend is 2/3rds grape juice and 1/3rd Armagnac. The bottles carry a standard handsome gold label with space at the foot for the individual producer to have his name and address printed. Production and sales have risen each year and now stand at nearly a million bottles.

The headquarters of the Floc de Gascoigne syndicat is Rue des Vignerons, 32800 Eauze. The Academie des Dames du Floc de Gascoigne is at 9, Place d'Armagnac, also in Eauze Tel. 62.09.85.41. The academy was formed in 1980 with a view to promoting the Floc aperitif, through all the regional restaurants and through stars of cinema and radio. Floc is recommended with melon, foie gras, strawberries and cream, pastries and gâteaux.

Cocktails and recipes

Armagnac is also recommended in certain cocktails.

- The 'Side-Car' is ⅓ Armagnac, ⅓ Triple Sec, ⅓ lemon juice.
- Armagnac '75' consists of ¼ Armagnac, ¼ lemon juice and ½ of champagne or good quality sparkling wine.
- Armagnac 'sour' is ¼ Armagnac, ½ lemon juice plus a mixture of soda, slices of sugared lemon and ice cubes.

There are many splendid recipes needing Armagnac, including 'Poulet sauté à l'Armagnac and 'Tarte aux pommes flambées à l'Armagnac'. Armagnac is also blended with many different fruits in pre-mixed bottles by Sempé, amongst others.

Leading Armagnac producers

Janneau Fils S.A. B.P.55, 32100 Condom. Tel. 62.28.24.77 is probably the largest producer. It was founded in 1851 by Pierre Etienne Janneau. Five generations later the company is run by

Michel Janneau with Etienne, his son, in charge of exports. Their three main brands are TRADITION, at least 5 years old; VSOP, a blend of 12 year old brandies; and Janneau XO. Their single vintage, A.C.Bas Armagnac, comes from their estate Domaine de Mouchac.

Visitors are welcome at 50 Avenue d'Aquitaine in Condom. No notice is required from 1st July to 15th September between 10.00 a.m. — 12.00 noon and 2.30 p.m. — 7.00 p.m. At other times of the year please telephone at least 24 hours beforehand. Visitors are shown some of the old warehouses dating back to 1851, blending vats, bottling hall, the stone-floored Tonnellerie, the old cooperage and have an opportunity to taste Janneau Armagnac. They can see a splendid example of the old 'ambulatory' pot still on wheels, similar to the one in the Armagnac museum in Condom. If you go there make sure you see the ancient bell to warn field workers of an approaching thunderstorm; the Alambic de Fraudeur, in which Armagnac was illicitly distilled; and a Bidon de Fraudeur, a large metal container shaped like a fat man's stomach, for smuggling the distilled spirit through customs.

Armagnac Larressingle is owned by Etab. Papelorey, 32100 Condom, Tel. 62.28.15.33. They own the Château de Larressingle, built in the thirteenth century for the Bishop of Condom. Five generations of Papeloreys and four generations of maîtres de chai have masterminded the production of Armagnac Larressingle – Three Star VSOP, Napoleon, Hors d'Age and Millésime. Also, in Condom is Armagnac Ducastaing Saint-Vivant, Route de Nerac, Tel. 62.93.88.84. In Condom, at La Table des Cordeliers restaurant, try 'foie gras au naturel parfumé au viel Armagnac', and 'oie en daube'.

The well known Marquis de Montesquiou brand is owned by Societé des Produits d'Armagnac Campagne d'Armagnac on the outskirts of Eauze, Tel. 62.09.82.13. The family descended from the noble family of the eleventh century when the Comte de Fezensac gave his second son the title of Baron de Montesquiou. In the seventeenth century D'Artagnan, the leader of the musketeers, was the son of Francoise de Montesquiou. Now they stock 2800 casks of superb Armagnac, equivalent to nearly 2 million bottles, of Monopole, Napoleon, XO and Soleil.

Nearby is the Marquis de Caussade Armagnac, Route de Cazaubon, Eauze, Tel. 62.09.94.22, who proffer a unique 'Chansons de Geste en Armagnac', an audio-visual presentation of the region, with free entry *and* tasting of their Armagnac.

J. de Malliac, who are to be found in Montreal, introduced the 'Hors d'Age' label early in the twentieth century and now put distillation *and* bottling date on all their bottles. 'Folle Blanche Grand Bas Armagnac' was distilled in 1963, bottled in 1984 – a single grape variety single year vintage.

Armagnac Sempé is in Aignan-en-Armagnac 32290, Tel. 62.09.24.24. Their VSOP is more than five years old and their Napoleon more than 6. Sempé also have 10 and 20 year old blends as well as an exotic range of 16° Fruits à l'Armagnac: Plums, Greengages, Mandarines, Chestnuts, Grapes, Pears and others. Their 'La Sabazia' is a special blend of Armagnac à l'orange, and their 'Bagheera' is a combined gascon Armagnac cocktail. Rudyard Kipling would have approved of the elegant, dangerous black panther on the label amidst the exotic jungle.

Ets. Gelas & Fils Armagnac, 48 Ave. Edmond Berges, is in Vic-Fezensac 32190, Tel. 62.06.30.11. The family trace their origins back to 1246 and have been producing Armagnac since 1875. They market a five year old, a VSOP Reserve, a Reserve Antique Hors d'Age, a vintage 1952, 1962, 1968 and a 25 year old Reserve. They also bottle Clementines, Cerises (cherries) and Cocktail des Fruits in Armagnac. The Gelas family, who are descended from the de Batz (d'Artagnan) family, have stocks of nearly 500,000 litres of old Armagnacs.

The family firm of Grassa at the Château de Tariquet, southeast of Eauze, have produced Armagnac for several generations as well now as increasing white wine interests.

In the Landes is the Domaine d'Ognoas at Arthez-d'Armagnac, 40190 Villeneuve-de-Marsan, Tel. 58.45.22.11 – a property and château owned by the département (which is unusual). Of the area owned of 540 hectares (1350 acres), 24 grow vines for production of Armagnac. Their old-fashioned but effective still is fired by wood from their own forests. Their brand is Grand Bas Armagnac Domaine d'Ognoas.

The Château de Lacaze Armagnac is in Parleboscq-en-Armagnac, just inside the eastern borders of the Landes. For three centuries a fine Armagnac has been produced here although the château dates back to the thirteenth century. The firm is run by an Englishman, Christopher Oldham. Jean-Louis Lafourcade, the oenologist and winemaker has introduced low temperature fermentation of the wines for distillation. Oak from four different forests are used for the barrels and matched to the four different grape varieties grown on the estate. The results are monitored on the château's computer system. Their style is smooth, with an unfiery nose and a mellowness on the palate in which the fruit comes through.

Just southwest of Labastide d'Armagnac in the Landes is the Château Garreau where there is 'Le Musée de Vigneron' which shows all the ancient distillery equipment and wine-making utensils in the 'Histoire de l'Armagnac'. Taste their Grand Cru Armagnac and look at their experimental vineyard and try the local food products, fruits, liqueurs, foie gras, confits and wines, Tel. 58.44.81.08.

One kilometre southwest of Nogaro is the powerful Cave des Producteurs Réunis, 32110 Nogaro-en-Armagnac, Tel. 62.09.01.79. This co-op was formed in 1963 and is the largest in the Armagnac area. The 500 small vigneron-members farm 2000 hectares (5000 acres) which produce 200,000 hectolitres of vin blanc Colombard, of which 50,000 hectolitres are distilled to make Armagnac. Their stock of Armagnac is equivalent to four million bottles. Besides Three Star, VSOP, eight year old, 12 year old and Hors d'Age, there is a fine range of single year millésimes, back to 1924. Their cheapest Armagnac inclusive of all local taxes is Francs 87 and their most expensive, a Pot Gascon of 2½ litres Vintage 1924 is Francs 2,777. They also market a wide range of Armagnac-related products: Le Mousquet liqueur, Le Pinkger aperitif, Le Floc of course, and Le Jarnac fruits in Armagnac. Their annual sales turnover is £5 million of which 20% is for export. They have a tasting caveau outside their main offices and chais and opposite a vintage ambulatory pot-still in working order.

59

Armagnac Croix de Salles is produced by the Dartigalongue family, and has been since 1838, at 32110 Nogaro, Tel. 62.09.03.01. They claim to be the oldest producer of Armagnac.

Panjas is a village on the Gers/Landes borders where the co-op produces Armagnac Cles des Ducs, one of the best known brands in France. In Lavardac is another noted Armagnac Castarede at Pont de Bordes, Tel. 58.67.50.06. Chabot Armagnac is on the Bordeaux road north of Villeneuve de Marsan, Tel. 58.45.21.76.

There are many other Armagnac producers – Domaine de Payroutin, Larée 32150 Cazaubon; Armagnac Pouchegu, R. Laporte 32440 Castelnau-d'Auzan; Domaine de Lagajan-Pontovat, Georgacaracos-Dulau, 32800 Eauze; Compagnie des Grands Armagnacs, 32440 Castelnau-D'Auzan; Claude Lacoste, 40190 Hontanx (Landes). All would welcome a visit to taste and buy a few bottles.

UK Sales Distributors

Janneau – Matthew Clark & Sons Ltd, 183/5 Central Street, London EC1V 8DR;
D. Rintoul & Co. Ltd, 13 Lynedoch Crescent, Glasgow, Scotland

Marquis de Montesquiou – J.R. Parkington, Pernod House, Great West Road, Brentford, Middlesex;
Dent & Reuss Ltd, Hertford

Larressingle Armagnac – Hawkins & Nurick Ltd, 27 Carnwath Road, London SW6

J. de Malliac – Deinhard & Co, 29 Addington Street, London SE1;
Rivinvend Ltd, Glasgow G62 7LN

Cles des Ducs – Carillon Wine & Spirit Shippers (IDV) 12 Brick Street, London W1

Cave des Producteurs Reunis – Nogaro – David Scatchard Ltd, 4 Temple Court, Liverpool

Armagnac Baron de Casterac – The Wine Society

Armagnac Château de Lacaze – Peter Dominic branches

Armagnac Marquis de Puysegur (CVGA) – W.E. Smith & Co.
Ltd./Christopher Piper

Armagnac Grassa – Thierry & Tatham and Eaton Elliott
Winebrokers of Alderley Edge

Armagnac Marquis de Caussade – George Morton Ltd & City
Vintagers Ltd

Armagnac Samalens – Eurobrands, 63 Windsor Avenue,
Merton Abbey, London SW19

Gelas Armagnac – The Bristol Brandy Co., Redland Road,
Bristol BS6 6YE

Armagnac Miguel Clement – K.F. Butler & Co. Ltd, East
Grinstead, Sussex

Armagnac Comtes de Cadignan – Paul Boutinot Wines

Armagnac St. Vivant – G. & J. Greenall, Warrington, Cheshire
& Harvey Prince & Co.

Armagnac Michel Faure – A.H. Colombier (Midlands), Ashby
de la Zouch, Leics.

Armagnac Vibrac – J.D. Vintners, Bragborough Lodge,
Daventry, Northants

Armagnac Patrice-Burcard – Bacchus Ltd, 9 Macklin Street,
London WC2

Vignerons de Floc de Gascogne – Michael Hall, 24 Baronsfield
Road, St. Margarets, Twickenham, Middlesex.

UK prices

The Oddbins chain market a wonderful range of Armagnacs
– easily the finest in the UK, which starts with Larressingle xxx
at £9.25, and includes Janneau, Cles des Ducs VSOP,

Malliac VSOP, Cachet du Roi XO, Larressingle Hors d'Age, Comtes de Cadignan 1966, Dupeyron 1961, Malliac Hors d'Age and finally De Mouchac 1960/2 at £32.99 from Janneau.

Oddbins state 'comparisons of the flavours of Armagnac and Cognac always class Armagnac as "rustic" with the implication that it is a coarser spirit. This is not the case as one of Armagnac's special distinctions is that it is marvellously smooth: it is usually darker than Cognac with a slightly less refined, more robust earthy style. But unquestionably its greatest delight and difference to Cognac is the great pungent smell which stays in your mouth or even in an empty glass for such a long time.'

Their favourite from their long list is Larressingle Hors d'Age at £13.99. Their sales of Armagnac have doubled in a twelve month period. Oddbins now claim to be the foremost Armagnac specialist retailer in the country today, and have added three single vintage Armagnacs of La Grindière to their range.

One of the most interesting specialist importers in the UK is the Bristol Brandy Company, Tel. 0272–745193. Apart from being agents for the Gelas wide range of Armagnacs, they have Ducastaing Armagnac of 1893 and 1900 and, most unusually a range of wonderful single Domaine Armagnacs from G. Pelat, Farbos, Massot and E. Durou – all supplied by Gelas of Vic-Fezensac.

Anthony Byrne Wines have a fine range of Alain Faget's Armagnacs – xxx, VSOP, Hors d'Age, '20 Ans' and 7 vintage years – all from £10.80.

Berry Bros. & Rudd sell Chateau de Labaude from £14.45.

Morris' Wine Stores sell Samalens xxx @ £9.25, their VSOP at £11.00.

Haynes Hanson & Clark sell Janneau Tradition xxx at £12.32, VSOP @ £14.64.

The Wine Society offer Baron de Casterac 1962 at £15.75, and Fine at £11.50.

K.F. Butler offer Miguel Clement VSOP at £9.75 plus VAT, Vieille Reserve (12 years) at £14.00 plus VAT.

Christopher Piper Wines sell Marquis de Puysegur Selection Privée at £18.85.

La Vigneronne sell Janneau XO at £20.75, Domaine de Mouchan 1974 at £33.75.

So do please try this splendid velvety, grapy, full-bouqueted brandy called Armagnac − from the heartland of the Three Musketeers.

In the autumn you may still see the travelling still, an ancient bronze railway engine wheezing away as it trundles from farm to farm. At work its glowing firebox is fed with oak branches day and night and the whole countryside can breathe the monster's fiery brandy fumes. If you are in Eauze on a Thursday look in on the Armagnac market. There you will see buyers and sellers arguing and bargaining in the narrow streets, sampling the brandy for sale or testing it just by rubbing a few drops between their palms and sniffing the aroma. They will show you how to drink Armagnac properly. First cradle your glass in the hollow of your hand and warm it for a short time. Then breathe in the scent and glorious aroma of plums and nuts which the fumes give off. Then taste and roll it round your tongue and against your palate and finally sip the whole glass slowly enjoying the sense of earthy warmth and the infinite comfort.

CHAPTER FIVE:
DISCOVERING THE DELIGHTS
OF GERS

This is one of the forgotten départements of France. There are no autoroutes in the Gers and also, thank goodness, no industrial pollution because there is no heavy industry in the area. The département is almost totally dependent on agriculture (by that I include Armagnac, a thriving wine trade and the goose byproducts). The population of 180,000 is scattered over 462 communes, with only Auch, the prefecture town, above a 10,000 population. The area covers 6300 sq km and the peaceful rolling countryside is well watered by small tributaries flowing into the Garonne to the north and the Adour to the west. There are 15 little rivers with 1000 km of waterways gently straggling through the Gers from the foothills of the Pyrenees. There are also 1000 km of Grandes Randonnées, pedestrian and equestrian: most of these footpaths are on the pilgrim routes to St. Jacques de Compostella, the GR 65, GR 653 and GR 652. The highest point of 380 metres is the chapel of St. Roch at Morlaux-Bernet on the southern borders with the Haute Pyrénées.

There is a good sprinkling of châteaux, medieval 'cités', romanesque churches, bastide towns, and relatively traffic-free quality minor roads on which to travel. In short – if you add the Gascon wines, food and hospitality – an ideal part of France to visit for the first time. You should not on any account miss visiting Auch, the dignified, musical town with its Musketeer traditions; Condom and Eauze, the centres of Armagnac production; Mirande for its fortified gothic church and museum; Larressingle, the walled, fortified and elegant medieval village west of Condom; and finally, visit one of the homes of my ancestors, the only circular bastide of Fources beside the sleepy River Azoue – most photogenic!

There are two alternatives. The first is to spend the best part of a week in Auch, the prefecture town, make a different circuit each day and returning each evening. Or one can spend six different days and nights in different regions. Both possibilities are now shown, and you'll need Michelin Map 82.

Tour One

With Auch as a base the first circuit is northwest on the N 124 for 7 km then north on the D 930 for 11 km to Labatisse. Then travel to **Lavardens** due east on the D 103 for 3.5 km to see the marvellous château of Mirabeu and due west on the D 103 for 1.5 km to **Jegun** to see the old bastide town – both are worth a detour. Continue on the D 930 for 7 km to **Castéràverduzan** to see this little spa town and the national museum of Lannelongue, and on by the same road through Ayguetinte, a small hamlet with a pelota court, another 11 km to **Valence sur Baise**, bastide town and museum, to see the wonderful Abbey of Flaran on the minor road D 142 northwest.

Now due east on the D 232 to the hamlet of Maignout-Tauzia to see the famous but ruined **Château de Tauzia**, southeast on the D 142 and pick up the signs for **St Puy**. The Château de Monluc on the hill in the village produces the only sparkling wine in Gascony (of which more later). Next continue northeast on the D 42 to Mas d'Auvignon and **Terraube**, a distance of 8½ km, where the fortified town and Gascon château are worth a look. (Briefly on Michelin Map 79.) Now north on the D 166 for 11 km, to **La Romieu** where the fourteenth century collegiate of St. Pierre plus cloister and frescoes is one of the sights of Gascony. East cross country on the D 266 and south on the D 36 following the course initially of the little river Auchie and then the larger river Gers into **Lectoure**. Architecturally, after Auch, this is probably the most interesting town in the Gers and you will need several hours to do it justice.

From Lectoure due south on the N 21 to **Fleurance**, although if you have time take a detour east to St. Clar where there is a unique bazaar-shop which stocks the widest range of wines, Armagnac and confit d'oie available in the Gers/Landes. Fleurance is a classic bastide town with a notable church of St. Laurent. The last homeward lap continues on the N 21 for 24 km via Montestruc. 8½ km south make a detour west for 1½ km to the château of Le Rieutort. Finally 5 km before one reaches Auch the airport is on the west side of the road.

Summary: The alternative to staying in Auch on this tour is Lectoure (pop. 3800) which is rather more interesting than Fleurance. The road distance is not great, approximately 125 km, but the many attractive stops will make this a very full day.

Tour Two

The eastern circuit is called the Route du Foie Gras dans les Côteaux de Gers. It starts on the main N 124 with a visit to the Château of St. Cricq or the Château of Montegut, both 3 km east of Auch: one is ½ km north of the road, the other south, across the railway and up the hill – a distance of 1½ km.

Continue east on the minor road D 509 north of and parallel to the N 124, which can be busy early in the morning, to **Marsan** where the seventeenth century château is worth a visit. Keep on the D 509 east for 5 km and due north on the D 928 keeping the river Arratz on the west side for 14 km to **Mauvezin** which is a fortified bastide with arcades and thirteenth to fifteenth century church. On the way east to Cologne, call in to see the Château de Bartas near St. Georges but bordering the D 654. **Cologne** is another bastide town with an arcaded central square. Southeast for 15 km past a large lake on the east side of the road through Monbrun to **Isle-Jourdan**, a bastide town with notable collegiate church. Now 19 km west on the N 124 across the rivers Save and Marcaoue to **Gimont**, a bastide town with a church of note, and on Wednesdays the most important market in the Gers. This is a centre for ham, duck and goose confits.

Due south for 19 km on the D 4 to **Samatan** and neighbouring **Lombez**. The former has half a dozen châteaux in the vicinity and the latter a fascinating red-brick Cathedral of Ste. Marie. Wellington's army stormed down the valley of the river Save. Follow the D 632 for 7½ km, turn right and north to **Simorre** on the D 566 and D 34 to see the fortified red-brick Toulousan-style church – a veritable fortress – with views to the southern Pyrénées. Parallel to little river Gimone on the D 12 north 9 km to **Saramon** with its Renaissance houses and 3 km on the D 626 to **Boular** to see the huge twelfth century gothic style Abbey. Northwest for 6 km on the D 626 to **Castelnau-Barbarens**, a typical Gascon village built originally in 1140.

On the remaining 15 km northwest on the D 626 to Auch, you pass through **Pessan** with three small châteaux nearby, a fortified town gate-tower and a twelfth century abbey.

Summary: The distance is about 150 km, most of it on deserted minor roads with a chance to enjoy the undulating countryside, the many small rivers, the unusual red-brick Toulousan architecture and a dozen Gascon châteaux. As a base l'Isle-Jourdain (pop. 4200) is the best place to stay.

Tour Three

The southwest section of Gers is called the Route des Bastides de L'Astarac. Take the N 21 south for 4 km and then the D 929 southeast following the river Gers to **Pavie** which has an interesting history. The thirteenth century bastide town has an attractive arched stone bridge across the river Gers, châteaux, windmills, a watchtower, convent and several churches. South through Orbessan and Ornezan which has a Gallo-Roman villa of St. Pé, and Labarthe – a distance of 25 km to **Masseube**, a thirteenth century bastide, with ramparts, moat and church. Due west on the D 127 on the old Roman Way 15 km via St. Elix-Theux, which has a Gallo-Roman domaine (although all the important finds have been removed to the museum of St. Raymond in Toulouse), to St. Michel, a small hamlet noted for its fêtes (lily of the valley i.e. Mothers' Day, and Caillaou).

Turn north on the D 939 for 7 km to **Berdoues** and look at the ancient Cistercian abbey overlooking the river Baise. 4 km further on the same road is **Mirande**, a thirteenth century bastide, where there is a tower, château, pilgrim hospital, pigeonniers and a famous church and museum.

Then southeast on the N 21 via St. Maur 14 km to Mielan passing the large lake of the same name on the east side of the road. **Mielan**, a bastide town, was the scene of constant fighting during the Hundred Years War. Due west on the N 21 for 2 km and then north on the D 3 for 19 km to Marciac via Tillac. If you continue on the N 21 for 3 km towards Rabastens-de-Bigorre and Tarbes, the view of the Pyrénées from the Puntous de Laguian is superb.

Stop in Tillac after 6 km to admire the curious 'village-rue' with several towers and old houses. The English couple Brian and Freda Beacham run a cafe here dispensing French and English food (and tea). Follow the course of the river Boués by the D 3, leaving the imposing ruined feudal château of Monlezun on the west side of the road, into **Marciac**. This bastide town is worth a stop for its châteaux, fourteenth century church and natural history museum. It is famous throughout France for its jazz festival on the 15th August each year.

Continue along the wide valley of the rivers Boués and Arros on the D 3 towards Plaisance via Beaumarches, noted for its gothic church and Anglo-Arab stud breeding farms. **Plaisance** is another fourteenth century bastide town where the Black Prince behaved rather badly in 1355. Noted too for its musical organ festival, its goat-cheese market, and for being a centre of the local wine industry.

Back on our tracks on the D 3 for 3½ km and east in Beaumarchés on the D 943 – a winding pretty road along the hills 16 km to **Bassoues**. The fourteenth century crenellated keep of the Archbishop's château is one of the major tourist attractions in the Gers and is well worth a visit. Now continue 5½ km east to **Montesquiou**, a very pretty village on a hill and home of the descendants of the old Dukes of Gascony.

Isle-de-Noé is in the confluent of the valley of the rivers Auloue and Loustere, hence its name, and then 5 km on the D 943 to **Barran** on the old Roman way, which has an unusual collegiate church of St. Jean, Château de Mazeres (4 km north), windmills, and pigeonnier. Continue for 21 km back to Auch.

Summary: The distance is 165 km by quite easy roads. As a base Mirande (pop. 4800) makes an attractive halt.

Tour Four

The western circuit is designed for the wine buff. Take the N 124 west out of Auch and keep on it for 22 km crossing the rivers Auloue and Baise to **St. Jean Poutge**. Another 8 km takes one into **Vic-Fezensac**, a bustling town, which is the centre of the bullfighting area, has a wine co-operative in the northern suburb, and nine châteaux within easy range. Keep due west on the main road N 124 through Demu to **Manciet**, a distance of 23 km. There are feudal moats, an amphitheatre, a pilgrim hospital, a modern pilgrimage site and it is Armagnac country. A distance of 9 km into **Nogaro**, the principal town of feudal Armagnac, dating back to 1060 AD. The eleventh century romanesque church, canon's house and cloisters are worth a visit. So too is the excellent co-operative for Armagnac and Côtes de Gascogne wines. The championship of the Courses Landaises for the whole of Gascony is held here in October. Keep on the N 124 for 20 km to **Barcelonne-du-Gers** via Luppé-Violles.

Aire sur l'Adour is a few hundred metres into the neighbouring département of the Landes. It is a most attractive town and the pivot of the main wine growing areas of Gascony. To the south west are the vineyards of Tursan and to the south east the vineyards of Madiran and St. Mont. Five tributaries of the river Adour water this fertile area – the Gros-Leese, the Lees, the Larcis, the Saget and the Bergons. There are a dozen little wine villages covered in the appropriate chapter, but I would recommend a visit to the magnificent wine Co-op at St. Mont.

From Barcellone-du-Gers keep east south east on the D 935 for 7½ km to St. Germe and take the minor road D 262 south for the Co-op at St. Mont to taste their range of wines and buy some bottles. Then 5½ km due east parallel to the river Adour on the D 946 to **Riscle** which has a fourteenth century gothic church, and has many fêtes, fairs, firework displays and Courses Landaises. Back across the river on the

D 935 and east on the D 3 for 5½ km to see the huge soaring 'donjon' keep and museum on the hill north of the road, of Termes d'Armagnac. Continue north east on the D 48 10 km to **Aignan**, once upon a time the capital of Armagnac and the parliamentary seat of Gascony. Here there is a twelfth century romanesque church, three châteaux, another good Co-op linked with St. Mont, and Courses Landaises.

In the rectangle formed between Auch, Vic-Fezenac, Aignan and Plaisance – roughly 40 km by 20 km – there are village names ending with the word d'Anglés, pronounced Anglais (i.e. English). There is Cazaux d'Anglés and Castelnau d'Anglés, both north west of Montesquiou. There are the **Peyrusses, Grande** and **Vieille** with eleventh and twelfth century romanesque priories and churches worth a detour. **Lupiac**, a little fortified hamlet on a hill, is surrounded by D'Artagnan memories. His château of Castelmore is just north on the D 102. His uncle's Château de la Plagne is just north east on the D 37. Other hamlets which have a story attached to them are Biran, St. Arailles and Le Brouilh.

Now there is a choice of routes. Continue north east on the D 20 and D 263 10 km to Demu on the main road and return eastwards on the same road at the commencement of this tour 40 km to Auch.

For the brave traveller who wants to explore the hinterland which the English dominated for three hundred years (and who has not only Michelin Map 82 but also a good map reader and patient driver in the car) try one of these routes:—
- There is the northern route taking in Le Parre (D 157), Castelmore château (D 102 south), Lupiac, east D 37 to Belmont, **Tudelle**, Bazian, le Brouilh, south to Laubare, north to Biran via the 'Tour Gallo-Romaine' and back on the main road N 134 14 km south east to Auch.
- There is the southern route taking in, via the D 155, Castelnavet, St. Pierre d'Aubezies, Peyrusse-vieille, east via the D 252 to Peyrusse-Grande and continue south east to Castelnau d'Anglés, east to St. Arailles, southeast on the D 179 to Mirannes and back on the D 934 to Auch via Barran, Bonnefont, Embats and Tufferis.

Either route is 40 km as the crow flies from Aignan to Auch.

Provided the weather is good this is an ideal opportunity to see the real unspoilt France. You are unlikely to encounter other tourists as you drive through river valleys where our ancestors fought, lived, and died many centuries ago. There are seven little parallel rivers to be crossed – the Riberette, the Douze, the Azoue, the Guiroue, the Osse, the Baise and the Auloue, all running from south to north. None of the hills are above 250 metres high, the roads are empty and usually well-signed and the hamlet of Tudelle (E–6) is famous locally for its wine!

Summary: The distance covered, depending on the final return lap, is about 180 km. As a base either Vic-Fezensac (pop. 4200) or Nogaro (pop. 2200) make attractive and interesting places in which to stay.

Tour Five

For the grand tour of the Armagnac area to the north north west of Gers from Auch you will need not only Michelin Map No 82, but also No 79 to the north as well. (Condom is on both.)

Take the familiar N 124 west for 29 km to St. Jean-Poutge and go due north on the D 939 on the west bank of the river Baise. The famous château of Herrebouc is 2 km and merits a detour. At St. Paul de Baise west on a minor road to **Marambat**, a small fortified village with ramparts, north on the D 35 to Mourède, west to **Lannepax** with the thirteenth century Château de Gajan, north on the D 118 to **Courrensan**, another 'village perché' with ramparts and château-fort.

Five km north on the D 113 brings us to **Gondrin**, a small town with a thirteenth Gascon château, windmills and a wine co-operative that is worth a visit. West on the main road for 13 km to **Eauze**, one of the most interesting small towns in Gascony. This is the heart of Armagnac country and there are many 'chais' in the town. The fifteenth century cathedral of St. Luperc and the archaeological museum are both worth a visit. There are half a dozen Gascon châteaux within a 5 mile radius and the area is famous for its gastronomic specialities. There are a dozen small towns and villages with the word

71

'Armagnac' as part of their name – Caupenne, Salles, Campagne, Bretagne, Mauléon, Monlezun, Castex etc.

From Eauze west on the D 626 and after 3 km fork right and northwest 18 km to **Cazaubon**, a small town with a wine co–op, seven churches and also seven Gascon châteaux within a short radius. **Barbotan-lès-Thermes** is 4 km north east on the D 656 and this is the major spa town in the Gers. The thermal baths and small town devoted to the '*curistes*' is encircled by an exotic park with tropical plants and trees. Well worth a visit even if you have no medical need! On the D 656 again and east on the D 15/D 36 to Castelnau d'Auzan which has a cave co-operative, several Gascon châteaux, five little churches and two so-called 'fountains of devotion' for various cures. East to Montreal which is 25 km from Barbotan. **Montreal** is a classic fortified bastide town. The Gallo-Roman mosaics in the nearby village of **Séviac**, southwest 2 km, and two churches and Gallo-Roman museum in the town are all worth visiting.

Northeast from Montreal 5½ km on the D 29 is one of the homes of my ancestors, the village of Fources, once Forces, on the river Azoue. The circular bastide with arcaded houses, mostly well restored, and a much repaired château make this an enchanting place. Take the minor road D 114 south east to **Belarin** to see the château and church. Back on the D 15 and 8 km eastwards is my favourite archaeological site in Gascony. **Larressingle** is 1 km south of the main road and is designated the Carcassone du Gers, being a high walled fortified château-fort of the old Bishops of Condom. Parts date from the fourth century but mostly from the thirteenth century including the exquisite fortified romanesque church. You can buy there Armagnac Larressingle, Floc de Gascogne and other refreshments.

Condom (pop. 8000) is 8 km east on the D 15 and is the centre of the Armagnac business. The Cathedral of St. Pierre, mainly sixteenth century, as are the cloisters, plus the churches of Ste. Germaine and St. Antoine de Lialores, plus a score of Gascon châteaux and the Museum of Armagnac make Condom an essential visit. There are many interesting sites plus visits to the leading Armagnac producers to warrant a stay of several days.

Returning towards Auch take the D 931 south (signed for Eauze) and after 4 km, the D 208 2½ km for **Cassaigne**, a hamlet boasting two thirteenth century Gascon châteaux of note – both worth a visit. Next west on the D 208 for 3 km to **Mouchan** to see the romanesque church with a clock tower dating from the eleventh century, called St. Austréségile. Then south on the D 35 for 5 km and southeast on a minor road to **Mansencôme**, a small hamlet with two Gascon châteaux, that of Busca-Maniban with its own chapel, being worth a detour.

From Mansencôme south east on to the D 939 parallel to the river Baise south for 27 km back to St. Jean-Poutge and the N 124 south east back to Auch.

Summary: The distance is about 230 km – perhaps a little too much for one day – so on balance the recommendation is to stay in Condom (pop. 8000) where there is a good choice of modest hotels and restaurants, and lop about 50 km off the circuit total.

In terms of ranking I would put the tours in the following order of descending interest — five, four, one, three and two respectively.

CHAPTER SIX:
TOWNS AND VILLAGES OF GERS

Aignan (C–6) This fortified little town dominating the valley of the river Midour was once the capital of Armagnac and the parliamentary capital of Gascony. Now it has three Gascon châteaux, two romanesque churches (q.v) and a cave co-operative. Monday is the day for markets and fairs. The Ferme-Auberge Château Lassalle has an excellent Francs 85 menu including wine and coffee.

Aubiet (H–7) Saint Taurin was martyred here in the fourth century.

Auch (G–7) Known originally as Elimberris, capital of the Ausci who defended themselves, in vain, against Caesar's legions in BC 50. Then renamed Augusta Auscorum, the region was evangelised by St. Taurin and St. Orens. The 'oppidum' on the top of the hill overlooking the valley of the river Gers was impregnable from the east, vulnerable from the west. It became a bishopric after the destruction of Elusa (Eauze) and subsequently an archbishopric. The ninth century saw the peaceful occupation by the younger sons of the Kingdom of Navarre and the creation of the first Dukes of Gascony. Later it became a fief of the powerful Counts of Armagnac (whose daughter married a direct ancestor of mine early in the eleventh century), who for the most part sided with the English during their three centuries of Gascon rule. In 1473 the town was taken and pillaged when the Armagnacs lost their power struggle with the Burgundians. The main sights are the fifteenth Cathedral of Sainte Marie (q.v), the fourteenth century Tour d'Armagnac, 40 metres high (now a prison) at the summit of the stone staircase of 370 steps from river to town summit. Half way up as you take breath there is a splendid statue of the swashbuckling D'Artagnan, Capitaine des Mousquetaires du Roi. The préfecture, which was the archbishop's palace in the eighteenth century, the hotel de ville of the same period and the fifteenth century maison du tourisme, all cluster together in the main square near the cathedral. There are two museums of note (q.v) and Auch is a cultural city. The music festival is held in June and concerts in the cathedral in August and October. An exhibition of local artisans' products is held in July and August. There are flea markets and antique fairs. There are fêtes galore: including firework displays at the end of June, beginning of July. The fête patronal is the second Sunday in September, the fête of the departure for the pilgrims of St. Jacques de Compostella is in mid-July, and carnival takes place in the first fortnight of April. Auch is a jolly, bustling centre with lots of activities, a gastonomic centre for food, wine and Armagnac. It has several low cost hotel-restaurants and easy parking at the top of the hill in a large park in the Allées d'Etigny leading northwest towards Condom from the main Place de la Liberation. There are a dozen notable châteaux gascon within a few kilometres, including Marin and St. Cricq. Auch has an exceptionally mild climate particularly in autumn and spring – ideal times for a visit.

Aurensan (A–7) is a small thermal spa with warm mineral waters from the Maska and the rivers Larcis and Leez.

Auterive (G–7) Several Gallo-Roman villas with mosaics have been discovered here.

Barcelonne du Gers (A–6) is a fortified bastide town created in 1316. Originally known as Gosset it took its Spanish name in 1343 – it is also nicknamed the 'Porte du Gers'.

Barbotan lès Thermes/Cazaubon (B–3) These two quite disparate towns are twinned. The former is one of the leading spa towns in the southwest of France, able to take 2000 '*curistes*' at a time. Set in a large tropical park with banana trees, palms, and lotus plants, it is a curious mixture of ancient and modern. Some of the ramparts are fourteenth century, the main town gatehouse is sixteenth century, but the spa complex and hotels are distinctly modern. Neighbouring Cazaubon has a noted renaissance church, a wine co-op, and many local Gascon châteaux. Well worth a visit.

Barran (F–7) An old fortified village before it became a bastide in 1279. Ramparts, fortified gatehouse, bridge, moats, a noted pigeonnier of Bonnefort, several windmills, and Gascon châteaux plus a notable church, make Barran of interest to the visitor. It is west of Auch on the D 943.

Bassoues (D–7) A thousand years ago St. Fris died here leading his Christian troops in a rare victory over the invading Saracens. Later the Archbishop of Auch created a bastide here in the thirteenth century and the famous donjon (castle keep q.v) was built by the military-minded Archbishop Arnaud Aubert, nephew of Pope Innocent VI. The saint's tomb and basilica is still a pilgrimage point. Bassoues is an archaeological gem, west of Montesquiou on the D 943. The Hostellerie du Donjon, Tel. 62.64.90.04, has menus from Francs 41.50 including wine. Ask for 'civet de lièvre' or 'salmis de palombes'.

Bazian (E–6) is a tiny fortified hamlet, south of Vic-Fezensac, west of the D 34, which boasts a watch tower, château of St. Yors, a fortified town gate with interesting facades and roof, as well as old windmills.

Beaucaire (E–4) has several prehistoric sites and latter Gallo-Roman finds, including a villa, mosaics, a necropolis for the slain barbarians and other early medieval unfortunates!

Beaumarchés (C–7) This bastide was founded in 1240 by King Philippe le Bel and has a notable church (q.v), an Anglo-Arab stud, windmills, the Tower of Marseillan and a view of the Pyrenees. Mid-summer candle-lit concerts are held here.

Beaumont (E–3) A hamlet which belonged to Louis XIV's mistress de Montespan. The château and romanesque church are of note (q.v).

Belloc-Saint-Clamens (F–9) 'Belloc' means 'beau lieu' in French. A pagan sanctuary is the original site of the present romanesque rural chapel of St. Clamens (q.v).

Beraut (F–4) is just southeast of Condom, an old fortified village owned by King Edward I in 1286. There are three Gascon châteaux here including Lasserre (q.v).

Berdoues-Ponsampère (F–8) Southeast of Mirande, this Cistercian abbey founded in 1137 is one of the ecclesiastical sights of Gascony (q.v).

Bézéril (I–8) This hamlet south of Gimont has a noted seventeenth century château and thirteenth century romanesque church.

Biran (F–6) Fourth century Roman coins were found in this picturesque fortified village northwest of Auch. The Tourraque de Lacouture is the name of the Gallo-Roman pile. The town gate, belfry and ramparts, remains of a stronghold and three romanesque churches can be seen still in Biran.

Blanquefort (I–6) This tiny hamlet harbours a pigeonnier of Maupeu dating from the mid-nineteenth century of toulousan style, which is rare in the Gers.

Blaziert (F–3) A temple to Apollo exists at Lauriac, part of a huge Roman encampment.

Bonas (F–5) The Marquis de Bonas lived here in the château (q.v). He was the first Armagnac distiller about 1800.

Boular (H–8) The abbey of this name (q.v) was built in AD 1140 by the Archbishop of Auch and the Count of Astarac.

Bretagne-d'Armagnac (D–4) was an important halt for the pilgrims coming from Brittany in the eleventh century. Later it became a bastide in the thirteenth century called 'Villa Comitalis'. F. Lacave produces Floc in this village.

Campagne-d'Armagnac (C–4) There is an exhibition of the Armagnac wine society at the château.

Cannet (B–7) is a hamlet near the rivers Bergon and Arrioutor where vineyard production of AOC Bearn and Madiran is being increased.

77

Castelnau-d'Auzan (C–3) West of Condom on the D 115 this picturesque medieval village has three Gascon châteaux, five churches and two sacred fountains. There is a cave co-operative which you can visit, as well as Armagnac Pouchego owned by M. Laporte, Tel. 62.29.20.88, Armagnac Damblat, Tel. 62.29.21.11, Armagnac La Plêchade from M. J-P Caron, Tel. 62.29.20.70, and Maison Lafontan, Tel. 62.29.23.80. The Courses Landaises arena is in a corner of the public gardens opposite two 'chais d'Armagnac'.

Castelnau-Barbarens (H–7) Another picturesque Gascon village rebuilt in AD 1140 after encounters with the barbarians. The Gallo-Roman villa of Taros has mosaics, thermal baths and furnishings of the first century. A pagan sanctuary is part of the rural chapel of Pépieux nearby.

Castéra-Lectourois (G–3), due north of Lectoure, was built on the Roman road. The church and 'château fort' are thirteenth century but the manor houses and watermill are early eighteenth century.

Castéra-Verduzan (F–5) Flavius Vegelius wrote in the third century of the thermal baths in their Roman camp. Later the village was owned by the Templars and later still by the Counts of Armagnac. The Marquis of Miran was responsible for establishing the fame of the thermal spa in the reign of Louis XV. The rivers Auloue and Baise produce the mineral and sulphuric waters, not from the Adour, as with all the other spas of Gascony, but deriving from the Garonne. Professor Lannelongue, President of the Academy of Medecine in France, also promoted the virtues of Castéra-Verduzan early in this century. It is a 'village fleuri' with Courses Landaises, horse racing and many gastronomic specialities. The Restaurant le Florida, Tel. 62.68.13.22, has menus from Francs 52. M. Ramouneda's Francs 98 menu includes 'la petite salade au boudin tiède (black pudding), le feuilleté de ris de veau grand-mère (braised calf's sweetbreads in pastry), assortiment de légumes, la pintade fermière sautée à l'ail comfit (guinea fowl with garlic) et les desserts'. You *will* need a cure after that!

Cazaubon (B–3) see Barbotan-lès-Thermes.

Cazeneuve (D–4) The fourteenth century fortified keep of Lamothe-Gondrin dominates this little village which has a Gascon museum with archaeological finds, and local paintings and regional costumes. The association 'sauvegarde des monuments et sites de l'Armagnac' is based in Cazeneuve. So is M. Gimet's Le Roy des Armagnacs distillery, and Domaine de Saas, Tel. 62.09.90.36.

Cologne (J–6) is on the eastern border with the Tarn et Garonne. The French King Philippe le Bel built this classical bastide in 1286. It has a pretty central square with arcades, a fourteenth century wooden market-hall with fifteenth century grain measures. Ditches surround the walls, there is a presbytery, a château, a windmill and an interesting church. Cologne is on the road from Mauvezin southeast to L'Isle-Jourdain.

Condom (E–3) is bisected by the river Baise, which for centuries transported its Armagnac brandy northwards to the Garonne and the sea. In the ninth century an important Benedictine abbey was built, then destroyed by the Normans and rebuilt again. The Cathedral of St. Pierre and cloisters (q.v) are superb. Condom, besides its fame as one of the two centres of the Armagnac business (particularly Janneau near the station on the D 930, and Larressingle, rue des Carmes), has 16 other churches (q.v) and 21 Gascon châteaux (q.v), a cave co-operative and the Museum of Armagnac. There are several low cost hotel-restaurants in Condom and a welcoming tourist office. In mid-August there are fêtes 'nuits musicales de l'Armagnac', and the Cathedral is floodlit every night on summer weekends. Condom merits a visit and indeed a stay, since there is much to see and do.

Cravencères (C–5) Charles Samaran, the leading Gascon writer and historian, lived in this little village, east of Nogaro, in the heart of Armagnac country. The fête communale of St. Vincent, patron of the wine growers is celebrated on the 22nd of January. Additionally there are two annual banquets here – the fête de l'Armagnac and the fête du Floc de Gascogne.

Armagnac Guy Dutirou, Tel. 62.08.52.53, is produced here.

Eauze (C–4) Caesar's lieutenant named Crassus conquered the Elusates in BC 50 and Elusa knew great prosperity in the third century. Rufin, the prime minister to the Emperor Theodosius, lived here, as did the Saints Philibert and Luperc. Although the barbarians, vandals, Francs, Moors, Normans, Huguenots and the English, continually burned and destroyed the town it remains prosperous and bustling. It is half the size of Condom. The ramparts and some manor houses date from the fifteenth century, as does the Cathedral of St. Luperc (q.v). There are five Gascon châteaux, several old windmills, the Eauze cave co-operative (60 Rte. de Nogaro) and the Elusate archaeological museum to see. There are many fêtes and foires, including St. Marc, aux Armagnacs and foie gras. There are several hotel/restaurants within budget. The Henri IV, 1 Place Saint Taurin, Tel. 62.09.75.90, offers a four course menu at Francs 40 including 'rognons madère with pâtes' (kidneys and noodles with madeira wine sauce) and half a litre of local wine. L'Armagnac, Bd. Saint Blanat, has a huge choice in their Francs 38 menu including 'pintade fermier' (beef marinated with vegetables, wine and Armagnac) or 'daube gasconne' (peasant recipe for guinea fowl). The Armagnac chais of San de Guilherm is in nearby Ramouzens (D–5) run by Alain Lalanne, Tel. 62.06.75.02; Armagnac Marquis de Caussade is on the Route de Cazaubon, Tel. 62.09.94.22, as is the Armagnac Marquis de Montesquiou, Tel. 62.09.82.13 (open for visits in the morning). The headquarters of the Armagnac aperitif called Floc is at the Maison des Producteurs, 9 Place Armagnac, Tel. 62.09.85.41. Other well known Domaines locally are Le Tariquet owned by the Grassa family; de Juglaron at St. Amand 2½ km north, owned by the Duffau family; and the Gentilhomme de Gascogne brand at the Domaine de Lagajan-Pontouat. A week of fêtes in early July includes balls, bandas, ballet, corridas, opera, fishing and flying competitions, a Gascon soirée and a 'nuit Andalouse'. Eauze, like Condom, is an essential visit and an excellent place to stay.

Escorneboeuf (I–6) On the Roman way from Toulouse, Auch and Bordeaux, this was a Gallo-Roman town with finds of Roman amphora. A first century statue of Jupiter has also been discovered.

Fleurance (H–4) When Hannibal fought two wars against Rome, he brought with him the tribe of Sibillates who, about 200 BC, settled here in the 'Plaine d'Aygueral'. The visigoths, vascons and other northern invaders were assimilated in this verdant valley of the river Gers. In 1272 King Phillippe authorised the building of a bastide, and there are many traces to be seen in the central square. In 1292 the Albret family, strong English supporters, acquired the town. There are many Gascon châteaux, manor houses, windmills and churches including the gothic St. Laurent (q.v). The town's name derives from the multitude of wild flowers to be found locally although curiously it is not a 'ville fleuri'. It has an appropriate town motto 'Florencia floruit, floret semperque florebit'. There are many low-key fairs, markets and fêtes.

Fourcés (D–3) was an English bastide founded by King Edward I in 1289. It was the home of my Gascon ancestors and in my admittedly biased view is quite the prettiest bastide in Gascony. Beside the sleepy lily-clad river Auzoue, across a bridge alongside the fifteenth century Gascon château is the only *circular* bastide, with arcaded half timbered houses, a noted clock tower and town gatehouse, with plane trees everywhere. There are fairs six times a year. Well worth a visit from Montréal or Nérac on the D 29.

Frégonville (J–7) Some form of bastide was erected here in the eleventh century. On the first Sunday in September is the communal fête, entitled the 'Castagnade', when chestnuts and 'vin nouveau' are offered to all.

Gaudonville (I–4) was originally known by the Romans as 'villa Gaudens' i.e. 'maison de plaisance' (a country seat). The chapel Notre Dame de Tudet is the oldest pilgrimage point in Gascony and this still takes place on the 9th August.

Gazaupouy (F–3) The English built a château (not a bastide)

81

here at the end of the thirteenth century, which still stands with towers and keep.

Gimont (I–7) The Abbot of Planselve and the Count of Toulouse erected a bastide here in 1265 for the French king. There are seven Gascon châteaux, old windmills and a church (q.v). The Wednesday markets are the most important in the Gers, mainly for ducks, geese and foie gras.

Gondrin (D–4) Apart from a Gascon château and a roman-esque church, the two attractions are the wine co-operative and the annual pilgrimage to the chapel of Tonnetau on the 15th August and 8th September. The Domaine du Bourdieu, Tel. 62.28.41.37, at neighbouring Lauraet (D–3) produces Armagnac and Floc. The Domaine des Cassagnoler, Tel. 62.29.12.75, on the D 931 produces excellent Cépage Gros Manseng Côtes de Gascogne, as well as Armagnac and Floc from Messieurs Cardeillac and Baumann.

L'Isle-Bouzon (H–4) is a hill-top village with a watch tower, ramparts, Gascon manorhouses and a rare sixteenth century circular pigeonnier.

L'Isle-Jourdain (K–7) St. Bertrand, Bishop of Comminges, died here in 1123 and the town was made into a bastide in AD 1230. The pilgrim route, now known as the Grande Randonée No. 65, passes through, as does the river Save which meanders – hence the town's name. Originally known as Buconis, on the Roman Way from Bordeaux to Jerusalem, the name signified 'le pays qui avoisine les grands bois' (wooded countryside). Later the chevalier and crusader Jourdain gave his name to the place. The bastide has arcades, a classic 'Halle', Hotel de Ville and a notable church (q.v). In the summer there is a Carnival, a musical spring festival, a 'Corso fleuri' and a four day fête. At the beginning of November is the week-long fête of Saint Martin.

Jegun (F–5) was originally a Celtic village, taking its name from 'ju' meaning tree, and 'guen' meaning wine. The barbarian tribes left their dead behind in the necropolis of Combis and Gallo-Roman finds were made at Peyrelongue.

Bernard IV, Count of Armagnac, fortified a bastide here in AD 1180. There are many Gascon châteaux, windmills and churches to look at. The restaurant Le Bastion, Tel. 62.64.54.57, run by Mme. Fauqué, offers excellent menus from Francs 44 including wine. (She is a member of the Academie Gastronomique de Gascogne.) The Château de Lavardens (q.v) is very close to Jegun.

Ladevèse-Ville (C–8) The word 'devize' in Gascon means 'defence', but still the English destroyed the village in the Hundred Years War. It is now a 'village fleuri' on the D 14 south of Plaisance.

Lagarde (G–3) has a large fifteenth century stable house with a pretty tower: the village, which is surrounded by ramparts, is being carefully restored.

Lagraulet du Gers (D–4) The dolmens here at the site called Hourés are notable. The Lapisse family grow and sell 'Le Dolmen' Armagnac nearby. There is also a small cave co-operative.

Laguian-Mazous (E–9) The panoramas are superb here from the N 21 looking south to the Pyrénées from a site called Puntous. The Hostellerie des Puntous, run by the Chevillon family, Tel. 62.67.52.51, has menus from Francs 40 and the views are free.

Lamazère (F–8) This feudal hilltop hamlet has Gallo-Roman sites called La Tourraque d'Ortolas and En-Peyroulet – both of note. The Gascon château and church of St. Blaise both date from the twelfth century.

Lannepax (d–5) On the hill of Ario, Crassus the Roman army commander, took control of the Novempopulanie, hence the name signifying 'land of peace'. The fortified bastide, the château of Gajan and the church date from the thirteenth century. In the valley of the Auzoue there are subterranean caves and grottos called Oeuil-du-Diable and Pont de Diable. Co-incidentally there are several good Armagnac distilleries in Lannepax including Cavé Frères, Dauriac fils and Armagnac Delord.

Larressingle (E–3) was recognised by the twelfth century Popes Alexander III and Innocent IV as belonging to the Abbeys of Agen and Condom, being the fortified village with high walls, deep moat, drawbridge and watch tower, in which the inhabitants of the neighbouring towns could take refuge. The ramparts of over 270 metres in polygonal shape encircle an acre and a half of early medieval life. The romanesque church and the keep are in the centre – the former magnificent (q.v), the latter battered but standing proud. There is a 'village fleuri' (village decorated with flowers) of the thirteenth century where you can drink Armagnac Larressingle in the courtyards. This is the jewel in the crown of Gascony. Do visit it.

Lectoure (G–3) was the capital of the tribe of Lactorates, and in the Gallo-Roman era was the centre of the pagan cult of Cybele (bull worship). Together with Auch and Eauze it is one of the oldest towns in the Gers. A hundred sarcophagi and a thousand or more archaeological finds, including Gallic wells in the Pradoulin plain, have been unearthed. In the fifth century it was a Bishopric, and was then destroyed by the Visigoths, despite its walled fortifications on the hill above the river Gers. Reconstructed in the tenth century it became the capital of Lomagne. King Edward I visited the town on 4th March 1273 to inspect the new cathedral (q.v). The powerful Barons of Armagnac were granted fealty of the town in 1325, and it became their capital until Louis XI recaptured Lectoure in 1473. There are still many Gallo-Roman sites – streets, sarcophagi, tauroboliques altars and finds of coins and ceramics of that period to be seen in the archaeological museum (q.v). The thirteenth century fountain of Diana, ramparts, Tower of Bourreau and Albinhac, and the remains of the château of Armagnac are today's evidence of the early Middle Ages. The Cathedral of St. Gervais et St. Protais of the fourteenth century (q.v) and many Gascon châteaux, churches and convents make Lectoure the centre of archaeological history in Gascony. Well might Lectoure be called the city of art and history. More mundanely there is a cave co-operative and several good value hotels and restaurants. An essential visit.

Lombez (I–8) is near Samatan; both are situated on the D 632 between Toulouse and Tarbes. The valley of the river Save flows through the southeast part of the town. The Romans occupied the region in BC 56 when it was known as Lumbarium, and the province was one of nine composing the new 'Novempopulanie' of Caesar Augustus. A vagrant called Majan settled near Lombez as a hermit and, in company with the Saints Clair and Prim, evangelised the region of the Saves. One story has it that Majan or Méen was the Bishop of Antioch and that he terrified a local dragon and caused its hasty exodus. After the Romans came the centuries of Barbarians. A Benedictine abbey was built in the ninth century by St. Thibery, and from the beginning of the tenth century it prospered with the passage of tens of thousands of Compostella pilgrims. Lombez has always been a religious centre and Pope John XXII in 1317 elevated the town to a Bishopric. During the Hundred Years War the Black Prince stayed in Lombez in 'Le Moulin' (the windmill), now part of the Cathedral of Sainte Marie (q.v). Much later Wellington's troops were briefly quartered in Lombez. Occasionally the town is flooded after heavy winter rains in the Pyrénées swell the river Save. The fête of St Majan is on the 1st June. Other fêtes are on the third Sunday in August and the 31st May.

Lupiac (D–6) The D'Artagnan family lived in this region of hills and the rivers Douze, Auzoue and Gelise, in the Gascon châteaux of Castelmore and La Plagne. Look for roads D 37 and D 102.

Manciet (C–5) is on the D 931 northeast of Nogaro and has an amphitheatre, two feudal moats, a twelfth century Templar hospital for the pilgrims and is still a pilgrimage site of St. Jean de Malaurey for patients with eye and ear problems.

Marciac (D–8) was a French bastide of 1298, has Gascon châteaux, watermills, a church of note (q.v) and a Jazz festival (the largest and best in southwest France). The Plaimont wine co-op has a Marciac Jazz label on a St. Mont wine. The restaurant La Péniche, run by the Levrel family, has menus from Francs 39 – by the side of a 75 acre lake.

Masseube (G–9) This English bastide was built in 1274, and still has ramparts, half timbered houses, a central square with arcades, market hall and windmills. There are non-commercial thermal springs and a local gastronomic item is green nut jam!

Mauvezin (I–6) is on the D 654/D 928 crossroads in the valley of Arrats near the river Gimone. The town was the frontier between Aquitaine to the west and Narbonne to the east and was capital of the region known as Fézensaguet in the tenth century. The English bastide town was built in 1275 and was fortified. It qualifies as a 'village fleuri' and the centre square with arcades, town hall, narrow streets, Maison de Jeanne d'Albret, various châteaux and a noted church (q.v) make Mauvezin an interesting port of call. Jeanne d'Albret, a fervent Protestant, ensured that Mauvezin became a centre for the Huguenots, and it became known as La Petite Genève. Opposite the nineteenth century Protestant temple in the Rue des Justices is the restaurant La Rapière run by the Fourreau family, Tel. 62.06.80.08. Menus start at Francs 50 and that at Francs 85 consists of 'potage, salade Gersoise, escalope de saumon au vin blanc de cépage armagnacois (salmon escalope cooked in white wine from Armagnac area), confit de canard avec ses légumes (duck conserve), fromage and coupe Rapière (glass of sparkling wine and Armagnac)'.

Miélan (E–9) is on the N 21 southwest of Mirande, close to the large lake of Miélan and the rivers of Bouès and Osse. A French bastide built in 1284 it was captured and destroyed by the English troops in 1370, rebuilt and finally recaptured by the French in 1450.

Miradoux (H–3) is in the northeast of Gers and, founded as a bastide by the English in 1253, claims to be the oldest in the Gers. The thirteenth century church is noted (q.v).

Mirande (F–8) was founded as a bastide in 1281 by the Count of Astarac and Bishop of Berdoues. Now on the N 21, the main Auch-Tarbes road, it is a classic bastide, with arcaded central square, ramparts, the Tower of Rohan, château of the old counts of Astarac, a pilgrim hospice, convent and several Gascon châteaux. The fortified gothic church of Notre Dame (q.v) and adjacent Museum of Beaux Arts (q.v) make Mirande an essential visit. Many of the neighbouring villages have saints' names – St. Maur, St. Martin (2), St. Médard, St. Clamens, St. Michel, Ste. Dode, St. Jaymes, St. Elix-Theux, St. Arroman – all clustered in the river valleys just south of Mirande.

Monfort (I–5) is another thirteenth century English bastide with noted châteaux (q.v) and church (q.v).

Monguilhem (a–4) An English bastide built by King Edward II in partnership with Annet de Toulouse. The King's seneschal was called Guillaume de Montegut, hence the town's name 'mon guillaume'.

Montaut-lès-Créneaux (H–6) is a few kilometres northeast of Auch and has a feudal château (q.v), pigonnier on stone pillars, and romanesque church.

Montesquiou (E–7) is on the D 943 west southwest of Auch, and is a picturesque hill village with prehistoric tumuli of Céridos and la Turraque, and Gallo-Roman villas called Céridos and Liebra. There are three Gascon châteaux including La Motte and the sinister Tour-des-Sorcières. The powerful family of Montesquiou produced field marshals, an abbot, a poet and D'Artagnan's mother. The fête of St. Jean is on 24th June and that of St. Martin is on the 1st November.

Montréal-du-Gers (D–3) The Gallo-Roman villa of Seviac dates from the fourth century and its polychrome mosaics, thermal baths, coins, tiles and furnishings make this one of the archaeological treasures of the Gers. The English bastide was created in 1289 on the site of a Celtic 'oppidum'. Montréal is a classic bastide with central arcaded square, seven Gascon châteaux (q.v) seven churches (q.v) and a Gallo-Roman museum. Most of the wine grown locally is distilled by the Armagnac firms of Lagrouera (Cardeillac & Fils), Bouillon (Ed. Michaud), Bordeneuve (Jean Michaud), Montréal Armagnac (Pierre Massartic), Roget Gimet; Jean-Pierre Labenne; and Roche Frères. The restaurant Chez Simone run by the Daubin family, Tel. 62.29.44.40, has menus from

Francs 55 including wine. The Francs 120 menu is 'grattons de canard, salade gasconne au foie gras mi-cuit, confit de canard maison avec sa garniture, croustade à l'Armagnac'. Madam Simone Daubin is a cordon bleu Gascon chef.

Nogaro (B–5) was known as Nogarolium (lieu planté de noyers, i.e. walnuts). St. Augustine, Archbishop of Auch in AD 1060, founded the church (q.v) and financed the growth of the town which grew prosperous from the Compostella pilgrims. It was a focal meeting place in Aquitaine for the councils of clerks and magistrates. Two convents were built, that of St. Vincent in 1250, and later in 1620, one of the Capucin order. Now known for its Armagnac (the large co-operative, Tel. 62.09.01.79) and Croix de Salles (H. Dartigalongue et Fils, Tel. 62.09.03.01) for its championship courses and corridas and for its car racing Grand Prix Paul Armagnac held in September. There are many fairs, fêtes and markets held in Nogaro. Well worth a visit.

Ordan–Larroque (F–6) is on the N 124 northwest of Auch. It has many Gallo-Roman sites: Lasserre, Larroque, Encassou, Mengot, En-Cassagne and Macaut with Merovingian necropolis, mosaics, thermal baths, furnishings and villas. The hill-top village is classified as 'amenagé et fleuri' and has eight Gascon châteaux and four churches plus a small archaeoogical museum.

Panjas (B–5) is in the heart of Armagnac country. This village has several Gascon feudal age houses, a château and the romanesque church of St. Laurent with Roman frescoes. The Cave Co-operative produces 'Cles des Ducs' Armagnac.

Pavie (G–7) was known as Esparsac from the Gallo-Roman villa named Spartacus. The French King Phillipe le Bel founded this bastide in 1281 as a rival to Auch, owned by the English 5 km to the north. This shows the curious No Man's Land effect in the Gers where the French and English Kings built and garrisoned small bastide towns almost indiscriminately. A pilgrimage to Notre Dame du Cédon at the twelfth century presbytery is made each year on the 25th March.

Pessan (G–7) is on the D 626 southeast of Auch. A Benedictine abbey was built here in the ninth century and a bastide in AD 1270 which has a fortified gatehouse. There are four Gascon châteaux, several Middle Ages half timbered houses, a church (q.v) and a museum (q.v). On the third Sunday in May is the procession of 'Nus-Pieds'!

Plaisance (C–7) was once known as Ripa Alta and became a French bastide in 1322, but the town was partly destroyed by the Black Prince in 1355. It is the chief town of Côtes de St. Mont wines: the cave co-op of Plaisance being one of the Plaimont group. A 'village fleuri', it is noted for its grand organ concerts. The Hotel D'Artagnan, run by the Marratt family, Tel. 62.69.30.37, offers menus from Francs 50 with wine and coffee included! Their Francs 75 menu consists of 'garbure (Gascon meat and vegetable soup), chariot de hors d'oeuvres, poisson, cuisse de canard grillé (grilled duck), croustade à l'Armagnac (brandy flavoured pastry)'.

Puycasquier (H–5) is a village 20 km northeast of Auch which has had many Gallo–Roman and Merovingian finds. The Count of Fezensaquet built the fortified bastide for the English in the thirteenth century with ramparts and a square called 'La Breche des Anglais'. The market hall, Château de St. Pé and thirteenth century church are of interest. The fête patronale of St. Ardon is on 30th July. The pilgrimage of Gaillan is on 27th April. The Relais Gascon run by the Fourcade family, Tel. 62.65.16.06, offers meals from Francs 45 including wine and coffee.

Réjaumont (G–5) just west of the N 21, north of Auch, was an English bastide founded in 1292 with a charter identical to Fleurance.

Riscle (B–6) The word 'risclo' in Gascon was used for a stone barrier to funnel fish into a net. Riscle is in wine country, with Madiran due south and St. Mont and Tursan due west. It is classified not only as a 'village fleuri', but better still it is a 'village que j'aime'. There are many large fairs and fêtes including the fireworks of St. Jean on 22nd June, fête des fleurs on Ascension day, courses and corridas. Being on the river Adour there are fishing competitions and 'sports nautiques'. Worth a visit.

La Romieu (F–3) Prehistoric finds and site called La Nauterie prove that this was a very old Iberian town. Now known for two châteaux (q.v) and the fourteenth century collegiate church and cloisters of St. Pierre (q.v). For an ecclesiastical small town it is surprising to find Mardi gras celebrated at Easter, on the 30th September, on the 1st November and at Christmas as well as a Cavalcade (a historical événement) held on Palm Sunday. There are two restaurants here – Le Grenier d'Alexane run by M. About, Tel. 62.68.22.33 with a menu from Francs 48 wine included and Le Camp de Florence run by the Mijnsbergen family, Tel. 62.28.15.58 with menus from Francs 43 including wine. This Dutch couple offer the Francs 75 menu with 'potage, salade Florence, moules gratinées (mussels with hot cheese sauce), confit de poule, légumes, table de desserts.' La Romieu is one of the major sights of the Gers – an essential visit.

Roquebrune (E–6) is west of the D 4, south of Vic–Fezensac. The third century temple of Mont-Joie dates from Gallo-Roman times, dedicated to the Eastern deities of Cybèle and Mithras.

Roquelaure (G–6) The oppidum of La Sioutat dates from the Iron Age. A Gallo-Roman villa of the same name has frescoes of the Pompeian style and furnishings dating from the first century BC to the second century AD. The château is noteworthy (q.v).

Saint Clar (H–4) is an English bastide town founded in 1289 by the Bishop of Lectoure. There are many Gallo-Roman sites here called Frans, Empourruche and Bénazide. Saint Clar knew prosperity in the seventeenth/eighteenth century due to its manufacture of 'sargette' or cotton-tape. More recently, with Mauvezin, it shares the honours of leading producer of garlic. On Thursdays is held the second largest garlic market in the whole of France. Visit 'Art Village' near the market which sells the widest range of Armagnacs, table wines, Floc and confits d'oie in the whole of Gascony, Tel. 62.66.48.22.

In Saint Clar try the restaurant Hotel Rison run by Mme Petit, Tel. 62.66.40.21 with a menu from Francs 45 including wine, 'potage, hors d'oeuvres, pot au feu (baked beef and vegetables), rôti de veau (roast lamb), légumes et dessert.'

Saint-Elix-Theux (F-9) has many traces of the Roman occupation: in the villa la Grange dating from the first century AD are mosaics, an altar, sculpted heads, pottery and ceramics. It recently won the 1st prize for 'village fleuri' in Aquitaine. The cult of St. Eutrope, patron of handicapped persons, have a religious fête here on the 30th April.

Saint Lary (F-6) is the Gascon version of St. Hilaire. This little fortified hamlet is on the D 930 northwest from Auch. A Gallo-Roman pile eleven metres in height and a fourteenth century Gascon château are of interest.

Saint Médard (G-2) has many Neolithic and Gallo-Roman remains including the mosaics of Le Gleyzette. The chapel of Notre Dame d'Esclaux is still a pilgrimage point in May of each year. This 'village fleuri' is on a hill overlooking the river Gers.

Saint Mont (A-6) A small hillside village with picturesque Gascon houses, an eighteenth century priory (on the tenth century site), two Gascon châteaux, a noted church (q.v) and of course the well known wine co-operative of Plaimont (Plaisance-Aignan-St. Mont). The Hotel Restaurant Auberge du Village run by the Iceta family, Tel. 62.69.62.59, offers a menu from Francs 45, wine and coffee included. 'Garbure (Gascony meat and vegetable soup), charcuterie (assorted pork derivatives) or crudités (sliced raw vegetables), poule farcie (stuffed chicken), légumes, fromage ou dessert'.

Samatan (J–8) like Lombez was a pilgrim halt. It now has five châteaux including Latour (q.v) and Pradel (where the writer Belleforest lived and worked, who probably supplied William Shakespeare with the plot for Hamlet and other plays). Samatan is nicknamed 'The Mecca of Gras' due to its foie gras markets held on the first and third Monday of every month. These are the largest in the whole of the southwest of France. There are many fêtes, fairs, concours and marchés in Samatan.

91

Saramon (H–8) A fortified village with the arcaded central square, old market hall and several renaissance houses.

Sarragachies (B–6) The curious name derives from the Latin word for 'colline couverte de menthe' (mint). It has the accolade 'Coq d'argent "village de France"'. The pilgrimage to Notre Dame de Laleugue takes place on the 15th August.

Sarrant (J–5) was the Gallo-Roman town of Sarracis and it is still an interesting fortified village with polygonal shaped walls, fourteenth century town gatehouse and two fifteenth century Gascon châteaux. It is on the border with Tarn and Garonne near the rivers Gimone and Sarrampion. The restaurant Auberge du Donjon run by the Durville family, Tel. 62.06.99.50, has meals from Francs 45 including wine and coffee.

Sauveterre (I–9) Prehistoric fossilised mastodens were found in this hill top village. The chapel of St. Christopher among the cypress trees is a scene of pilgrimage each year by car owners!

Seissan (G–8) is on the D 929 south from Auch. It has many Gallo-Roman sites, at le Glisia with mosaics, tiles, bricks and a villa. There are three Gascon châteaux, one with a twelfth century keep and romanesque chapel. The Thursday markets for foie gras from November to February are well known. The Hotel des Pyrénées run by the Note family, Tel. 62.66.20.35, offers meals from Francs 46 with wine included. Their Francs 100 menu includes 'soupe, salade gasconne, brochette de coeurs d'oie (goose hearts on skewers), magret (sliced goose in aspic) or confit d'oie (goose liver) et dessert.'

Solomiac (I–5) is a fourteenth century bastide village and 'village fleuri' on the D 928 on the eastern borders of the Gers.

Tillac (E–8) is a small pretty fortified bastide on the D 3 northwest of Miélan. Technically it is now a 'village-rue' because of its shape. It has a keep, the Tour de l'Horloge, fortified town gates and several half timbered houses. Worth a visit.

Valence-sur-Baise (E–4) has the Gallo-Roman site of Glézia, mosaics, coins, pottery and Roman weights and measures (museum q.v). The thirteenth century fortified bastide was founded in 1274 by the Count of Armagnac and the Abbot of Flaran for the English, although the town was held alternately by both sides. The main square, Hotel de Ville, the town gates 'Espagne', the tower du Guardes (one of four Gascon châteaux) and above all the incomparable abbey of Flaran (q.v) are excellent reasons for a visit.

Vic-Fezensac (E–5) The words 'le Vicus' mean large village in Gascon. It is a bustling town known for its Armagnac (Gélas, Trepout) and at Pentecost its corridas, cavalcade and horse breeding (and horse fair). Its Fête de la Saint Mathieu is in the third week of September. There are nine Gascon châteaux and the romanesque church of St. Pierre. The wine co-op is near the rugby ground and race course north of the town on the way to Condom.

CHAPTER SEVEN:
GERS PAST AND PRESENT

The Gallo-Roman period has left many traces behind in the Gers. The hundreds of feudal 'mottes' still to be seen (Lannux for example) are ditches with the earth forming a minor defensive barrier, probably with château fort on top. Practically all of them are overgrown with grass, bushes and occasionally trees. The Gallo-Roman 'piles' are at Biran, Roquebrune, St. Lary and Lasserre (Ordan-Larroque). Amongst many villa mosaics the most colourful are probably at Séviac (Montréal) but see also St. Elix-Theux. In Auch, Eauze and Lectoure the pagan bull-worship altars can still be seen. Pagan temples are scattered over the region including Escorneboeuf and Montjoie. Many of these artefacts and finds are to be seen in the score of museums mentioned at the end of this chapter.

The romanesque ecclesiastical art-form in the Gers does not scale the heights of Burgundy since the Gascons have never been rich. Nor have they had the stone available to construct superb buildings in quantity. Finally, though all France has suffered horribly at the hands of foreigners and their own inter-tribal wars (political and religious), the southwest had the extra tribulations of the barbarians (whose fleets arrived *every* spring for several hundred years) and the Hundred Years War with the English. These endless wars have taken their toll of the early architectural sites. So what is left? The abbey of Flaran is an excellent example of the Cistercian architecture. Romanesque churches of note include Sabazan, Vopillon, Mouchan and Lialores: amongst the village churches Luzannet, Bouzonnet and Ste. Germaine are notable. The large town cathedrals at Lectoure, Condom, Mirande, Eauze, Fleurance and La Romieu should be on everybody's travel list, as well as the two redbrick Toulousain style abbeys of Lombez and Simorre.

Arnaut de Moles was a famous Gascon artist who was born at St. Sever in 1465. His stained glass windows can be seen still in half a dozen fine churches in the Gers including Auch Cathedral, Fleurance, Simorre and others. His pupils who followed his style left their mark too in churches such as Gimont, Lombez and Seissan. His rich colours range from traditional reds and blues to a marvellous golden-yellow which is rarely seen elsewhere.

Architectural feast

There are such a wealth of architectural sights in the Gers (and the Landes) that only MH (Monument historique) or IMH (inscrit à l'inventaire des Monuments historiques) sights have been included. In many of the small villages the church is frequently shut, and the key may be with the 'voisin', the 'forgeron', 'à l'auberge', but all the village will know *who* has the key

The département of the Gers has more bastide towns than any other département in France. About two thirds were built by the English in the period 1250–1315 and the remainder by the French (mainly by Philippe le Bel at the end of the thirteenth century). Amongst the dozens mentioned in this book one can single out Montreal, Mauvezin, Gimont, Cologne, Valence and Fleurance which have retained the classic architecture of the rectangular grid pattern of streets and houses, with a central square, usually with the 'Halle' which is a stone built, occasionally wooden covered market place, and a fortified church. Each corner of the square will have cornices and arcades. The exception to the rule is the circular bastide of Fources. Some bastides will have remnants of the town walls or ramparts and gatehouses. Some of the best examples of the fortified villages or keeps (donjons) that guarded them are to be found at Bassoues, the tower of Termes, the superb fortified village of Larressingle and the château of Herrebouc (at St. Jean de Poutge). Typical Gascon châteaux in the no mans land between English Gascony and the rest of France are to be seen at le Tauzia, Mansencome and Balarin. Rarely were the château-forts built for beauty and comfort. They were down to earth strong solid defensive structures in which the frightened peasant farmers sheltered when the Black Prince was on one of his 'chevauchées', or simply if the local baron changed his mind. A 'pot' or two of gold and some promises, and an Armagnac, Albret, Foix or Montesquiou would be leading his troops in a different direction. Many villages still have half timbered houses, windmills and occasional watermills. The eighteenth century classic 'hotels' or town mansions can be seen in Auch, Condom and Lectoure. Some villages are being actively restored with care and taste, such as Fourcès and Lagarde-Fimarcon.

Châteaux and castles

Bassoues (D–7) The château of the Archbishops has an imposing fourteenth century fortified keep (donjon), 38 metres high, whose five storeys tower over the fortified bastide. This is the finest example of military architecture in the Gers. There are buttresses, ramparts, a curtain wall, and fourteenth century well (indispensable). There are panoramic views of the Pyrénées from the keep's platform.

Béraut (F–4) the sixteenth century château of Lasserre just southeast of Condom is worth a visit.

Bonas (F–5) The eighteenth century château is approached by an alley of cedars. The facade, entrance hall, library, interior staircases, and the 'salle de César' are of interest.

Cassaigne (E–4) The château was built in 1247 as a country house for the Bishops of Condom. It has a huge vaulted kitchen, wine cellar, renaissance windows and many original thirteenth century walls. It is due south of Larressingle near the D 931. See also the nearby Château de Léberon of the same period with three circular towers.

Caussens (F–3) The original château of Mons was built in 1285 for King Edward I. It was then owned by the Bouzet family, and more recently by Maréchal Lannes, one of Napoleon's favourite generals, who fought in Egypt, Spain, Jena and Austerlitz. Now owned by the Chamber of Commerce of Gers it produces commercial and experimental wine varietals and Armagnac. Open 1st July to 30th September.

Cazaux-Savès (J–8) The sixteenth century Château de Caumont was owned for many years by the Dukes of Epernon. Set in a park it has three main battlements around a fortified courtyard, six watch towers of various shapes and sizes, and four pepper-pot towers. It is one of the classic large scale Gascon châteaux, overlooking the valley of the Save, 2 km northeast of the village.

Condom (E–3) Neighbouring châteaux of note include Goalard, du Luc, Cahuzac and Peyriac. There are another dozen within a few miles radius.

Flamarens (H–3) This fifteenth century château is being restored. It is a few kilometres east of Saint Mère in the north east of the department. Some of the original twelfth century battlements can still be seen. Gascon lords who have owned it include the Viscounts of Lomagne, Durfort, Galard and Grossoles.

Fources (D–3) The fifteenth century château by the side of the river Auzoue is being restored.

Lagardère (E–4) A thirteenth century typical château gascon on three floors – a bit battered but worth a visit, just east of the D 35, south of Condom.

Lannepax (D–5) has the thirteenth century château of Gajan with crenellated keep.

Larressingle (E–3) is a few kilometres west of Condom. The high walled ramparts tower above the moat, encircling a small medieval village reached only by a drawbridge and fortified gatehouse. The twelfth century keep has four walls and staircase on three levels. Open all the year round, no entrance fee, a visit to this exquisite medieval castle-village is essential.

Lavardens (F–5) On the remains of a tenth century château

97

gascon has been implanted an elegant seventeenth century residence of the Maréchal de Roquelaure (1620). It has unique Moorish-Arab flagstones. This is a huge dominant castle on a rocky hilltop overlooking the valley of Guzerde, reached by the D 148.

L'Isle-Bouzon (H–4) Three km due east on the D 178 is the castle of Gramont which is a few hundred metres outside the Gers. Now restored and repaired, this elegant château belonged to Simon de Montfort in 1215. Well worth a visit.

Maignaut-Tauzia (F–4) Just south of Condom the thirteenth century château of Tauzia has a square keep with sixteenth century facade. Although battered it is worth a visit.

Mansencome (E–4) This hamlet south of Cassaigne has the fourteenth century Gascon château of the same name and the classic seventeenth century Château de Busca-Maniban (and noted chapel) set in huge gardens.

Marsan (H–6) Just north of the N 124 east of Auch, this mainly seventeenth century château set in a park was owned by the Montesquiou family for centuries.

Mas d'Auvignon (F–4) Near St. Puy this thirteenth century English-built château still has four hexagonal towers, a gate-house and walls standing.

Miramont-Latour (H–5) The thirteenth century Château de Latour is on the D 21, southeast of Fleurance; and the Château de Miramont, nineteenth century (and hexagonal pigeonnier) is of note.

Monfort (I–5) is on the D 654 northwest from Mauvezin. The Château d'Esclignac is mainly fifteenth century set in a park with lake. Two huge courtyards, a drawbridge and several towers flanking the main buildings make this an interesting stop.

Montréal (D–3) has the thirteenth century Gascon Château de Balarin and there are six others in the vicinity.

La Romieu (F–3) The Cardinal's palace dates from the fourteenth century, the Château de Madirac and de St. Aignan are both sixteenth century.

St. Avit-Frandat (G–3) The Château de Lacassagne is seventeenth century. The 'salle des Chevaliers de Malte', in good condition, is where the Order of St. Jean of Jerusalem met 'en grand conseil'.

St. Georges (J–6) The Château du Bartas was constructed in 1568 by the Gascon poet Guillaume Saluste du Bartas' family. Six other châteaux are near this little hamlet.

St. Jean-Poutge (E–6) is on the N 124 northwest from Auch. The fourteenth century Château de Herrebouc, built of golden yellow stone, was a watch tower in the valley of the river Baise. Restored in the sixteenth century it is worth a visit.

Ste. Mère (H–3) is on the N 21 north of Lectoure. Perched on a hill overlooking the valley of the Gers and with a view of the Pyrénées, this Gascon château was built by the Bishop of Lectoure in AD 1280, and subsequently was owned by the Dukes of Leynes. It is in surprisingly good condition and merits a visit.

Samatan (J–8) The Château de Latour is seventeenth century with good furnishings, pictures, chapel and pigeonniers. Quite close is the Château du Pradel, where the writer Belleforest lived and worked.

Termes-d'Armagnac (B–6) Thibaut d'Armagnac, Baron de Termes, was a Gascon follower of Jeanne d'Arc and fought for her at Orleans against the English. The high keep on six levels, 36 metres high, can be seen from afar. There is a museum in the same building and 'Le Relais de la Tour' restaurant in the village. During the summer the Tower is illuminated and concerts and exhibitions take place in the grounds.

Terraube (G–4) is southwest from Lectoure on the D 42 and the thirteenth century Gascon château has been repaired and restored in the sixteenth, seventeenth and eighteenth centuries. It is a strong square building with terraces and stables set in formal gardens. There are guided visits.

Other châteaux of note are Marin and St. Cricq, both near Auch, Beaumont (E–3), Bellegarde (G–9), Betplan (D–9),

Bézéril (I–8), Cazeneuve (D–4), Clermont-Savès (J–7), Laas (I–8), Lagarde (G–3), Loubersan (F–8), Lupiac (D–6) (Château de Castelmore), Magnas (H–4), Montesquiou (E–7) (Château de la Motte), Pouylebon (E–8), Puycasquier (H–5) (Château de St. Pé), and Roquefort (G–5).

Cathedrals, abbeys and splendid churches

There are nearly 500 towns and villages in the Gers. They all have a church and many have two, three, even seven. A town like Condom has twenty one, including the cathedral, a convent and chapels. So it is a difficult task to condense the ecclesiastical sights to a manageable size. There are 28 Monuments Historiques and another 28 IMH churches, and the final choice has been made from this short list of rather over 50.

Auch (G–7) The fifteenth century Cathedral of Ste. Marie stands fair and square at the top of the hill at one end of the main square overlooking the river Gers. The tombs of the evangelised saints of Taurin, Austinde and Leothade are here. In this huge flamboyant gothic church, measuring 105 metres long and 40 metres wide, the two unusual features are the Arnaud de Moles renaissance stained glass windows – 58 kneeling figures – and the 1500 sculpted wooden biblical characters in the choir stalls. The grand organs, the crypt and the sixteenth century eastern facade are of note. Also in Auch one should see the Carmelite chapel (now a library), the chapel of the Jesuit College (now a school), the priory of St. Orens and the convent of the cordeliers (with cloister and chapter house) and the Jacobin convent with chapel and cloisters.

Barran (F–7) The old collegiate of St. Jean is mainly sixteenth century, but has a fortified clock tower with an unusual spiral slated roof with gables. Barran is an interesting fortified bastide village with ramparts, bridge, moats and crenellated town gates, on the D 943 west of Auch.

Beaumarchés (C–7) The fourteenth century gothic church in Philippe le Bel's bastide village (on the N 946 southeast of

Plaisance), has a polygonal chevet, a nave with five traverses and a massive unfinished clock tower.

Belloc-St. Clamens (F–9) is a hamlet southeast of Mirande. The romanesque eleventh century rural chapel of St. Clamens has a white marble sculpted coffin used as the altar and a fourth century 'Cippe' funeral sarcophagus.

Berdous-Ponsampère (F–8) In 1137 a Cistercian abbey was built here south of Mirande, and the chapel, part of the old cloister and a staircase are of note.

Bernède (A–6) is on the Gers/Landes borders, a hamlet with sixteenth century church of flamboyant gothic style. The clock tower is 32 metres high and towers above the valley of the Adour.

Boular (H–8) is a hamlet on the D 12 southwest of Gimont. In AD 1140 the order of Fontevrault built a huge abbey here under the auspices of the Archbishop of Auch. It is still in sound condition. One of the old towers is reserved for abandoned infants.

Caillavet (E–6) is southwest of St. Jean Poutge, a hill-top village of 160 souls. Besides a nineteenth parish church of no architectural interest there are two MH chapels, de Tabaux and also St. Orens de Laas, both of twelfth century romanesque style.

Caupenne-d'Armagnac (B–5) is northwest of Nogaro and has a curious 'Annexe-eglise d'Espargnet' of the twelfth century with a romanesque north door and fourth century white marble paleo-Christian sarcophagus, now serving as the tomb of the fourteenth century Bishop of Aire.

Condom (E–3) The renaissance Cathedral of St. Pierre was built between 1506 and 1531 and has a large single nave without a crossing. The crenellated clock tower and cloisters are of note. Also in Condom one should see the twelfth century church of Ste. Germaine, that of St. Anthony of Lialores and the Carmelite church (let alone the other 17 in the immediate neighbourhood!).

101

Eauze (C–4) The gothic Cathedral of St. Luperc was built by Benedictine monks with Gallo-Roman masonry and finished in 1521. The stained glass east window is by Arnaud de Moles.

Fleurance (H–4) The gothic fourteenth century church of St. Laurent has three naves, many pilgrim cockleshell sculptures and three 'vitraux' by Arnaud de Moles. The fourteenth century facade has withstood the ravages of the religious wars.

Gimont (I–7) The fourteenth century church is built of stone and brick, but it is the sixteenth century church Notre Dame de Cahuzac that has stained glass windows attributed to Arnaud de Moles.

L'Isle-Jourdain (K–7) in the farthest eastern corner of the département on the river Save has a classic collegiate church, mainly eighteenth century but with a fifteenth century clock tower from the original pilgrim church.

Larressingle (E–3) Inside this medieval jewel is a small fortified twelfth century romanesque church, originally dedicated to St. Sigismond, King of the Burgondes, who was martyred here by Clodomir, King of Orleans, son of Clovis about AD 516–523. It is a simple chapel-church in a beautiful setting.

Lectoure (G–3) Until the French Revolution the quadrangular clock tower of the thirteenth century Cathedral of St. Gervais et St. Protais soared up to a height of 90 metres. Now the spire is only 50 metres high, but still can be seen for many miles around. Originally built on a pagan temple site, the church just survived the ravages of King Louis XI's troops in 1473 battling with the Counts of Armagnac, when the population was butchered. The church was reconstructed and the nave is gothic of the late fifteenth century, and is 21 metres high. The choir dates from the sixteenth and seventeenth centuries and is pure flamboyant gothic style, opening onto nine chapels.

Lombez (I–8) The handsome red brick Cathedral of Ste. Maria was built in 1317 on the model of the Jacobin church in Toulouse. The treasury and font are of the thirteenth century.

The hexagonal clock tower has 12 bells and measures 43 metres in height.

Marciac (D–8) The fourteenth century church is of note as is the fifteenth century convent chapel of the Augustins which has an octagonal church tower, facade, doors and cloister dating from the fourteenth century.

Mirande (F–8) The fortified fifteenth century gothic church of Notre Dame has strong flying buttresses and a clock tower of note.

Monfort (I–5) The romanesque thirteenth century church has an octagonal clock tower, single nave and polygonal choir of note.

Montréal (D–3) has two churches of note: one fifteenth century gothic and the other the twelfth century romanesque St. Pierre de Genens.

Mouchan (E–4) is southwest of Condom. The romanesque church of St. Austrésegile dates from the eleventh century (clocktower) being the oldest in the original archbishopric of Auch. An order of Cluny dependant on St. Orens-d'Auch was responsible for building this church. Prayer to the Saint is said to help nervous ailments.

Nogaro (B–5) The eleventh century romanesque church also has a cloister of note.

Peyrusse-Grande (D–7) is on the D 102, east of Plaisance. The eleventh century romanesque priory of St. Mamert has rich sculptures and roman windows. Peyrusse-Massas (G–6) and Peyrusse-Vieille (D–7) also have small romanesque churches.

Le Romeiu (F–3) The fourteenth century collegiate church of St. Pierre, east of Condom is one of the finest ecclesiastical sights in the Gers. The sacristy is covered with gothic frescoes and the cloister also dates from the fourteenth century. An essential visit.

Saint Mont (A–6) The priory founded in AD 1050 by Bernard

103

Tumapeler, Count of Armagnac, has been restored, and the village church is half eleventh century romanesque and half twelfth century gothic style.

Sainte Dode (E–9) is east of Miélan on the D 127. The church has frescoes, reredos, bas-relief and old paintings of note.

Simorre (H–9) The thirteenth century red brick fortified church was built in the Toulousan architectural style with octagonal clock tower, sculpted choir stalls and several stained glass windows attributed to Arnaud de Moles.

Tasque (C–7) is situated in the valley of the Arros north of Plaisance. The original Benedictine abbey was destroyed, rebuilt and destroyed by the barbarians, but the church still standing has an eleventh century romanesque nave, a twelfth century church door with sculpted tympan, capitals and Byzantine cross on the cemetery gate.

Valence sur Baise (E–4) is due south of Condom on the D 930. The Cistercian abbey of Flaran is set in woods with a large formal garden. The Order of Citeaux built this fine romanesque church and cloisters in 1151. Much damaged in the Hundred Years War, in the religious wars and by the citoyens of the French Revolution, it has been carefully repaired and restored. Open for visits all the year round except Tuesday.

Other churches of note are: Aignan (C–6), Arblade (B–5), Aubiet (H–7), Beaumont (E–3), Castéra-Verduzan (F–5), Cazauban (B–3), Faget-Abbatial (H–8), Labejan (F–8), Lahitte (H–6), Lasserade (C–7), Lussan (H–7), Magnan (B–5), Manas-Bastanous (E–10), Mont d'Astarac (G–10), Mauvezin (I–6), Miradoux (H–3), Pessan (G–7), Riscle (B–6), St. Anthoine (I–2), St. Arailles (E–7), St. Christaud (E–8), St. Créac (I–4), Toujouse (A–5) and Tournecoupe (I–4). They are ALL classified churches with unusual features (murals, frescoes, chevets, sarcophagus etc.) or simple romanesque or gothic classic architecture!

Museums

Auch (G–7) Museum of Art and Archaeology in the Musée des Jacobins (convent). Closed Monday.
Museum de la Résistance, rue Pagodeoutes. Closed Monday, weekends.

Bassoues (D–7) Museum of the Gascon Village.

Belmont (D–6) Village musée scolaire – ask at Mairie.

Campagne-d'Armagnac (C–4) Wines and Armagnac exhibition at the Château.

Castéra-Verduzan (F–5) Musée Lannelongue, natural history, beaux arts.

Cazeneuve (D–4) Musée Gascon, archaeology, regional paintings, costumes.

Condom (E–3) Museum of Armagnac production and history.

Eauze (C–4) Museum of local archaeology, Gallo-Roman finds.

Flamarens (H–3) Ecology museum of the Lomagne.

Gimont (I–7) Musée cantonal.

Jégun (F–5) Musée rural.

Lectoure (G–3) Musée Lapidaire Gallo-Roman (see collection of tauroboles).
Salle du souvenir Maréchal Lannes in Hotel de Ville (Napoleon's general).

Marciac (D–8) Museum of Natural History.

Mauvezin (I–6) Musée archaeologique.

Mirande (F–8) Museum of Beaux Arts (excellent collection of paintings).
Musée of local history.

Montréal (D–3) Museum Gallo-Roman finds.

Ordan-Larroque (F–6) Museum Gallo-Roman finds.

Pessan (G–7) Museum Gallo-Roman finds.

St. Michel (F–9) Museum of taxidermy (local wild animals).

Sauveterre (I–9) Museum of cavalry (at Ressequies).

Seissan (G–8) Museum of art and local traditions.

Simorre (H–9) Musée paleontologique.

Valence-sur-Baise (E–4) At the Abbey of Flaran, museum of St. Jaques de Compostella.

In the small villages ask at the Mairie or Syndicat d'Initiative for times of opening, and in the larger towns at the tourist office. Some of the smaller museums open only in the summer. The larger ones shut usually on Tuesday, occasionally on Monday.

CHAPTER EIGHT:
THE FRUITS OF THE VINE

A decade or two back most people would not have heard of the wines of the Gers département. The wine trade dismissed them as being thin and acidic and, being mainly white, fit only for distillation into Armagnac.

Now due to a variety of recent events the situation has changed dramatically. The major retail supermarkets, and leading wine chains such as Oddbins, Roberts & Cooper and Peter Dominic, and specialist importers such as the Wine Society, Berry Bros & Rudd, Lay & Wheeler, Haynes, Hanson & Clark, Bordeaux Direct, Majestic Wine Warehouses, all have one thing in common. They import and sell the white wine called 'Vin de Pays des Côtes de Gascogne' for a price well under £2.50 per bottle. Wine writers describe it as 'perfumed fruit, soft and a really refreshing green taste.'

The second phenomenon is quite simply called 'Madiran', which was granted Appellation Controlée status in 1948 and has very strict controls including a minimum maturity of a year before shipment. This fine red wine is slowly becoming known in the UK. Finally the Côtes de Saint Mont was given VDQS status as recently as 1981 and is now being imported into the UK.

Behind the totally altered situation lie the endeavours of several individuals and their wine-growing companies – a fascinating story.

Production figures

The total annual production of wine in the Gers is 2 million hectolitres of which about 160,000 hectolitres are distilled to

107

produce 40,000 hectolitres of Armagnac. Rather over 20,500 hectares (50,000 acres) of vineyards are under cultivation. Madiran accounts for 45,000 hectolitres from 1200 hectares (3000 acres), Côtes de St. Mont 28,000 hectolitres from 600 hectares (1500 acres), Côtes de Gascogne 40,000 hecto-litres from 600 hectares (1500 acres) and the rest is ordinary vins de Pays. Of the total amount the twenty co-operatives produce 35% of the total production and 15% of the Appellation Controlée wines. Their annual production is nearly 700,000 hectolitres of which 25% is distilled for Armagnac.

Main co-operatives

Towns	Hls.	Tel. No.
St. Mont (61,000) Plaisance (25,000)		
Aignan (50,000) called Plaimont	136,000	62.69.75.04
Condom, Lectoure & Montestruc	115,000	62.28.12.16
Eauze	111,000	62.09.82.08
Nogaro	100,000	62.09.01.79
Cazaubon	80,000	62.69.50.14
Vic-Fezensac	64,000	62.06.31.01
Panjas	62,000	62.09.07.11
Castelnau d'Auzan	8,000	62.29.22.29

The Federation des Caves Co-op du Gers is at 32190 Vic Fezensac, President M. Dauge, Tel. 62.06.31.01.

The areas of vignobles are mainly in the southwest of Gers around Riscle and St. Mont and in the northwest around Condom, Eauze, Nogaro and Panjas.

The cépages (grape varietals) are Ugni blanc, Colombard and Listan for Côtes de Gascogne blanc. For Côtes de Gascogne rouge, the Tannat, Cabernet and Fer Servadou; for Côtes de Saint Mont the red cépage is the same, with Tannat 70%, Cabernet Franc 10%, Cabernet Sauvignon 10% and Fer Servacou 10%; finally the cépages for Madiran are Tannat 60%, Cabernets 20% and Fer Servadou 20%.

The Cave des Producteurs Réunis, 32110 Nogaro, Tel. 62.09.01.79, is situated 1 km west of the town on the

Route d'Aire N 124. There is a splendid vintage 'alambic' mobile still, and the caveau dégustation in the main courtyard. The co-op was formed in 1963 and they have 500 member vignerons farming about 1500 hectares (4000 acres) and an annual production of over 100,000 hectolitres, of which nearly half is distilled to produce 12,000 hectolitres of Armagnac. Although they produce an excellent vin de Gascogne blanc Colombard, their main business is in Armagnac (de Castelfort) and derivatives, cocktail Gascon, aperitif Pinkger and Floc, and various fruits in Armagnac. The Directeur General is M. Jean Claude Gaillard and the export director (20% of sales) is M. Jacques Barthe, Tel. 62.09.01.79. David Scatchard Ltd., 4 Temple Court, Liverpool L2 6PY are their UK agents.

The Union des Producteurs Plaimont, Saint Mont (A–6), 32400 Riscle, Tel. 62.69.78.87, is the most sophisticated co-operative in Gascony, perhaps in southwest France. M. Andre Dubosc is the Directeur Commercial. The original co-op of St. Mont was formed in 1947, and Aignan and Plaisance in 1951. The three were linked together in 1974 and now have 1350 viticulteur members farming 2000 hectares (5000 acres) and collectively producing 136,000 hectolitres. They aim to produce 200,000 hectolitres in the not too distant future. They produce no Armagnac but concentrate (1) on Madiran (180 hectares out of a total of 1,200) and with 9000 hectolitres have a 20% share of that market, (2) on Côtes de St. Mont and with 95% of this market were themselves responsible for obtaining VDQS status in 1981. They have 600 hectares (1500 acres) under production of Côtes de St. Mont producing just under 25,000 hectolitres (80% red) and finally (3) Côtes de Gascogne Vin de Pays grown on 1200 hectares (3000 acres) up to 90,000 hectolitres of mainly white wine. They claim to have nearly 80% of the Côtes de Gascogne wine market. Their Colombard from 150 hectares is well known in the UK and is sold by Marks and Spencer, Fuller Smith and Turner, Master Cellar of Croydon, Lay & Wheeler and Haynes, Hanson & Clark. It is described as 'fresh, flowery, slightly peardroppy nose and light apply fruit on the palate'. Their Côtes de St. Mont is stocked by Tesco. Their wines ex-caveau

109

are priced from Francs 3.80 a litre for ordinary vin de table, the VDQS Côtes de St. Mont at Francs 7.30 per bottle, the VDQS Côtes de St. Mont Tradition at Francs 11.50 the bottle and Madiran from Francs 15 the bottle. Vintage wines were 1983, 1984, and 1985. Quality control is paramount at this co-op. They are maturing and blending a variety of wines – Côtes de Gascogne, Côtes de St. Mont and Madiran from half a dozen cépages and over 1300 vinyards. Lay & Wheeler describe the Côtes de St. Mont blanc as 'lively, dry and firm. Remarkably elegant for an inexpensive wine', and the rouge as 'mouthfilling, juicy red – a well-made quality wine.' The UK Agents are Castle Growers Ltd., Anglia Vintners, 109 Unthank Road, Norwich NR2 2PE, Tel. 0603 625917.

The Co-operative Armagnacaise Viticole d'Eauze, 60 route de Nogaro, 32800 Eauze, Tel. 62.09.82.08, founded 1947, is one of the four largest co-ops in the Gers, with production of about 110,000 hectolitres each year. They have 400 vigneron members cultivating 1000 hectares (2500 acres). Their stock of maturing Armagnac eau-de-vie is 7,000 hectolitres. Their brand name is Le Chevalier Gascon. They also produce the aperitifs Lou Traouc and Floc de Gascogne and an orange Armagnac liqueur called Ambrée.

The Cave Co-operative Condom-Lagraulet-Gondrin, Avenue des Mousquetaires, Condom, Tel. 62.28.12.16, have the usual range of vins de pays from Francs 3.75, Côtes de Gascogne from Francs 7.85 and their own Côtes du Condomois from Francs 9.50, as well as Armagnac and Floc de Gascogne. Their annual production of about 115,000 hecto-litres puts them in the top four in Gers.

Independent vineyards

Now we turn to the individual growers in the region. The family of Grassa own the Domaine du Tariquet, 32800 Eauze, an attractive property about 15 km southeast of the town. Their other Domaines are De Pouy, des Landes, le Prada (selected for the Wine Society), Domaine de la Jalousie (ASDA), Domaine de Rieux (Berry Bros and Findlater, Mackie Todd), Domaine de Planterieu (Waitrose) and Domaine

THE FRUITS OF THE VINE

D'Escoubes (Tesco). Founded in 1912, the family farm 65 hectares (170 acres) and produce 7000 hectolitres of which 4500 are Côtes de Gascogne. The company is run by Yves Grassa, and his dynamic daughter is the sales director responsible for making wines of the Côtes de Gascogne so popular in the UK. The cépages are Ugni Blanc, Colombard and Gros Manseng, and the wine is described as 'attractive, fresh, lively white wine with a fragrant, lemony nose, a soft fresh fruity, lemony palate with a good grassy-fruity finish. Very characterful wine from a usually characterless grape'. Waitrose Supermarkets stock Domaine Planterieu 1986 and retail Marie-Thérèse Grassa's wine at £2.15 described as 'light dry grapy with slight petillance enhancing its freshness'. The Domaine du Tariquet 1986 Cuvee Bois sells at £3.95 described as a 'well made dry full-bodied wine with depth of flavour from being matured in the wood'. UK stockists include Threshers, Bibendum, Morrisons, Tanners, Arthur Purchase, Peatling & Cawdron. Their Agents are Thierry & Tatham.

Other noted growers of Côtes de Gascogne blanc include Domaine Mesté Duran supplying Sainsburys in Magnums retailing at £4.95; and Domaine d'Aula of Condom also owned by Patrick Aurin and shipped by Etab. Gelas; Domaine Moureou at Maumusson 32400; Domaine d'Entras at Ayguetinte; and Château de Cassaigne owned by the Faget family. Majestic Wine Warehouses describe their Côtes de Gascogne blanc as '... and if you thought Gascony was all onions and berets ... this surprisingly sophisticated dry white will change your mind'.

The Château de Mons at Caussens near Condom (between the D 7 and D 654) is owned by the Chambre d'Agriculture and produces from 64 hectares (170 acres) Armagnac, Floc de Gascogne and red, white and rosé Côtes de Gascogne table wines. This estate is comparable to Ognoas in the Landes – a sensible experimental estate offering help and information to other growers, Tel. 62.29.12.75. J. Cardeillac & C. Baumann of Camaradon supply Domaine de Cassagnoles to Bordeaux Direct. Dulong Frères of Floirac, Gironde supply Majestic Wine with a Côtes de Gascogne blanc retailing at £1.99 a bottle. Côtes de Gascogne rouge is shipped by the negociant

Yvon Mau, 33190 Gironde to Oddbins retailing at £2.19.

Madiran is correctly known as the 'Vin des Pyrénées' since it covers a circular area of 1200 hectares (3000 acres), partly in the départements of the Pyrénées Atlantiques, the Hautes Pyrénées and the Gers. The southernmost village is Lembeye, the western Moncla, the northern Maumusson-Laguian and the eastern Madiran itself. There are 23 small villages altogether. It is a pleasant and attractive area to visit after leaving St. Mont by a minor road south to Maumusson-Laguian (B–7), and then by the D 164 7 km south to Madiran.

The red wine (45,000–60,000 hectolitres) comes from the Tannat grape (which gives its robustness) and Cabernet (which gives it bouquet and finesse). Even before the Compostella pilgrims made much of Madiran in the eleventh–thirteenth centuries, mosaics found in the Gallo-Roman villa of Taron (dating from the third century) show a grape bunch and vine leaves. However the official historical credits go to the Benedictine monks of Marcillac who left Burgundy in the eleventh century and founded the Abbey of Madiran. They grew the wine to use at Mass and the thousands of pilgrims appreciated it. Legend has it that the same monks created the famous Clos Vougeot red wine of Burgundy!

The white wine of the area is called Pacherenc du Vic Bilh and is truly a Pyrenean wine, mainly produced by the Co-op of that name with a small production of 1500 hectolitres from six cépages – Arrufiac, le Gros and le Petit Menseng, le Courbu, le Sauvignon and le Semillon.

One of the reasons why so little Madiran is seen in export markets is that it is relatively expensive. The co-op of St. Mont, who produce 20% of the annual production of Madiran, offer the standard AOC ex caveau at Francs 15, the 1983 vintage at Francs 25, the 1980 vintage Médaille d'Or won in Paris at Francs 29 a bottle. The wine is often kept in oak casks for between four and eight years and is most definitely a wine of quality which compares favourably with many second and third growth clarets from the Gironde.

The most dynamic independent grower in the region is M. Alain Brumont who owns the Château Montus of 31 hectares (75 acres) and the Domaine de Bouscassé

29 hectares (70 acres). Both are near Maumusson, Tel. 62.69.74.67. Including a 5 hectare vineyard to produce Pacherenc du Vic Bilh white wine, the total area under production controlled by M. Brumont is now 64 hectares producing about 44,000 hectolitres per annum. About 1000 oak casks age these fine Madiran wines served by many of the nation's top-class restauranteurs. The Château Montus dates from AD 1330: one of the early Christian martyrs, Sainte Libérale, was crucified in the fourth century in the nearby woods. The wine from this vineyard can age well up to 20 years or more, and comes mainly from the Tannat grape. The Domaine Bouscasse is made up of 60% Tannat, 25% Cabernet Franc, 10% Cabernet Sauvignon and 5% Fer Servadou. Production is 50 to 55 hectolitres per hectare and the wine can mature up to 10 years. Exports now account for 25% of M. Brumont's production and several UK importers sell Alain Brumont's wines in the UK. Sookias & Bertaut sell his Tradition 1982 at £3.95, his Domaine Bouscassé 1982 at £4.30 and the Château Montus at £4.95. Anthony Byrne Wines sell his 1983 and 1984s for between £4.16 and £5.26 a bottle.

Each year there is a Concours des Vins de Madiran organised by the Syndicat des Viticulteurs. The most recent had 65 entries, of which 33 were for the title of Grappe d'Or for the vintage wines of 1985 and 32 for the Bouteille d'Or for the vintage wines between 1976 and 1982. M. Brumont's Château Montus won the Grappe d'Or and he entered his neighbour (Domaine Marty of 2 hectares) and won the Bouteille d'Or award. The St. Mont co-op was fifth.

The 'Chevaliers du Madiran' are a group of 18 producers clustered around Maumusson-Laguian (Gers) owning 300 hectares (750 acres) and producing nearly 2 million bottles a year (15,000 hectolitres). The Brumont family are members. Other leading vignerons are Marc Lafitte owning Domaine Teston (18 hectares) shipping to Prestige Vintners; Jean Ducournau owning Domaine Moureau; and Maurice Captmartin owning Domaine Barejat (13 hectares). M. Crouzet owns Château du Perron (8 hectares) and M. Auguste Vigneau owns Domaine de Pichard (12.5 hectares).

113

The co-op of Vignerons Reunis du Vic-Bilh with 170 hectares is in Crouseilēs-Lembeye in the Pyrénées! Lay & Wheeler import their Madiran wine into the UK.

The last word must be with the French wine writers who describe the red Madiran wines as 'sensuels, charnus et charpentés, avec des arômes de pain grillé, des vins 'virils' par excellence.'

St. Puy (F–4) is a small village of 670 inhabitants on the D 654 between Condom and Fleurance. On the hill over-looking the village is the sixteenth century Château de Monluc which was owned by three English Kings: in 1287 by Edward I, 1307 by Edward II and in 1327 by Edward III. Finally in 1415 Charles V's French troops recaptured the château from the English. The Lassus family own the château and run the firm of Sica-Monluc, Tel. 62.28.55.02. They produce from the Ugni blanc cépage 600,000 bottles a year of an excellent sparkling wine (Vin Sauvage and Brut de Brut). The latter is made by the méthode champenoise and has a label showing the famous Blaise de Monluc (1500–1577) who chased and killed many thousands of wretched Huguenots in Gascony. The Lassus' also produce a Gascon cocktail called Pousse-Rapière which is made of one proportion of their liqueur-Armagnac to six proportions of their Brut de Brut. Purchased locally Vin Sauvage is Francs 23 and Brut Blanc de Blanc Francs 30 per bottle. The liqueur Pousse-Rapière, 24°, sells at Francs 80.

Some French sparkling wines do not travel well. There is no doubt at all that Gascony's 'Vin Sauvage' or Monluc Brut Blanc de Blanc does, since 35% is exported. It tastes like a good second class champagne for a fraction of the price. In the UK Richard Kihl Ltd. are the agents and stockists include Buckingham Wines, and Gerrys Wines, 74 Old Compton Street.

Patrick Aurin, who owns the Domaines of Aula and Mesté-Duran near to Condom, Tel. 62.28.12.98, besides producing Vin de Coteaux de Gascogne, also produces a 'vin mousseux méthode champenoise'.

CHAPTER NINE:
A ROOF OVER YOUR HEAD,
FOOD ON YOUR PLATE

Modest hotels and restaurants

Those noted will have a double bedroom, breakfast and a main meal for about Francs 230 per couple.

Auch (pop. 23,000) The préfecture town has ten hotels and a wide choice of restaurants from the famous Hotel-Restaurant de France where M. André Daguin's exquisite meals wil set you back several hundred francs, to the Brasserie Rugby-Bar. There are four within budget shown in the summary at the end of this chapter: the Paris, the Modern, les Trois Mousquetaires ('cuisine régionale, poissons, paella), and de la Gare. The following restaurants serve meals for around Francs 50 per person. The Lion d'Or, the Paris, les Trois Mousquetaires, de la Gare, les Grenadines ('cuisine régionale'), Les Darolles, Le Palerme, Le Rimbaud, Le Cyrano, Le Montebello, Le Petit Gascon, La Dent d'Oche, Le Gersois and Le Warda. A wide choice, with most of them serving regional dishes. For instance, M. Patrick Bembaron, Restaurant les Grenadines, 165 rue Victor Hugo, Tel. 62.05.48.96, will serve you a Francs 65 menu inclusive of wine, of mixed salad with ham and goose liver, hearts of duck on a skewer and apple pastry.

Condom (pop. 7800) There are three hotels here within budget: the Continental, du Midi and the Lion d'Or. The Restaurant Au Petit Gascon run by the Meulemans family, Tel. 62.28.28.42, offers menus from Francs 50 including soup, duck mousse, grilled chicken with shallots and desert.

Eauze (pop. 4400) The Hotel Henri IV, the L'Armagnac and the Auberge du Guinlet are within budget. At the latter the

Larrouy family, Tel. 62.09.85.99, will offer you menus from Francs 40, wine included. Their Francs 60 menu includes choice of soup, pork derivatives, ragout of guinea fowl, grilled chicken and brandy flavoured pastry.

Fleurance (pop.5800) The Hotel Capelli and Le Chantpie are within budget. The restaurant Chez Pujade, Place de l'Eglise, Tel. 62.06.02.23, offers a menu from Francs 43 with wine included. M. Alphonse Pujade's Francs 75 menu includes 'garbure, omelette aux cèpes, pintade flambé à l'Armagnac, légumes, salade, patisserie.'

Lectoure (pop. 3800) The Hotel-restaurant Le Bellevue, Le Gascogne, La Gare and de France are within budget. The Restaurant Auberge des Bouviers, run by the Dubois family, Tel. 62.68.71.69, offers you menus from Francs 52: 'soupe des Bouviers, salade Etable, grillade de boeuf, fromage ou dessert'.

Mirande (pop. 4800) The Hotel Metropole, Gascon and des Pyrénées are within budget, as are three restaurants Chez Roberte, Au Bon Acceuil and Auberge de l'Astarac.

Map Ref.	Town	Hotel (Rooms)	Tel.(prefix 62)
C–6	Aignan 32290	Le Vieux Logis, r. des Arts (5) du Centre (8) Chez Mimi (5)	09.23.55 09.25.10 09.24.16
G–7	Auch 32000	de Paris, 38 av. de la Marne (22) Modern, 10 av. Mendès-France (10) Les Trois Mousquetaires, 5 rue Espagne (6) de la Gare, 2 av. Mendes-France (6)	63.26.22 (closed Nov) 05.03.47 05.13.25 05.02.83
B–3	Barbotan-lès-Thermes 32150	Hotels usually pension terms only — closed in winter Six are in the rue des Thermes; Les Cygnes, Les Kakis, Petit Versailles, Rocher, A Noste and Bellevue-Faig. Two are in Avenue Henri IV; Beausoleil and Dalma.	
A–6	Barcelonne 32400	du Centre, r. Jeanne d'Albret (6) Délos, r. Jeanne d'Albret (5) Chez Pomies (6)	09.44.87 09.44.23 09.44.39 Routiers
D–7	Bassoues d'Armagnac 32320	du Donjon (9)	64.90.04 recommended
B–5	Bourrouillan 32370	Moulin de Comte (10)	09.06.72
E–3	Condom 32100	Continental (18) du Midi, 32 r. Bartlet (20) du Lion d'Or (9)	28.00.58 28.24.10 28.23.50
F–5	Castéra-Verduzan 32410	Ténorèze (22)	68.10.22 (closed Nov & Feb)
B–3	Cazaubon 32150	Du Centre, Pl. de la Mairie (35) Le Gai Logis, Pl. Alban (15) Dulhoste	69.51.62 09.50.44 (closed winter)
B–7	Cahuzac 32400	Relais des Pyrénées (6)	69.73.03

117

C-4	Eauze 32800	Henri IV, 1 Pl. St. Taurin (16)	09.82.32
		L'Armagnac, Bd. St. Blanat (10)	09.88.11
		Auberge du Guinlet (7)	09.85.99
H-4	Fleurance 32500	Capelli, 72 r. Gambetta (22)	06.11.88
		L'Etape Gascon (6)	06.15.28
		du Midi (12)	06.11.79
		Le Chantpie (20)	06.10.95
I-7	Gimont 32200	Prefaure (10)	67.71.11
		de France, 8 Pl. du Marché (8)	67.72.93
D-4	Gondrin 32330	Le Pardaillan, du Lac (11)	29.12.06 recommended
G-3	Lectoure 32700	La Bellevue, 55 r. Nationale (12)	68.80.06
		de France, 106 r. Nationale (18)	68.70.65
		Le Gascogne, Rte. d'Agen (10)	68.77.57
F-7	L'Isle de Noe 32300	Auberge de Gascogne (7)	64.17.05 recommended
K-7	L'Isle-Jourdain 32600	du Centre (12)	07.00.23
		de France (8)	07.00.04
I-8	Lombez 32420	Chez Maryse, Pl. l'Eglise (6)	65.31.32
B-6	Luppé-Violles 32110	Le Relais d'Armagnac (10)	09.04.54
D-8	Marciac 32230	des Promenades (10)	09.38.13
		Le Belvédère (7)	09.38.29
G-9	Masseube 32140	du Parc (10)	66.00.32
I-6	Mauvezin 32120	Auberge du Cheval Noir (9)	06.83.94
		de France (8)	06.81.45
F-8	Mirande 32300	Metropole, 32 r. Victor-Hugo (14)	66.50.25
		des Pyrénées, 5 Ave. Etigny (20)	66.51.16

D-3	Montréal 32250	de la Gare, Rte. d'Eauze (6)	28.43.37
		Les Ramiers (10)	28.43.07
G-5	Montestruc 32390	Cante-Gril (10)	62.27.02
B-5	Nogaro 32110	du Commerce, 2 Pl. Cordeliers (16)	09.00.95
		des Arènes, Pl. des Arènes (12)	09.03.33
		Dubroca, r. d'Artagnan (12)	09.01.03
G-7	Pavie 32000	Chez André, Rte. Lannemezan (5)	05.29.14
C-7	Plaisance 32160	d'Artagnan, r. de la Porte (9)	69.30.37 recommended
		de l'Amagnac, r. Armagnac (7)	69.40.79
		La Pergola, Allée des Ormeaux (5)	69.30.22
H-5	Puycasquier 32120	Relais Gascon (6)	65.16.06 recommended
B-6	Riscle 32400	de la Paix, Pl. Libération (17)	69.70.14
		Relais du Pont d'Arcole (12)	69.72.30
		Relais de l'Auberge, Pl. l'Eglise (10)	69.70.49
E-6	St. Jean de Poutge 32190	de la Baïse (21)	64.62.11
A-6	Saint-Mont 32400	Auberge du Village (9)	69.62.59 recommended
J-8	Samatan 32130	Maigné/du Midi, 7 r. Noilhan (15)	62.30.24
		de la Poste, 9 bd. Castres (3)	62.39.15
		Tiffes, r. Belleforest (6)	62.30.63
A-7	Ségos 32400	Minvielle, près l'Eglise (6)	09.40.90
G-8	Seissan 32260	des Pyrénées (7)	66.20.35 recommended
		Samaran (5)	66.20.32
E-5	Vic-Fezensac 32190	Le d'Artagnan (10)	06.31.37
		Le Relais de Poste (10)	06.44.22
		Le Midi (8)	06.35.17

Gîtes ruraux

There are no less than 550 in the Gers. From September to June there is a discount of 30% from the high season tariffs of July and August. There are seven regions: (1) Armagnac, which includes Nogaro, Eauze, Vic-Fezensac and Cazaubon-Barbotan, (2) Astarac, which includes Mirande, Marciac, Miélan, Masseube and Montesquiou, (3) Auch includes Jégun, (4) Côteaux du Gers, which includes Isle-Jourdain, Cologne, Gimont, Samatan, Lombez, Simorre and Saramon, (5) La Lomagne, which includes Lectoure, St. Clar, Fleurance, Mauvezin and Miradoux, (6) La Rivière-basse (or more romantically Pays Vert d'Artagnan), which includes Riscle, Plaisance Aignan and Lupiac, and (7) La Ténarèze, which includes Condom, Montreal and Valence-sur-Baise.

Each gîte varies in size (6–10 people), in comfort and in style. As a rough indication the recent prices in Armagnac in high season per family ranged from Francs 740 to Francs 2410 per week.

For a full list write to Relais Gersois des Gîtes de France, Route des Tarbes, BP 99, 32003 Auch Cedex, Tel. 62.63.16.55, or Maison du Gers et de l'Armagnac, 16–18 Bd. Haussmann, 75009 Paris, Tel. (1)42.46.91.39. Each Gîte has a code number for ease of reference.

Gîtes d'etapes/fermes equestre

This is a mixed bag ranging from modest farms to elegant châteaux with one thing in common – the opportunity to have a riding holiday.

Lasseube-Propre, centre de vacances, pony club for 32 children	Ref. 050
Pessan, 'La Rochette', 10 places in a château	051
Lussan, 'En Peybrouste', 18 places in a farm	052
Lartigue, Moulin de Mazères, 16 places in a converted windmill	066
Samatan, 'Galabar', an equestrian farm with own 'camping'	055
Condom, 'Trois Epis', an equestrian farm with 10 places	053

Chambres d'hote

These are bed and breakfast lodgings, usually in the country-side in or near a village. Main meals by arrangement. There are 100 of them in the Gers. Each region has its Syndicat d'Initiative to whom to write, although a master booklet can be obtained from U.D.O.T/S.I. 32700 Lectoure, Tel. 62.68.76.98.

The main regions are as follows: (1) Armagnac, write to S.I. Mairie, 32800 Eauze, Tel. 62.09.85.62, (2) Asterac, write to S.I. 32300 Mirande, Tel. 62.66.68.10, (3) Coteaux du Gers, write to Office de Tourism, 32600 L'Isle-Jourdain, Tel. 62.07.14.39, (4) Auch, write to S.I. 32000 Auch, Tel. 62.05.22.89, (5) Rivière-Basse, write to S.I. 32400 Riscle, Tel. 62.69.70.10, and (6) Ténarèze, write to S.I. 32100 Condom, Tel. 62.28.00.80.

There are three categories: de luxe – comfortable – normal. Prices vary considerably and high season in some cases is double that of the period September-June inclusive

Fermes auberges

These are farmhouses where you live 'en famille' and have usually excellent meals. Some examples follow:

Ferme-Auberge Château Lassalle, Mme. Arlette Thorignac, Aignan, Tel. 62.09.24.21, with three menus from Francs 85 including Floc, 'feuilleté au foie gras, pintade au poivre vert, légumes, salade, dessert', wine and coffee included.

Ferme-Auberge Bourrouil, Mme. Maite Mathe, Faget-Abbatial, Saramon, Tel. 62.65.42.61 offers two menus at Francs 98 and 140. The former includes 'salade des bergers avec fromage de chèvre chaud, tarte aux légumes, poularde à la Pacherenc, dessert maison, pain maison'. Ferme-Auberge 'La Clauzade', Mme. Sheila Rogers, Gaujan, Simorre, Tel. 62.65.32.45, menus at Francs 85, 110 and 160.

Ferme-Auberge Ruat, M. Desbarats, Lupiac, Aignan, Tel. 62.09.26.33 offers menus from Francs 80 and 140.

Ferme-Auberge Jouars, M. Lacome, Pessoulens, St. Clar, Tel. 62.66.42.15, offers menus at Francs 60, 80 and 95.

Ferme-Auberge La Baquere, M. Barret, Preneron, Vic-Fezensac, Tel. 62.06.42.75, offers a Francs 80 menu 'Floc de

121

Gascogne' as apéritif, 'soupe paysanne, assiette fermière, demi-magret grille ou confit, légumes, dessert maison (tarte aux myrtilles) vin et café'.

There are less than 20 Fermes-Auberges in the Gers. For information write to Loisirs Accueil Gers, Maison de l'Agriculture, BP 99, 32003 Auch, Tel. 62.63.16.55.

Generally speaking expect to pay Francs 150 or so for a couple in a comfortable bedroom.

Villages de vacances – holiday camps

32100	Condom	31 bungalows	Tel. 62.28.17.32
32330	Lagraulet	60 bungalows	Tel. 62.29.11.11 (except Jul/Aug)
32700	Lectoure	19 bungalows	Tel. 62.68.82.33 (except Jul/Aug)
32270	Marsan	15 bungalows	Tel. 62.65.60.11
32120	Mauvezin	33 gites	Tel. 62.06.81.45
32170	Mielan	26 gites familiaux	Tel. 62.67.51.76
32130	Samatan	18 gites familiaux	Tel. 62.62.51.90

Stations vertes

These are villages or towns where the municipality tries very hard indeed to be helpful to holidaymakers and receive the above accolade.

Aignan – Barbotan les Thermes – Condom – Eauze – Isle Jourdain – Masseube – Mauvezin – Panassac – Plaisance du Gers and Riscle.

Camping in farms

There are 48 in the Gers divided into eight regions.

(1) Armagnac (10 farms) Info. from S.I. 32100 Condom Tel. 62.28.00.80
(2) Ténarèze (6 farms) Info. from S.I. 32250 Montreal Tel. 62.28.43.18
(3) Cazaubon-Barbotan (4 farms) Info. from M. Jacques Castandet, 'Soubiran', 32150 Cazaubon
(4) Pays de la Save (5 farms) Info. from Mairie/S.I. 32130 Samatan Tel. 62.62.30.19
(5) Pays de la Lomagne (7 farms) Info. from Mairie de St. Clar, 32380 St. Clar Tel. 62.66.40.45

(6) Miradoux (3 farms)   Info. from Mme. Laville, 'Biran', 32340 Miradoux
                             Tel. 62.28.64.65
(7) Auch region (9 farms)   Info. from Mme. Jean-Louis, Club Camping,
                             Tourist Office, Auch
(8) Vic-Fezensac (4 farms) Info. from S.I. 2 Rue de la Filature, 32190
                             Vic-Fezensac Tel. 62.06.34.90

Camp sites

There are 35 municipal camp sites in the Gers, including two
nudist. They range in quality from one to three stars and the
rates vary accordingly. The majority are near a lake, river or
have a large swimming pool, and have tennis, fishing and
restaurant. Some are open all the year round, others from
either 15th March or 1st June to the autumn and close in the
winter.

Map ref.	Address	Telephone	Places
G–7	32000 Auch		
	*** Ile Saint-Martin	62.05.00.22	200
C–3	32800 Castelnau-D'Auzan		
	* Du Lac	62.29.23.43	100
F–5	32410 Castera-Verduzan		
	* Des Thermes	62.68.13.41	50
		62.68.13.11	
A–6	32400 Barcelonne-du-Gers		
	* Camping Municipal	62.09.44.21	50
B–3	32150 Barbotan-les-Thermes		
	*** De l'Uby	62.09.53.91	600
E–3	32100 Condom		
	*** De Gauge	62.28.17.32	225
C–4	32800 Eauze		
	** Du Pouy	62.09.86.00	60
B–4	32240 Estang		
	*** Lac de Courtès	62.09.61.98	300
H–4	32500 Fleurance		
	* Camping Municipal	62.06.10.01	150
I–7	32200 Gimont		
	** Camping Municipal	62.67.70.02	150
D–4	32330 Gondrin		
	* La Rochelle	62.29.12.06	100
F–7	32300 L'Isle-de-Noé		
	** Camping Municipal	62.64.17.21	–

K–7	32600 L'Isle-Jourdain		
	*** Camping Municipal	62.07.14.39	160
F–3	32480 La Romieu		
	** Camp de Florence	62.28.15.58	60
G–3	32700 Lectoure		
	*** Lac des Trois Vallées	62.68.82.33	1200
	* La Croix Rouge	62.68.70.22	75
I–8	32220 Lombez		
	* La Grange	62.62.32.20	50
D–8	32230 Marciac		
	* Bèzines	62.09.38.03	100
J–7	32490 Marestaing		
	* Camping Municipal	62.07.03.77	20
H–6	32270 Marsan		
	* Emmarques	62.65.60.11	100
G–9	32140 Masseube		
	*** Julie Moignard	62.66.01.75	400
I–6	32120 Mauvezin		
	** Camping Municipal	62.06.81.45	90
E–9	32170 Miélan		
	*** Du Lac	62.67.51.76	210
F–8	32300 Mirande		
	*** L'Isle du Pont	62.66.64.11	150
E–7	32320 Montesquiou		
	*** Chateau du Haget	62.64.95.80	–
G–9	32140 Panassac		
	* Le Grillon	62.66.05.23	100
C–7	32160 Plaisance-du-Gers		
	** L'Arros	62.69.30.28	100
G–6	32000 Roquelaure		
	* Le Talouch	62.65.52.43	150
B–6	32400 Riscle		
	*** Pont de l'Adour	62.69.70.10	200
J–8	32130 Samatan		
	** Camping Municipal	62.62.30.19	50
G–8	32260 Seissan		
	*** Laverdure	62.66.21.76	100
J–6	32430 Thoux-Saint-Cricq		
	*** Du Lac	62.07.03.29	210
E–4	32310 Valence-sur-Baise		
	* La Cale	62.28.51.89	100
E–5	32190 Vic-Fezensac		
	** Les Acacias	62.06.30.08	100

Naturisme/Nudist Camps
C–1   32290 Aignan
          *** Castex Camping..............................62.09.25.13 140
I–4   32380 Gaudonville
          *** La Devèze....................................62.66.43.86 400

Gastronomic delights

Besides the well known delights of Armagnac brandy and Floc aperitif and the wines of the Côtes de Gascogne, St. Mont and Madiran, 'la cuisine gasconne' in Gers has many traditional dishes to offer, many of which have been included in the menus shown in this book.

'La garbure' (bacon and cabbage soup) often starts the meal, followed by charcuterie (various porcine delights) and jambon (ham) de pays. Foie gras of ducks or geese is cooked in a variety of ways, including with grapes or with apples. Besides 'confits' (conserves of goose or duck), regional meat dishes include 'daubes' (braised beef), 'alicuits au pot', 'poitrines de veau' (breasts of veal) 'farcies', and poultry dishes of 'dinde' (turkey) and 'poulets' (chickens).

Vegetables and fruit of the region include asparagus, garlic, melon, strawberries (particularly from Lectoure), and vineyard pears. Ecrevisse (freshwater crayfish), salmon, trout, pike, perch, carp and sandre (perch-pike) come from the many rivers threading their way through the Gers.

The autumn dishes and recipes will include caille (quail) and perdreaux (young partridge), and cèpes (large, flat tasty mushrooms) and palombes (wood pigeons) either roasted or 'en salmis' (ragout). Patisserie includes pastis (aniseed flavoured pastry) and croustades.

There are many specialist producers of ducks, geese, rabbits, snails, garlic, biscuits and goat cheese (le Gascon, le Magret, la Tome de Lomagne, la Fontine Fleurantine).

A Gascon recipe book is on sale at the Syndicats in Gers, priced at Francs 25. There are 60 recipes covering Soupes – Escargots – Sauces Gasconnes – Champignons – Rotis – Gibiers (game) – Desserts. It is called Editions Recettes.

Specialist food producers

Croustades Elusa, Patrick Stammier, 24 rue Pourtic, 32800 Eauze.

Biscuiterie Caperan, Le Dollar Gascon, 30 rue d'Etigny, 32000 Auch.

Maison Darquier (Foies Gras), Domaine d'Archan, 32240 Castelnau-d'Auzan.

Jean Pierre Laulan, Asparagus canner, 47170 St. Maure de Peyziac.

Escargots (tinned – many recipes) G.I.E. Helicicole de Montesquiou.

Garlic/Ail Co-op Gersail, rue des Bastides, 32380 St. Clar de Lomagne.

Codigers (Co-ops, turkey, rabbit and poultry), R.du Chemin Neuf, 32130 Samatan.

Gerlap Co-op les Silos Vicois (rabbit co-op) 32190 Vic-Fezensac.

Goat Cheese. Elevage de Dauzère, St. Puy 32310 Valence-sur-Baise.

Gascon Cheeses, Le Saoubie 32700 Terraube.

Gascon Cheeses, GIE Chevre Gers, Z.I. Alimentaire, Rte. Fleurance 3200 Auch.

Mail order

The widest range of foie gras, pruneax du vigneron (plums in wine or armagnac), cèpes (large mushrooms), morilles (small yelow mushrooms), local fish souffles, cassoulets (many varieties), tripes, daube de lomagne, patés, salmis de palombes, civet de canard, bibelotte de lapin, pot au feu, garbure au confit, Armagnacs, Floc, twenty different local jams, etc. can be ordered from Art-Village, BP 5, 32380 Saint Clar.

Market days in the Gers

Monday
    Samatan — Mauvezin – Aignan – Mirande

Tuesday
>Fleurance – Solomiac (2nd & 4th of each month)

Wednesday
>Auch – Gimont – Castelnau-d'Auzan (a.m.) – Condom

Thursday
>Auch – Jégun (2nd & 4th of each month) – Eauze – Miélan – Plaisance (p.m.)

Friday
>Seissan – Vic-Fezensac (p.m. – Lectoure – Riscle

Saturday
>Auch – l'Isle-Jourdain–Cazaubon (a.m.) – Nogaro

Sunday
>Estang (a.m.) – Bassoues

Some fairs and fêtes in the Gers

May	Foire aux Eaux-de-Vies d'Armagnac in Eauze
July 13–18 August	A la Mecque, journée Foie Gras at Samatan
July 14	Foire aux fromages de chèvres (goat cheese) in Plaisance
July 22	Journée Armagnac Noir at Manciet
July-December	Garlic market in Mauvezin (p.m. only)
August 11	Garlic market in Saint Clar
August 24	Journée de la Vigne et du Vin, at the Tower of Thermes d'Armagnac at Riscle
September 11	Fête des Vendanges, Tour de Lamothe at Cazeneuve
September 24–27 Auch	'Gascogne-Expo', in the park 'Endoumengue',
winter	Foie Gras markets in Samatan, Gimont, L'Isle-Jourdain (11 Nov), Condom (25 Nov), Montreal (Monday before Christmas). Mirande (Monday before St. Catherine's Day), Riscle (11 Nov and 31 Dec)

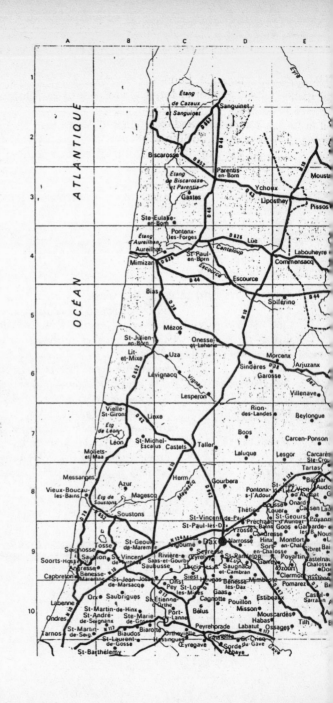

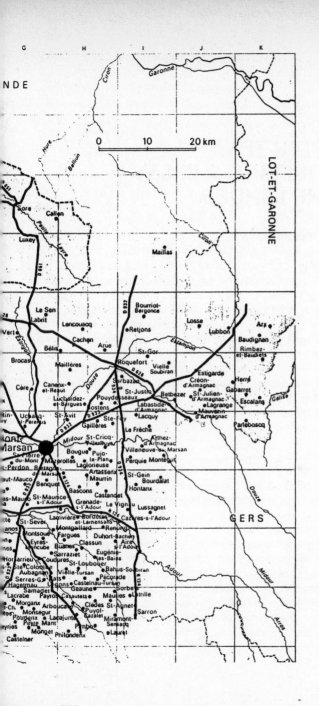

CHAPTER TEN:
UNCOVERING THE LAY
OF THE LANDES

This département is the most complex in the whole of France, since it has three totally different characters. The triangular region in the southeast formed by the Mont de Marsan, Aire sur l'Adour and Bayonne to the southwest (the latter being just outside the Landes) is a continuation of the Gers to the east. So expect to find rivers, small hills, woods, maize fields and occasional vineyards. Sprinkled about in this triangle are scores of delightful towns and villages boasting superb romanesque churches such as St. Sever, St. Girons (Hagetmau), St. Paul-lès-Dax, and the abbeys of Arthous and Sorde. The treasure in the museum of Brassempouy, the unique Dame à la Capuche, must be seen. The food and wine reflect the character of the Gers. The Tursan wines are particularly good value.

Natural beauty

The west coast of the Landes consists of nearly 200 km of golden sands, with 21 'stations balneaires' – the plage town of Capbreton in the south to Biscarosse in the north. Ideal for the young, and the young at heart, provided attention is paid to the bathing regulations. Mimizan and Hossegor are two of the traditional resorts as are the other two just mentioned. Nearly three quarters of the land mass of the Landes (9300 sq km) is made up of the largest forest in France, which includes the Parc Naturel des Landes de Gascogne. This huge area is bisected by small rivers and attendant lakes and is ideal for nature-students. It makes a complete contrast to the bustling resorts.

The population of 300,000 is spread over 331 communes. Mont de Marsan and Dax/St. Paul-les-Dax are the largest towns with populations each of 30,000. In addition there are six others with a population over 5000 – Biscarosse, Mimizan, Aire sur l'Adour, Tarnos, Morcenx and Soustons. The main river is the Adour with its dozen or so tributaries watering the south and east of the département. Another six small rivers are to be found in the west and north. The highest point is a mere 234 metres at Lauret, a hamlet on the southern border with Pyrénées-Atlantique.

The Landes is noteworthy for many reasons: its sandy beaches and plage towns; its Spanish connections (Courses Landaises and pelota); and its gastronomic delights (Tursan wines and a share in Armagnac production). The three pilgrimage centres should be visited by aficionados of Rugby, Cycling and Courses Landaises. The English links are many since more than 30 bastide towns date back from the English occupation in the twelfth to the fifteenth centuries.

The Landes welcomes tourists and has a sophisticated network of good value low cost hotels and restaurants which will be examined in subsequent chapters. The three regional tours which follow give only basic information about each stop, which is covered in some detail elsewhere in the text.

Regional tours

Tour One

From Mont de Marsan take the D 932 northeast 10 km and at a major junction fork right and northeast on the D 933 for 4 km and take a very minor road due north for 3 km to see the fine romanesque church of Ste. Marie in the hamlet of Bostens.

Next due east for 2½ km to Pouydesseaux, a village on the pilgrim route, and south for 1 km to the **Centre Jean Rostand**, a new ecological centre, Tel. 58.93.92.43. Back on the D 933 and keep east for 7 km to St. Justin, a bastide village with several local châteaux and manor houses. The church of Argelouse has a romanesque choir and capitals.

Take the D 626 east for 4 km to **Labastide d'Armagnac**, which is one of the little architectural gems of Gascony. It is a

131

classic bastide town founded by King Edward I with the Count of Armagnac in 1284. The Place Royale or central square, despite the Catholic Monluc's ravages, is still beautiful. Look at the Gallo-Roman villa, and the romanesque church. Three kilometres outside the village, the **Chapel of Géou** beside the little museum are both dedicated to the modern day cult of cycling. Every winner of the Tour de France either visits the chapel or hands over his 'maillot' to the museum or both. This is Armagnac, confits and foie gras country (Château Garreau).

Back into Labastide d'Armagnac and take the minor road D 11 west and south west via Le Frèche to **Villeneuve-de-Marsan**, a distance of 14 km. This bastide town is the centre of the Bas-Armagnac brandy and agricultural producers. The Château d'Ognas, Tel. 58.45.22.11, is to the east near Arthez d'Armagnac and is the Armagnac domaine and chai owned by the département.

Alternatively visit the Château de Ravignan in **Perquie** southeast of Villeneuve de Marsan – one of the most elegant in Gascony (Louis XVIII style). Stay on the D 934 due south for 21 km towards **Aire-sur-l'Adour**. This town has a dashing Spanish ambience, was the scene of one of Wellington's smaller but quite decisive battles, and has a superb church crypt of Sainte Quittérie. It is the centre of the foie gras area, of Tursan wines and Armagnac. One of the most interesting towns in Gascony, set beside the river Adour.

Now southwest on the N 134 for 3 km and west on the D 2. Just to the north is the pretty little spa town of Eugénie-les-Bains. Keep on the D 2 to **Géaune** and visit the co-op and taste their interesting wines, Tel. 58.44.51.25. This bastide town was founded in 1318 by King Edward III and it still has a massive romanesque keep. The church is Languedoc gothic style and the Tower of Augustins is notable.

Most of the little local wine villages – Castelnau Tursan, Sorbets, Urgons, Bats and Vielle Tursan were English bastides, and have romanesque churches. Vielle Tursan was famous for its wine in the seventeenth century.

Now west, still on the D 2, for 11 km to **Samadet**, which was always famous for its china and earthenware. This is corrida country and arenas are to be found in Aire sur l'Adour, Duhort-Bachen, Eugénie-les-Bains, Bahus, Soubiran, Géaune, Pimbo (bastide), Arboucave, Samadet, Urgons, Vielle-Tursan and St. Loubouer (château).

From Samadet north mainly cross-country to Grenade sur l'Adour via the villages of Aubagnan, Coudures, Sarraziet, Bahus and Montgaillard. Most are Tursan wine villages and all were English owned in the Hundred Years War.

In a triangle south of Grenade sur l'Adour are several architectural sites of interest, near Fargues, Buanes and Classun. So is **Larrivière**, which is on the D 11 on the river banks of the Adour facing Grenade, and has the Roman camp of Thun. Nearby is another modern pilgrimage site – this time for Rugby players – called Chapelle de Notre Dame de Rugby. It is also a Tursan wine village, with Courses Landaises held during the summer. Across the river is **Grenade sur l'Adour**, an English bastide in 1322, which was a scene of skirmishes by Wellington's troops in 1814.

From Grenade take the minor road D 406 6 km to **Bascons**, another English owned town with a delightful thirteenth century church. The chapel of Bostens (2 km north) houses the sanctuary of Notre Dame des Courses Landaises, and appropriately the small town has a museum for devotees of the local sports of Courses and Pelota. From Bascons northwest via Bostens to the D 30 and northwest into Mont de Marsan.

Summary: The total circuit is about 135 km and the most interesting places are Labastide d'Armagnac, Aire sur l'Adour, Géaune with its nearby wine villages, and the three curious modern sanctuaries and sites of pilgrimages for the Cyclist, the Rugby players and the Courses Landaises followers. Aire sur l'Adour makes an attractive place to stay from which to make the circuit.

Tour Two

From Mont de Marsan south on the N 124 and after 8 km turn west on the D 351 to **Benquet** to see the 'Château-Vieux' where Jeanne d'Albret and her famous son King Henri IV once lived. West on the D 404 to the main road D 933 and southwest for 9 km to **St. Sever** on a hill, which is the archaeological centre of the Landes and was an early medieval city. The eleventh century Benedictine Abbey, cloister and archaeological museum are amongst the best in Gascony. On the first Sunday of July there is a Gascon festival and many other activities, including Courses and foie gras markets.

Keep due south on the D 933 via Dumes, where King Edward I built a château in 1289, for 12 km to **Hagetmau**, where the romanesque crypt of St. Girons is one of the finest sites in Gascony. It is now a bustling town where Wellington stayed after the battle of Orthez and before his final victory over Marshal Soult at Toulouse. (The famous crypt is on the western outskirts of the town on the D 18.)

Keep south on the D 933 and take the D 58 signed for **Brassempouy**, which was an English bastide and is famous for its prehistoric grottos and 'Femme à la Capuche', one of the thousand treasures of France. The Prehistoric Museum here is worth a visit, Tel. 58.89.04.60. Due west is the Château of **Gaujacq**, and then drive south across the two rivers, known as 'Luy de France' by the D 21 to **Amou**, which was occupied by the Vascons, the Romans, the Saracens, the Normans, and then for three centuries, by the English! The seventeenth century château and fourteenth century church with the royal chapel of the Plantagenets are worth a detour.

Now northwest on the D 15 for 9 km to **Pomarez**, considered to be the 'Mecca of the Courses Landaises'. M. Pussacq, Tel. 58.89.32.67, will show you his famous 'ganaderia', but not in July/August when his fighting cows are fighting elsewhere in the Landes.

Drive north on the D 7 across the river Luy to **Castelnau Chalosse** where the 'Trésor de Gibret' was found in 1860, to **Montfort en Chalosse**, another thirteenth century English bastide with half a dozen châteaux and twelfth century romanesque church and the most important market in *Europe* for foie gras. There are also two museums here, devoted to local arts and traditions and the Chalosse region.

Now northeast on the D 32 for 9 km to **Mugron** which has the wine co-operative of the Haute Chalosse, Courses

Landaises, and pelota. Next west to **Laurède** where La Hire, companion to Joan of Arc, lived. Here the romanesque church and seventeenth century Maison de Peyne for the Compostella pilgrims is worth a visit. West to see the château at **Poyanne** (Louis XIII), on to meet the D 7 and north to **Tartas**, a town with several historic houses, convent and cloisters, occupied by the English for three centuries, and back by the N 124 via Meilhan and Campagne to Mont de Marsan.

Summary: The circuit covers about 150 km. Most of the architectural and archaeological treasures of the Chalosse will have been seen and the wine town of Mugron. St. Sever or Hagetmau would make agreeable stop-over towns.

Tour Three

This time starting out from Dax (and assuming that St. Paul-lès-Dax and Lac de Christus have already been visited) start northeast on the N 14 for 6 km to **St. Vincent de Paul** to see the Saint's birth-place, called 'Le Bercau', on the north side of the main road. Continue for 5 km north on the D 27 to **Buglose**. Here the church clock tower produces a carillon from 60 bells, has a fifteenth century stone virgin in polychrome colours and a treasury of note. The diocesan museum of Sacred Art is open every weekend in the afternoon, Tel. 58.89.91.02. The celebrated Ganaderia Labat is near Buglose, Tel. 58.89.91.05.

Next east on the D 130 for 5 km to **Pontonx sur l'Adour**, which was once a port on the river Adour, and south across the river by the D 10 to **Préchacq-les-Bains**. The Thermal Spa is north of the village near a bend in the river. South on the D 368 to **Hinx** which has the Château de Castera, crossing the D 32 on the D 324 to Sort en Chalosse, Clermont, and via the D 15 across the D 947 and the river Grand Arrigan to Mimbaste, which has a prehistoric necropolis, and southwest on the D 322 to **Pouillon** which is surrounded by minor Gascon châteaux. South on the D 22 for 6 km to the main road the N 117.

Keep on the N 117 east, parallel to the River Gave de Pau to Labatut and cross the river at Lahontan and turn west to

St. Cricq du Gave and **Sorde l'Abbaye**. The former has a twelfth century château and grottos and the latter is an essential sight for everyone visiting southern Gascony with its archaeological treasures, Roman villa, spa and mosaics and famous abbey. The old town is surrounded by ramparts and has a fine museum and pelota 'fronton'.

Now northwest on the D 29 across the A 64 autoroute and the river to **Peyrehorade**, the old Roman town. The châteaux of Aspremont and Montreal are worth a visit. The word 'Peyre' is Gascon for 'pierre' or stone. Sometimes the word can now mean a Menhir.

Cross over the river again on the D 19 to see the eleventh century Abbey and Museum of **Arthous** and west on the D 343 to **Hastingues**. As one might expect this was an English bastide town founded by Jean de Hastingues about AD 1300. Cross over the river, famous for its salmon-fishing, at the bridge of Peyrehorade. West to Orthevielle and northwest on the D 33 for 8½ km and north on the D 17 via **Orist**, which has several châteaux and a small ecological museum, and northwest across the Adour again to **Saubusse**, a little spa town. Northeast on the minor road D 70 to Rivière Saas et Gourby, a troglodyte shelter and warm mineral waters (not commercial) to another spa village of **Tercis-les-Bains** fed by the Adour, and by the D 6 northeast into Dax.

Summary: The distance is about 125 km and the highlights are the magnificent abbeys in the south and the spa towns on the Adour river. Peyrehorade would make an agreeable stopover place. It is close to the abbeys as well as many Roman camps and villas along the riverside.

CHAPTER ELEVEN:
THE TOWNS AND VILLAGES
OF LANDES

Aire-sur-l'Adour (I–9) Once the 'oppidum' of the tribe of Tarusates, it was conquered by the Romans and with Toulouse became the capital of the region under the Visigoths. Sainte Quittérie, the patron saint of Gascony, was martyred on the hill above the town. There is still a 'miraculous' fountain of Ste. Quittérie. For nearly three centuries the English ruled here until Charles d'Albret reconquered the town in 1425. Now it is a charming place near the banks of the river Adour, noted for being the centre of VDQS Tursan wine, of the foie gras area, and of the corridas and Courses Landaises. On Tuesday mornings the major market in France for foie gras is held in Aire. Amongst many fêtes, the fête patronale on the third Sunday in June should be visited. There are horse races, Courses, corridas, processions, firework displays, bands and general gaiety. (Church q.v)

Amou (F–10) After the Vascons, the Romans, the Saracens, and the Normans, this 'village fleuri' tolerated three centuries of English occupation. The local groupe folklorique is called Banda 'Loustutayres de la Técouère', and the local association is the 'amis du Vieil Amou'. Down in the deep south of the département, the town has views of the Pyrénées. It is situated on the river Luy de Bearn and has several archaeological sites, ramparts and towers. Courses Landaises take place, and pelota is played in Amou. It is noted for its fruit orchards, especially pears.

Angoumé (C–9) This hamlet has pre-Roman troglodyte shelters and a Roman oven in the Larras manor house.

Argelos (F–10) This hamlet has an old prior haunted by phantom monks.

Argelouse (F–3) With a population of 37 this little hamlet in the Parc Naturel des Landes has a rustic fifteenth century church, the ruins of a medieval redoubt and Roman camp, and a fountain of Sainte Marguerite.

Arjuzanx (E–6) meant 'terre basse', low-lying ground. After the Romans left, the Normans destroyed it in AD 850. Later it became English under the Sire d'Albret. It has lignite mines and is a thermal centre. (EDF) Visits, Tel. 58.07.81.15.

Arsague (E–10) was known as Arsac in the Middle Ages, and from the 'Laiterie de la Côte d'Argent' is produced cheese called 'Royal Landais'.

Arthez–d'Armagnac (I–7) The Domaine expérimental d'Ognoas is the départemental Armagnac producer. Visitors welcome, Tel. 58.45.22.11. Sited near the lake of La Gaube there are delightful views of the Pyrénées.

Aubagnan (G–9) has many Neolithic and Iron Age tumuli (Mesplède in particular), and a Gallo-Roman villa. Courses and fêtes from the beginning of March.

Audignon (G–9) English owned village and a halt on the pilgrim route.

Aureilhan (C–4) has a Gallo-Roman villa, two moated 'castrum', and is near the pretty lake of the same name fed by the rivers Escource and Canteloup.

Aurice (G–8) One of King Louis XI's Scottish guards built the château of Estignols here, which was destroyed on the orders of Louis XIII, but later reconstructed. Two pilgrimages take place in this village – that of Notre Dame des Pins and Notre Dame de Lagastet, both on the 15th August. The local Groupe folklorique is called 'Pastou et Pastourettes'.

Baigts (E–9) King Edward I confirmed the Seigneurie of Baigts in 1285. There are several archaeological sites of note here (Bouheben), numerous medieval houses, romanesque church, and panoramic views from the Château de Prulhe.

Bascons (H–8) Saint Amand, a Merovingian evangelist, founded a chapel here in AD 660, which became the site of the law-courts of the powerful Viscounts of Marsan. The English owned Bascons for three centuries. This is a 'village fleuri' and several fêtes (folklorique and vendange) and pilgrimages take place here (to Notre Dame de la Course Landaise on Ascension Day, and to the chapel of St. Amand on 15th August). There are Courses Landaises, and pelota is played in Bascons. (Church q.v)

Bastennes (E–9) The Romans worked the bitumen mines here, and they were still productive until the nineteenth century. The vineyards were important up to the nineteenth century until the phylloxera beetle destroyed them. The waters from the river Luy contain sulphur, sodium and calcium. The fête is on the last Sunday of August.

Bélus (C–10) A hill village where King Henri IV used to hunt. In 1898 the vine, a white hybrid called Baco 22A, was first grown and cultivated here. The Cave Co-op des Côteaux d'Orthe is in Bélus. At the fête on 15th August the local drum and bugle band called 'les coquelicots de Bélus' perform.

Benquet (G–8) The 'Château-Vieux' was a pied-à-terre of King Henri IV and his mother Jeanne d'Albret. Now it is an experimental centre of Artiguères for agricultural research.

Betbezer (I–6) was the scene of terrible battles in the Hundred Years War. Bernard de Pardaillan was the victor in 1345, but the Black Prince also took the town by storm and burned it. Its local Armagnac gained a gold medal for excellence in 1978.

Biscarosse (C–2) The Captal de Buch, one of the powerful barons who sided with the English, had his seat of power here and administered the royal justice in the communes of Parentis, Gastes and Ste. Eulalie-en-Born. Now it is a major resort in the midst of pine woods and the large lakes of Cazaux and Parentis. There are many fairs and fêtes. Nearby is the CEL, the centre of space research in the Landes.

Bonnegard (F–10) was a bastide founded in 1279 by King Edward I, and vestiges of the château of Castera can be seen.

Brassempouy (F–10) is celebrated for its extraordinary prehistoric grottos. Later it became a Roman camp and an unusual English bastide, in the shape of a herring bone 'arête de poisson', built in the thirteenth century. In the museum is the celebrated 'Tete à la Capuche' or 'Dame de Brassempouy', the prehistoric woman's face carved in ivory, dating from 23,000 BC.

Brocas-les-Gorges (G–6) On the 1st Sunday in July an evening fête is held here with illuminated boats on the lake of Brocas and river Estrigon.

Buanes (H–9) Megaliths and the menhir of Pierre-à-Pytchisé can be seen in this English bastide village created by King Edward II in 1346.

Buglose – see St. Vincent de Paul (D–9).

Capbreton (A–9) The sailors of this port discovered America before Columbus, when they named the island of Capbreton in the estuary of the Saint Lawrence River (Canada). Part of the old town in the Rues General de Gaulle and Jean Lartigau have medieval houses in Basque or Landes architectural style. The gulf of Capbreton with its submarine valley, its marina and high sand dunes make this 'village fleuri' worth a visit. The fête patronal is held on the 6th December, the fête of the sea in Mid-June and during June to September there is a non-stop series of regattas, bullfights, Courses, firework displays, pelota, parades and processions.

Carcarès-Sainte-Croix (E–8) Apart from its neolithic encampments, feudal moat, castle and windmill, this village has the co-op of honey producers of the southwest Landes.

Cassen (E–8) The word 'casse' in Gascon means 'chêne' (oak tree). King Henry III in 1243 purchased the lordship from the Viscount of Tartas. Once a thermal spa, it still has sulphur springs.

Castelnau-Chalosse (E–9) The 'Treasure of Gibret' was found here in 1860, consisting of jewelry, brooches and 800 coins (Gordien and Emperor Antoninus Pius). The small town is now known for its basket making.

Castelnau-Tursan (H–9) The Seigneurs of this name, allies of the English, built a bastide here in 1325. The view over the rivers Escoulis and Bas from the château keep known as Le Tuc, is breathtaking.

Castelsarrazin (E–10) was occupied in 1254 by King Edward I's troops.

Castets (C–7) was a neolithic site and many finds have been made of arrow heads, fossilized trees and a dolmen. The town knew prosperity when the Compostella pilgrims stayed in it. Louis XI made it a staging post for the Royal Mail, where horses were exchanged.

Cauna (F–8) The powerful seigneurial family of this name, after the battle of Tartas in 1442, handed over the region to the French King Charles VII.

Cauneille (D–10) Jean Rameau, novelist and poet, lived here and died in 1942, having owned the château of Cauneille. 'La Gloriette', 'Le Pourtaou' and the mausoleum are interesting (site classé buildings – well worth a visit). The panoramic view from the top of the church towards the Pyrénées overlooks the meeting point of the rivers Pau and Oloron. The kiwi plant is being encouraged commercially in this region.

Caupenne (F–9) The Seigneurs in the thirteenth century obtained from the English throne the right to establish a weekly trading market here and a decade or two later the Seignerie was made into a Barony – presumably in the New Years Honours list.

Cère (G–6) The first merino sheep were introduced into the Landes at Cère under the First Empire by the Baron Poyféré de Cère, Inspector of the Bergeries Imperiales.

Coudures (G–9) was formed into an English bastide in 1274.

141

Dax (D–9) The second city of the Landes was stormed by Caesar's legions in 17 BC. It became famous and prosperous soon afterwards, due to the popularity of its thermal baths. Emperor Augustus Caesar and his daughter Julia Augusta both took the spa waters at Dax. Nowadays 50,000 'curistes' arrive each year. Richard Coeur de Lion gave it a title of 'ville royale' after he had captured it at the beginning of the twelfth century. After the Treaty of Taillebourg in 1442 the town was handed over to the French crown after three centuries of English rule. It was a major halt on the pilgrim route to Compostella where the Bordeaux and the Mont de Marsan roads joined up. It is the regional capital of Gallo-Roman archaeology with fourth century ramparts and museum. The most famous local citizen was Charles de Borda, a scholar and navigator, after whom the museum is named. Now Dax is a sophisticated modern city with parks, corridas, pelota, casino and 'bateaux mouches' on the river Adour with delightful tours to Saubusse and Port de Lanne. Reservations Tel. 58.74.87.07.

Donzacq (E–9) Prehistoric and Roman sites with coins have been found at Pas de Saubot. The local springs of Eschourdes, which contain sulphur and calcium in the water, are known as the 'bouillons d'Arremblar' (boiling waters).

Duhort-Bachen (H–9) Originally a Roman camp, it became later on an English bastide. There are five local châteaux and a church, to which the pilgrimage of St. Leu is made on the first Sunday in September.

Dumes (G–9) King Edward I authorised Guitard d'Arambes to build a bastide here in 1289, but unfortunately Cardinal Richelieu ordered it to be destroyed in 1625.

Estibeaux (E10) Initially a Neolithic site, it was called Tastoa by the Romans. A pilgrim hospital was created here in the twelfth century. La Motte d'Estibeaux is a 'site classé' feudal moat/tower.

Eugénie-les-Bains (H–9) The small spa town was used by King Henri IV and later the Empress Eugénie made it even more popular and she lent it her name. The sulphuric waters from the valley of the river Bahus, a tributary of the Adour, are called 'Las Aygyes' in Gascon.

Eyres-Moncube (G–9) A paleolithic site where 250 Gaulish coins were found - now in the museum of St. Germain.

Gamarde-les Bains (E–9) Once there were Neolithic camps of refuge here, then a Gallo-Roman fort called 'camp de César', and amphora and ceramics have been discovered. The river Louts produced spa waters much in fashion from 1900–1930, but no longer. Now there are five small Gascon châteaux and manor houses left and breeder-farmers of the yellow maize-fed chickens of the Landes!

Garrosse (D–6) Just off the D 38 in the heart of the forests, the Riga (Latvia) pine tree was first introduced here at the beginning of the eighteenth century – ideal for ships' masts!

Géaune (H–10) King Edward II founded this bastide in 1318 and the small town has been linked with Tursan (the town and the wine) ever since. But for a century it was on the frontier between the English and the French troops. Definitely worth a visit to see the massive Roman keep, the gothic church and the excellent Tursan wine co-operative, Tel. 58.44.51.25.

Gousse (E–8) There was once a colony of disbelievers here for three centuries (eleventh–fourteenth) who were all carpenters by trade, living by the side of the river Adour.

Grenade-sur-l'Adour (H-8) An English bastide from 1322 made this a prosperous town until the French occupation in 1422. Wellington's skirmishers visited the town in 1814. Now known for its ortolans (garden buntings) and foie gras.

Habas (D–10) was a stronghold in the Middle Ages and was on the pilgrim route. It now has five Gascon châteaux, several manor houses and is a gastronomic centre – poulets des Landes, jambon de Bayonne. There is a ganaderia here – a breeding farm for fighting 'vaches'.

Hagetmau (G–9) This bustling modern town, once an important prehistoric site, is classified as a 'village fleuri' and a cultural centre for music, theatre, pottery and exhibitions. Corisande d'Andouins, one of Henri IV's mistresses, lived here. The fête during the last week of July has corridas, Courses, balls and processions. The famous St. Girons crypt is 2 km to the west of the town.

Hastingues(C–10) was an English bastide for three centuries and is one of the best preserved in the country. The town gatehouse, part of the fortified walls, the central square with its 'cornières' and twelfth century cellars, Maison des Jurats, and Maison du Gouverneur, plus the fabulous Abbey d'Arthous (q.v) make this small town an essential visit. The festival of music of the Abbeys is held in June and July.

Herm (C–8) A 'village fleuri', it is noted for its co-op of asparagus producers and for its communal fête of Ste. Madeleine with Courses Landaises and fireworks displays and procession of Fête-Dieu on the Sunday after Easter. The Hotel-Restaurant De la Paix run by M. & Mme. Junca offers menus from Francs 46. Their Francs 115 menu includes omelette norvegienne, Bayonne ham, asparagus, dove ragout, duck conserve and fried potatoes.

Josse (C–9) Once English occupied it has now a feudal moat and five very old manor houses.

Labastide-d'Armagnac (I–6) This classic English bastide of 1284 served as the model for Henri IV's Place des Vosges in Paris at the beginning of the seventeenth century. The Gallo-Roman villa with its mosaics, the arcaded place Royale, romanesque church, wine museum, nearby Chapel of Géou and the Armagnac chais (Garreau) make this small town an essential visit. The fête des vendanges and fêtes folkloriques are held in mid-September.

Labastide-Chalosse (G–10) was an English bastide founded in 1327 by King Edward I, destroyed in the Wars of Religion, but reconstructed again near Hagetmau.

Labatut (D–10) was once a stronghold in the Middle Ages and has five Gascon châteaux and the feudal moat and tower of Lamothe. M. Lacarrau at the Auberge du Bousquet will offer a

144

prix fixe menu at Francs 80 which includes garbure (the Gascon recipe soup), manchons de canard (ducks legs en croute) with vegetables, un gâteau basque, local wine, coffee and service included!

Labenne (A–10) is a small town linked with Capbreton. One of Napoleon III's bastard sons was made the Count of Labenne. In the summer there are balls, sardinades, pelota, firework displays and Courses Landaises.

Labouheyre (E–4) A Carmelite convent of 1150 ministered to the Compostella pilgrims. The historian and folklore specialist of the Landes, Felix Arnaudin, lived here. On the western border of the Parc Naturel, Labouheyre is linked to Sabres by a small train through the forests.

Labrit (G–5) The most powerful family in the Landes, the Albret's, lived here. An interesting family who fought for the English and became the Kings of Navarre in the fifteenth century and produced the gallant Henri IV. Labrit is now known for its race of sheep dogs!

Lacajunte (H–10) was an important prehistoric site with numerous tumuli, Iron Age sepulchres, prehistoric forge, jewelry, weapons and skeletons.

Lacabe (G–10) King Henry III vainly attempted to take this small village in AD 1253.

Lahosse (E–9) takes its name from the plague victims buried in 'La fosse' or, in Gascon, 'La hosse' (ditch/grave). The grottos of Maquenan have stalactites and stalagmites.

Lamothe (F–8) The Seigneurs were ardent supporters of the English cause. Two Gascon châteaux and Gallo-Roman camp and tombs to be seen here.

Larbey (F–9) The grottos and prehistoric caverns at Bourg-Arman are of interest. This was an important Seigneurie on the pilgrim route, and in the twelfth century Ferdinand II created a hospital for the pilgrims to be protected by the chevaliers of St. Jacques de l'Epée Rouge. Several very old

Gascon houses and windmills and a notable church are to be seen.

Larrivière (H–8) The Roman camp of Thun is one of the best conserved in Gascony. There are also numerous megaliths, particularly the 'pierre de Guillay'. See also the Chapelle Notre Dame de Rugby, national sanctuary for rugby players, Tel. 58.45.92.79.

Laurède(E–8) Many Gallo-Roman remains to be seen here including châteaux, caveries and Maison de Peyne, a pilgrim hostel. In the twelfth century there were two watch towers overlooking the river l'Adour and two 'relais' (stopping over points) called 'Espitaou'. Joan of Arc's companion La Hire lived and owned lands here. The romanesque church must be seen (q.v). This 'village fleuri' has Courses Landaises, open air theatre and a fête in May called 'La Mayade'.

Léon (B–7) was on the old Roman Way of Caesar Antonius and is well known for its tropical vegetation around the Lake of Léon, and the 'courant d'Huchet' from lake to ocean. There is a 300 acre national game reserve nearby called 'Cout de Montagne'. The ecological society is called La Sepanso. Léon is an ideal place for an open air holiday with gîtes ruraux, camp sites etc.

Lesperon (C–6) was owned by the English but in 1325 the château of Souquet was owned by brigands, possibly because Lesperon was an important halting place for Compostella pilgrims on whom they preyed.

Le Leuy (F–8) In 1878 4000 Roman coins were found here.

Levignacq (C–6) was on the Roman Way, and pre-phylloxera, was a considerable wine producing area, hence its name.

Lucbardez-et-Bargres (H–6) has a mysterious grotto 'des Manes' under the bank of the river Douze.

Lüe (D–4) is a hamlet in the pinewoods with an oak tree hundreds of years old, diameter 3 metres. An ideal place on which to base a tour of the Parc regional and the lakelands to the west.

Luglon (F–5) is just west of the N 134 south of Sabres, with Neolithic sites and a cemetery, where the invading Moors were buried. Mme. Dulau runs the restaurant Chez Laurence, Tel. 58.07.53.08 and offers a good prix fixe menu including wine for Francs 50. It includes garbure (thick Gascon cabbage soup), pâté, langue de boeuf forestière (ox-tongue), legumes, pastis-croustade des Landes (aniseed pastry). A glass of Armagnac is Francs 6.

Mant (G–10) The Cistercian Abbey of Pontaut was founded in AD 1115. In 1930 it was purchased by John D. Rockefeller and removed stone by stone, to be rebuilt in the USA.

Mézos (C–5) This once English owned village is noted for its fish breeding from a 24 acre inland lake fed by the Courlis. You can rent a boat to explore 50 km of small streams around Mézos-Contis.

Mimizan (C–4) Besides the curious Château de Woolsack, near to the beach is a monument erected in 1929 to the early aviators, Messieurs Assolant, Lefèvre and Lotti in their plane l'Oiseau Jaune. The town is 3 km inland from the resort, which has during the season a non-stop variety of entertainments - circus, pelota, concerts, folklore, Courses Landaises, sardinardes, tennis exhibitions, painting exhibitions, fishing competitions, sailboard championship.

Miramont-Sensacq (H–10) King Edward I caused this bastide to be built in 1276.

Momuy (F–10) Another English bastide built for King Edward III in 1341. The sixteenth century château houses a good collection of works of art.

Mont de Marsan (G–7) One of the very earliest bastides built in 1133 i.e. before the English occupation. The local sculptor Robert Wlerick lived here 1882–1944. Look for the Rue des Arceaux, the fourteenth century donjon (keep) of Lacataye, the twelfth century romanesque house in Rue Lacataye, the ramparts with three watch towers, the Hotel de la Prefecture and château of Nahugues. Besides churches (q.v) there are four museums (q.v). Mont de Marsan is a gastronomic centre and you will enjoy the food here. There are many fêtes and fairs but the Sainte Madeleine in July and Fête de St. Jean d'août are the most important. The superb park of Jean Rameau, of Nahugues and the several rivers threading through the town make Mont de Marsan an essential place to visit. The Tourist Office is very helpful, Tel. 58.46.40.40

Montfort-en-Chalosse (E–9) An English bastide town with many Gascon manors, which has two claims to fame. The largest market in Europe for goose and duck 'gras' on alternate Wednesdays; and the grandest 'toro-ball' in the Landes, a combination of Courses Landaises and fiestas. The main fête day is the 30th of August.

Montgaillard (G–9) A notable archaeological site with mega-lithic monuments known as 'Prince' and 'Thicot', where arms, coins, statues, tombs and mosaics have been discovered. There are also three Gascon châteaux near this English bastide.

Morcenx (E–6) This town has a week of fêtes in the middle of June including a Middle Ages cavalcade with 200 participants. During the season there are six classical concerts, eight balls, pelota, trotting contests, archery competitions and night time cycle races. The Courses Landaises vaches come from the local ganaderia, Larrouture. Every three years Morcenx stages a three-day 'Folklore International' in mid-July. Four hundred participants come from ten countries to show off their customs, dances and costumes, Tel. 58.07.80.29. The firework displays end the 'fêtes de la bière'!

Mugron (F–8) Noted in the Middle Ages for its sorcery and then and now for its wine. There are five Gascon châteaux; the wine co-operative de haute Chalosse should be visited. It is a major market for foie gras.

Nassiet (F-10) Commercial gas has been discovered here at a depth of 5600 metres.

Nerbis (F–8) A noted archaeological site with the prehistoric caves of the Grotto des Fées (fairies) as well as skeletons and workings tools of the Stone Age. Church (q.v).

148

Oeyreluy (C–9) King Edward I owned a château here in 1305 which he refused to sell to the local baron. Warm thermal waters are to be found at Castel-Franco but not commercially exploitable. Church (q.v).

Ousse-Suzan (F–7) King Edward III renewed the 'coutumes' (rights and duties) here in 1338. On the 29th September is the Foire de Suzan and pilgrimage to the three holy shrines attended by up to 20,000 people.

Ozourt (E–9) is noted for its speciality, the pastis flavoured gâteau des Landes.

Parleboscq (K–7) is an interesting village with seven churches (q.v) and seven 'quartiers' of Esperoux, Sarran, St. Cricq, Mura, Laballe, Bouau and Mauras. There are three Gascon châteaux and three windmills and metairies (small farms held on metayage system).

Peyrehorade (C–10) This 'ville fleurie' is noted for its châteaux (q.v) its fêtes and competitions (fishing, motor bike and sidecar rallies, pelota). The fish (salmon, pike and pibales) from the Gaves (rivers) Pau and Oloron are well known throughout Gascony.

Pissos (E–3) has three windmills, a noted church (q.v) and is in the centre of the Forest des Grandes Landes. Many open air activities are available on the rivers Eyre and Leyre.

Pomarez (E–3) considers itself the 'Mecca' of the Courses Landaises. Visit the ganaderia of M. Pussacq, Tel. 58.89.30.37. This is a gastronomic centre so try the Restaurant Pecotche, Tel. 58.89.30.37 with menus from Francs 57. There are many fêtes, fairs and markets – worth a visit.

Pontenx-les-Forges (C–4) was famous for its potteries, tile makers and foundries. The château is called 'de la Forge'. This 'village fleuri' has several pilgrimages to sacred fountains, fêtes, fairs and cultural events.

Pontonx-sur-l'Adour (D–8) One of the earliest aerodromes in France was built here. The area was a centre for the Resistance movement in World War II. Local warm water springs

149

'des Baignots de Castra' are not recognised as a thermal spa. Three kilometres on the N 124 towards Dax is the Restaurant Au Bon Coin where Madame Dieudé, Tel. 58.57.21.18, will offer you a prix fixe menu from Francs 35. Her Francs 52 menu includes potage, crudités, jambon de Bayonne, confit de canard with frites, salade and a choice of dessert. The best Tursan wine is Francs 24 the bottle. The Restaurant Val Fleuri run by the Pozuelo family, Tel. 58.57.20.75, has a menu at Francs 45 including wine.

Port-de-Lanne (C–10) is a pretty little non-commercial port on the river Adour noted for its salmon, shad, and racehorse-breeding. There are four Gascon manor-houses, pelota court and a bridge over the river (N 117). Les Croisières Fluvials bâteau mouche will take you down river via Saubusse to Dax.

Pouillon (D–10) has many Roman archaeological finds at the site of the Tuc de Benarrucq. There are three local châteaux, old farmhouses, windmills and a wine co-operative to be visited. The fête des vendanges is on the second Sunday in October. There are tourist activities on the nearby lake of Luc.

Pouydesseaux (H–6) is noteworthy for its ecological Centre Jean Rostand which is researching shellfish breeding on the lakes. M. Darre, Tel. 58.93.92.48.

Poyartin (E–9) Mammoth's teeth were found here in the ravine of Poupan, and separately many Roman coins.

Préchac-les-Bains (D–8) The Roman Sully exploited these thermal mud baths and it is still one of the noted spa towns in Gascony.

Renung (H–8) A typical small Gascon village perched on a hill. It underwent Roman occupation, and then became a fortified village in the Middle Ages. The Loupy family's restaurant 'Les Corsaires de l'Ile Bourbon', Tel. 58.45.46.69, will offer you a prix fixe menu from Francs 42.

Roquefort (H–6) This little town claims to have remained faithful to the Kings of France during the English occupation of Gascony. A little rewriting of history after the event. It is doubt-

ful if the massive fortified twelfth century church kept the
Black Prince's storm troopers out. Around the confluent of the
rivers Douze and Estampon there are the grottos of Las Hades,
du Cros and des Cagots.

Saint Agnet (I–10) This hamlet is known for its four sacred,
miraculous, spring water fountains.

Saint Aubin (F–9) An interesting Iron Age find was an atelier
(primitive workshop) of iron axes (haches). There are three
sacred fountains in the wood of Lauga.

Saint-Cricq-Chalosse (F–9) There are three Gascon châteaux,
several windmills and old manor houses here as well as a
modern wine co-op.

Sarron (I–10) **Serreslous** (F–9) **Saint Etienne d'Orthe** (C–10)
Saint Gein (I–8) **Saint Géours d'Auribat** (E–8) **Saint Julien
d'Armagnac** (J–6) **Saint Maurice-sur-Adour** (H–8) **Saint
Pierre du Mont** (G–7) **Saint Vincent de Tyrosse** (B–9) were all
English bastide towns.

Saint Géours-de-Maremac (C–9) Besides its fortified thirteenth
century church with crenellated clock tower, this little town
has a game farm, a smoked salmon cannery and a factory that
produces Basque pelota glove-baskets.

Saint Gor (I–6) Near the rivers Launet, Estampon and Vialote
are to be found the Grottos of the Chambre des Fées (fairies).
Local legends exist about these very old underground caves
where fossilised oysters and shell fish have been found preserved by the sulphuric and ferruginous springs.

Saint Jean de Lier (E–8) Visigoth skeletons were found in the
grotto du Saumon and des Fées. A noted ganaderia of fighting
cows is situated in this village.

Saint-Lon-des-Mines (C–10) There are half a dozen Gascon
châteaux and manor houses here, including de Mombet which
has a three century old park full of camellias – the first introduced into France.

Saint-Michel-Escalus (B–7) A temple to Jupiter was found
here on a site called Jioure.

Saint Sever (G–8) This ancient medieval city has many architectural finds of note and architecture of repute – châteaux, convents, half-timbered houses, windmills, particularly the Abbey (q.v) and museum (q.v). Saint Sever, 'ville fleuri' must come high on the list of essential places to visit. The Hotel Restaurant Du Commerce et des Voyageurs is run by the Galland Family, Tel. 58.76.00.24, with menus from Francs 38. This is a town for good eating and drinking. There are several farming co-ops and the confrérie gastronomique les Jabotiers in Saint Sever exists to have a jolly time promoting the food delicacies of the Landes.

Sanguinet (D–1) The Roman Way coincided with the pilgrim route in later centuries through this small town famous for its underwater Gallo-Roman distillery of resin products. On the neighbouring lake of Cazaux-Sanguinet there are regattas and fishing competitions. There are small bathing beaches by the side of the large lake.

Sarbazan (I–6) The Gallo-Roman villa of Mouneyres is one of the best known in Gascony. There is a Roman atrium, balneum (bath) and mosaics. Also Merovingian sarcophagi and funeral urns were found at Treize Pouys nearby. Some of the original Gallo-Roman stones were used to build a fortified romanesque church.

Saubusse (C–9) besides being a thermal spa town has a noted church (q.v) and an extensive farm raising horses, geese and ducks.

Solferino (E–5) was created in the middle of the pine forests in 1863 for some inscrutable reason by Napoleon III. Predictably there is a notable museum here (q.v). Over 12,000 acres of maize and strawberry crops have been planted with a special irrigation system.

Sorde-l'Abbaye (D–11) The site du Barat de Vin and many other archaeological finds, including a Roman villa with mosaics and its own thermal baths, make this ramparted small town one of the major sights of Gascony. In addition there is the abbatial twelfth century church (q.v), a museum (q.v) and wonderful views of several rivers and the Pyrénées in the distance. An essential visit.

Souprosse (F–8) In the Middle Ages there were four separate strong points here, and two Gascon châteaux and one romanesque church remain. A local ganaderia breeding fighting cows is situated near Souprosse.

Tartas (E–8) This 'ville fleuri' has many medieval houses, two convents, a château and a sacred fountain. There are seven factories producing by-products from the forests of Marsan.

Tercis-les-Bains (C–9) Another spa town, with the prehistoric grotto of Larroque and a pre-Roman 'oppidum' called 'La Source', near the confluent of the river Adour and Luy de France.

Tilh (E–10) is a small town on a hill where St. Vincent de Paul was the local curé for 20 years. Henri Meunier, a famous écarteur (Courses Landaises leaper/dancer), lived here. There are three Gascon châteaux and the arena named after the maestro.

Vielle-Soubiran (F–6) has several half timbered houses, a fortified church, a ganaderia and a gastronomic specialty 'la tourtière Jeanne' (heavily flavoured pastry).

Urgons (H–9) **Villenove** (E–6) and **Villeneuve de Marsan** (I-7) were English bastide towns. The latter is worth a visit to see the Gallo-Roman mosaics, a château, a windmill, a fortified fourteenth century gothic church, but also to see the Armagnac co-operative, Courses and local 'bandas'. The main fête is on the 1st August.

Every year in France there is a National Concours or contest for the towns and villages 'fleuris'. This is more than being the 'best kept' village. It means that well planted and well tended gardens (public and private) with flowers, shrubs and trees are assessed and marked to a formula. Of the final short list of 141 communes at national level four were from the Landes – Sainte Colombe (G–9) won 2nd prize, Bonnegarde (F–10) was in 4th place, and Castelner (G–10) and Serres Gaston

(G–9) shared equal 5th place.

Aquitaine also stages a similar contest and the Landes gained nine prizes! Amou, Habas, Herm and Pouillon earned 3 fleurs, and Cazalis, Dax, Mimizan and Mont de Marsan gained 2 fleurs each. In 1981 and again in 1986 the Landes were given the title of 'département fleuri'.

CHAPTER TWELVE:
IN TOUCH WITH THE PAST

Castles and châteaux

Remember that these have for the most part been working castles, i.e. not built for decorative and social purposes as in the Loire. Most of the solid Gascon castles, châteaux and manor houses (known as caveries) were held at one time or another by the English and their Gascon vassals. The finest are Bassoues, Ravignan, Estignols, Gaujacq and St. Pandelon (Château des Evêques).

Only exceptional or unusual buildings, classified as MH (Monument Historique) or IMH (Inscrit à l'Inventaire des Monuments Historiques) have been included. Would-be visitors are advised to check opening times either with the nearest tourist information office or with the Comité Départemental du Tourisme, 22 Rue Victor-Hugo, Mont de Marsan, 40005 Landes, Tel. 58.46.40.40.

Amou (F–10) A seventeenth century château with classic façades, mullion windows, pictures and panelling.

Arengosse (E–6) Château de Castillon, Louis XIII style (1625) with façades, gatehouse, roofs and classic gardens à la Francaise.

Arsague (E–10) Château d'Argoubet restored in the nineteenth century in Italianate style with portico and columns. Inside are Napoleonic souvenirs. The plane tree avenue leading to the château is attractive.

Aurice (G–8) Seventeenth century with a Scottish background. Tel. 58.76.01.60. Visit to Park only.

Biarotte (B–10) Château de Camiade has its main building flanked by two fortified towers. In the pretty park is a classic pigeonnier.

Caupenne (F–9) Classic seventeenth century château with emblazoned formal staircase, doors of sculpted wood, mullion windows, and the mosaics of Gleyzia.

Duhort-Bachen (H–9) Château du Lau was reconstructed in the fifteenth century and has moats, towers, guard room, frescoed kitchen and battlements. See also Châteaux de Bachen, de Souilh and de St. Jean-de-la-Castelle.

Gaujacq (F–10) Château de Sourdis is mainly seventeenth century with classic structure, façades and roofs, a cardinal's salon, library and other monastic buildings including a cloister. M. Casedevant is the caretaker, Tel. 58.89.01.01. Open all the year for tour groups, but for individuals July to mid-September. Well worth a visit.

Perquie (I–7) Château de Ravignan was restored in the nineteenth century and is a classic pure Louis XVIII style with furniture, works of art and costume collection. Tel. 58.45.22.04. Visits as for Gaujacq.

Peyrehorade (C–10) The sixteenth century château of Montréal has four round towers at the corners of its keep. A good collection of furniture.

Poyanne (E–8) A classic Louis XIII château, and until recently a minor abbey of St. Eustase, set rather forlornly in a small park. Bernard de Poyanne was one of Henri IV's captains.

Saint Pandelon (D–9) The Château des Evêques was the residence of the Bishops of Dax in the fifteenth century: octagonal tower, moats, fourteenth century keep. Tel. 58.74.85.69. In the same village area are the châteaux of Hercular, Haubardin, Laureta and Herran.

Cathedrals, abbeys and splendid churches

Between AD 361 and AD 363 Pope Sibere in Rome sent the evangelists Severus, Girons, Justin, Clair, Polycarpe, Jean and Babile to convert the heathen in Aquitaine to Christianity. Four were martyred and were canonized in due course for their courageous and successful efforts. As a result there are more than 200 romanesque churches and chapels in the Landes. The Association Culturelle de Dax, Tel. 58.74.74.33 or 58.74.45.25, devised a Festival des Abbayes each year in mid-June and also at the end of July. These ten sites, which include four Abbeys, are clustered together in the regions of the Chalosse and Orthe, south and east of Dax: St. Paul-lès-Dax, Dax, Cagnotte, Sorde l'Abbaye, Montfort, Pouillon, Hastingues, Montaut, St. Sever and Peyrehorade.

Of these the classic romanesque architecture is to be found at the Abbey of St. Sever, the crypt of St. Girons at Hagetmau, the church of St. Paul-lès-Dax and the two Abbeys of Arthous and Sorde. In addition along the line of the several pilgrim routes to Compostella in the eleventh and twelfth centuries were built many small romanesque churches which, miraculously, have managed to survive into the twentieth century. Many of the bastide towns had a fortified church in the main square with arrow-slits for the defending archers, and huge defensive walls.

Aire-sur-l'Adour (I–9) From the Roman town of Atura this has been a Bishopric until as recently as 1933. The Cathedral of St. Jean-Baptiste is basically twelfth century with both apse and façade rebuilt in the seventeenth century. It was built on the site of a Benedictine monastery and the chapterhouse is now the sacristy. Across the river and up a hill is the Church of Sainte Quittérie du Mas. From AD 629 onwards the relics of the martyred Visigoth princess have been a centre of pilgrimage. The present church dates from the eleventh century but has been repaired. The choir has six romanesque arches and capitals and the belfry soars high from its five storeys. The white marble fourth century sarcophagus has biblical scenes carved on it. Some of the figures wear Roman togas. The crypt has been cleaned and restored and is a masterpiece of genuine Roman art. Visits are difficult, so consult the Syndicat d'Initiative, Tel. 58.71.64.70.

Amou (F–10) The fourteenth century romanesque church has

157

a gothic clock tower, a fifteenth century keep, the chapel with the Plantagenet royal arms and a main altar of the eighteenth century in polychromed marble by Mazetti.

Audignon (G–9) The eleventh century romanesque church has a fifteenth century stone reredos, fourteenth century doorway with 'grotesques', and a belltower-keep with loopholes.

Bascons (H–8) This church is mainly thirteenth century and was fortified in the fifteenth century with a watch tower, gabled clock tower in a triangular shape, and arrow-slits. Later Louis XIII master altar and doors were added.

Bostens (H–6) The twelfth century church of Sainte Marie with choir, arches and clock tower of note. Frescoes of Christ in Majesty date from the same period. The presbytery has sculpted animals in a floral garden.

Brassempouy (F–10) This roman-gothic church with a fine fifteenth century spire dominates the English bastide village.

Carcarès-Sainte-Croix (E–8) The fortified church of St. Laurent de Carcarès, with belfry, loopholes, baroque altar is encircled by a cemetery (unusual in southwest France). **Carcen-Ponson** (E–7) has an identical church.

Dax (D–9) The Cathedral of Sainte Marie is of neo-Greek style of the seventeenth–eighteenth century, with a gothic outer door of the Apostles dating from the earlier thirteenth century cathedral.

Doazit (F–9) The twelfth century romanesque church of Aules has a gated-belfry, a chevet with blind arch, historic capitals and thirteenth century nave with pointed gothic arches.

Géaune (H–10) The fifteenth century church is gothic-languedoc style. The gated-belfry is on 4 pillars, with pyramidal tiles dated 1452. See also the gothic Augustin Tower.

Hagetmau (G–9) Since the ninth century the crypt of St. Girons to the west of the town has been a pilgrimage site, although the Saint evangelised this part of Gascony in the fourth century. The romanesque capitals are well preserved. The staircase to the crypt is tenth century. The vault is supported by 14 columns. The crypt is housed by a building of little provenance. One of **the** sights of Gascony.

Hastingues (C–10) The romanesque Abbey of Arthous and chapel date from the twelfth century. The very long nave has five bays; the chevet is richly decorated. This English bastide with its fine abbey and archaeological museum (q.v) is an essential visit.

Horsarrieu (G–9) The fifteenth century gothic church contains the oldest calvary in the Landes.

Laurède (E–8) Although restored in the fifteenth century, the interior decoration is superb as is the eighteenth century master altar in marble by the brothers Mazzetti. Nearby is the Maison de Peyne, an old pilgrim 'relais' restored in the seventeenth century. Try to visit Laurède if you can, perhaps between Mugron (wine) and Poyanne (castle).

Lesgor (E–7) The English fortified this romanesque church in the fourteenth century; its massive outer walls are pierced with arrow-slits and a staircase leads up to the defensive chamber below the roof, for the archers to make their plunging fire on the French troops below. From Begaar (E–8) with a roman-esque church housing a noted statue to the Virgin, west on the N 124 for 3 km and then northwest on the D 380 for 6 km takes you to Lesgor – remote and thus relatively undamaged. Continue on the D 334 to Laluque (D–7) another romanesque church, and due south on the D 27 to Notre Dame de Buglose.

Levignacq (C–6) The wooden ceiling of the nave and the mural wall paintings make this thirteenth century church in the pine forests worth a detour on the D 41 from Lesperon, just west of the N 10.

Magescq (C–8) The fortified romanesque church is near the river of the same name on the N 10.

Maylis (F–9) This small village which boasts two interesting churches is just south of the D 18 between Hagetmau and Mugron – worth a small detour.

Mont de Marsan (G–7) has a cluster of churches worth looking at – La Madeleine, St. Jean d'Août and St. Medard.

Montaut (F–9) has two notable churches – the fortified fourteenth century 'du Bourg' and the romanesque church of Brocas from the twelfth century. The latter has a fortified clock tower devised by the English military architects in the fourteenth century. Well worth a visit.

Oeyreluy (C–9 The eleventh century church has a superb romanesque main door and pre-Roman sculptures on the capitals.

Parleboscq (K–7) In this small village of 550 inhabitants there are seven churches to see: St. Cricq, Mauras, Sarran, Mura, Bouau, Espéroux and Parlesboscq, plus three Gascon châteaux and three Gascon windmills. The village is on the eastern borders with the Gers (at the foot of Michelin Map 79) between Cazauban and Montréal just south of the D 36.

Retjons (I–5) The chapel of Lugaut has a twelfth century choir and frescoes representing scenes from the Bible and the life of Christ. Retjons is just east of the D 932 and north of Roquefort.

Sabres (F–5) In the heart of the pine forests this eleventh century church has a triangular clock tower and a Renaissance main door with 5 curved arches and statues.

St. Laurent de Gosse (B–11) has a gothic church with the coat of arms of the Black Prince on the keystone of a vault. This small village is just northeast of Bayonne and also has four Gascon châteaux.

St. Martin-de-Hinx (B–10) The mainly fourteenth century church has capitals of an earlier date with the keystone representing three geese, the emblem of the Pays de Gosse. The village also has three Gascon châteaux and the gentilhommerie of Sorey.

St. Paul-lès-Dax (D–9) Tucked away on a hillside overlooking the large modern suburb of Dax is this famous romanesque eleventh century church. The apse is twelfth century with a rich decor of blind arches, historic capitals and a frieze with allegorical motifs which date from AD 1120. Worth a visit.

Saint Sever (G–8) The eleventh century romanesque Abbey and adjoining museum (q.v), despite extensive repairs, is an essential visit. On a hill top – the 'Cap de Gascogne' is remarkable. The saint's original shrine became a monastery in the seventh century, was burned in the ninth century and rebuilt in 1028–72 by Gregory of Montaner, Bishop of Lescar and Dax. The Benedictine style has a chevet with 6 apse chapels on each side, a nave with 5 bays, a clock tower and a host of marble columns, mosaics and capitals. Look also at the convent of the Jacobins founded in 1280 by King Edward I with its elegant cloister and museum (q.v).

Saubusse (C–9) Inside this fortified thirteenth century church is a fine statue of St. Michel and of Christ in wood.

Sorde-l'Abbaye (D–11) The twelfth century abbatial church has a romanesque chevet with two apses, a main doorway, nave and transept with flamboyant arches and mosaics – all of the same period. This is, with Arthous, St. Sever and St. Girons (Hagetmau), one of the essential ecclesiastical sites to see in the Landes.

Tosse (B–9) The Roman-Byzantine church is mainly eleventh century with a massive clock tower, apses and cornices with grotesque heads.

To indicate what a wide choice there is of interesting romanesque churches in the Landes, the following list of small villages boasting such churches may be of interest:
Arjuzanx (E–6), Arx (K–5), Baigts (E–9), Begaar (E–8), Beylongue (E–7), Biarotte (B–10), Biaudos (B–10), Bougue (H–7), Bourdolat (I–8), Buanes (H–9), Cagnotte (D–10), Caupenne (F–9), Commensacq (E–4), Escalens (K–6), Garein (F–6), Geloux (F–6), Horsarrieu (G–9), Lagrange (J–6), Larbey (F–9), Lespéron (C–6), Lit et Mixe (B–6), Mézos (C–5), Montfort-en-Chalosse (E–9), Moustey (F–3), Pimbo (H–10), Pissos (E–3), Port de Lanne (C–10), Rion des Landes (E–7), St. Géours de Maremme (C–9), St. Jean de Marsacq (B–10),

161

St. Justin (I–6), St. Pierre du Mont (G–7), Sarbazan (I–6), Uchacq et Parentis (G–7) and Vielle Tursan (H–9).

A series of concerts are given each summer – known as the Albret concerts. They are held at Bélis, Brocas Canenx, Cère, Labrit and Le Sen. Details from the Mairie de Labrit (G–5), Tel. 58.51.40.93.

Museums

The Landes is well off for a wide range of museums catering for all tastes.

Arthous Hastingues (C–10)	58.73.03.89	Archeology
Bascons (H–8)	58.45.90.31	Courses Landaise (closed in winter)
Biscarosse (C–2)	58.78.00.65	Hydroplanes (summer only)
Biscarosse-Bourg (C–2)	58.78.72.01	Nature (open Easter — Mid-Sept)
Brassempouy (F–10)	58.89.04.60	Prehistoric (open July/Aug afternoons only)
Buglose/St. Vincent de Paul (D–9)	58.89.91.02	Sacred Art (weekends only)
Dax (D–9)	58.74.12.91	Musée de Borda. History of Landes, local traditions
Labistide d'Armagnac (I–6)	58.44.84.35	Musée du Vigneron (Chateau Garreau) Musée des Arts et Traditions Populaires
Luxey (G–4)	58.08.01.39	Atelier des Produits Resineux (Weekends. All day summer)
Mimizan (C–4)	58.09.22.22	Local history, Arts and popular traditions (as above)
Montaut (F–9)	58.76.05.13	Prehistoric paintings (open July-Aug)
Mont de Marsan (G–7)	58.75.00.45	Sculpture Despiau-Wlerick (open all year)
		Dubalen Natural History (open all year)
		Musée de Plein Air (open all year)

Montfort-en-Chalosse (E–9)	58.98.69.27	Arts & Traditions populaires (July-2 Sept)
Parentis-en-Born (D–3)	58.78.41.03	Musée du Petrole (not Tuesday)
Sabres (F–5)	58.07.52.70	Ecomusée 'Marqueze' (Weekends. All day summer)
Saint-Sever (G–8)	58.76.00.10	Lapidary & mosaics museum of Jacobins (summer afternoons)
Samadet (G–10)	58.79.13.00	Faiencerie, porcelain, pottery (all year)
Sanguinet (D–10)	58.78.66.63	Archeology & Hydrobiology (summer afternoons)
Solferino (E–5)	58.07.21.08	Museum of Napoleon III (all year)
Sorde-l'Abbaye (D–11)	58.73.04.83	Lapidary & mosaics museum (summer afternoons)

There are minor museums at Aire sur l'Adour (I–9), Géou (I–6), Gouts (E–8), Hossegor (A–9) and Orist (C–9).

Some museums may not open on Tuesdays. Some museums are free, but others charge about Francs 10 for an adult and half that for students and children.

CHAPTER THIRTEEN:
THE SPARKLE OF THE SILVER COAST

The Côte d'Argent – the silver coast – is the name given to the 100 km coast within the borders of the Landes département. Another 100 km continues north into the Gironde and south into the Pyrénées-Atlantique. Michelin Map 78 will be needed.

This chapter concerns twelve major and three minor plages which have been linked up into a Grand Tour of the Plages and includes five lakes with some intriguing towns in between. There is no coastal road running overlooking the beaches and the D 652, which covers the whole length of the Côte d'Argent, is between 2 and 20 km inland. In a way this is a blessing in disguise in that there is no ribbon development spoiling the coastal views. The many modern hotels, apartment buildings and villas are inland, usually half hidden amongst pine woods but within walking distance of each plage. Usually there is a bathing strip on the sands of about 400 metres, which is under the eagle-eyed surveillance of a coastguard. Since the surf can be dangerous (good for surfers but bad for ordinary swimmers) the three coloured flags indicating the relative safety/danger of the waves must be rigorously obeyed. Having said that, the beaches are un-polluted, with huge sand dunes, and even at high tide have about one hundred metres of marvellous silvery sand, with no shingle, pebbles or rocks! There are several well-known inland river. 'Courants' (strong currents) at Huchet and Mimizan.

The resorts offer a whole range of social activities including cinemas, concerts, theatre, a casino or two, fêtes, fireworks and festivals: also corridas and Courses Landaises, sea fishing, bicycling, pelota, tennis, golf, walking tours, sail-boarding, and discotheques for the young. Generally speaking the standard of hotels and restaurants is high but every resort offers hotels and restaurants *within* budget!

Every town and village mentioned in this chapter was English-owned during the three centuries of rule from London. Several towns and villages are also mentioned in subsequent chapters in more detail, as indeed are the appropriate hotels and restaurants.

Assuming the traveller arrives from the north via Bordeaux, the D 216 crosses the border between the Gironde and the Landes at the Forest of Lagnereau. The same road now becomes the D 46 and brings one to **Sanguinet** on the old Roman Way and pilgrim route to Compostella. There are still vestiges of a Gallo-Roman distillery of resin products to be seen. To the west is the large inland lake of Cazaux and Sanguinet where many regattas take place in the summer. The road changes number to the D 652 and 13 km southeast to **Biscarosse**, a substantial town originally of Basque origins, which now separates two large lakes. One of these, the Parentis, has France's major 'offshore' oil rigs. Between Biscarosse and the sea is a huge 'Centre d'Essais des Landes' known as CEL (space research) and predictably, next to it on the south side, a forbidden military zone – all well concealed within the pine forests. The naval base of Hourtiquets offers boat trips around the lake.

Biscarosse-Plage is 9½ km northwest on the D 146 and is the northern-most plage town in the Landes. There are two châteaux and a fortified fourteenth century church here, and a legendary elm tree over 600 years old! There are two minor roads, the Avenue des Echassiers and Avenue Nue, which lead towards the beaches. This is a major resort with a wide choice of hotels and restaurants as well as campsites. The casino is on the Boulevard des Sables.

Back on our tracks to Biscarosse and southeast to **Parentis-en-Born** where in 1954 oil was first discovered. It is a quiet little town with a Petroleum museum, where Courses Landaises, corridas, summer dances in the streets, and even a music hall are staged.

South, west and south again on the D 652 via Gastes with views over the huge lake of Biscarosse and Parentis, and Ste.-Eulalie-en-Born towards the lake of Aureilhan, still on the pilgrim road, and **Mimizan**. It was originally known as Roman

Segosa, and now as the 'Pearl of the Côte d'Argent'! It is a curious mixture of ancient (thirteenth century Benedictine Abbey) and modern (a twentieth century château of Woolsack built in mock-Tudor by the Duke of Westminster after World War I).

Mimizan-Plage is 6 km away and has a rich assortment of plage-fêtes, pelota, firework displays, Courses Landaises, aero-club, seafishing and a casino.

From Mimizan-Plage back to Mimizan and 32 km south to St. Julien en Born via Bias on the old Roman Way. In the eighteenth century the dune encroachment was so persistent that the church of St. Michel was removed stone by stone 2 km inland, and rebuilt. 1½ km before one reaches St. Julien is the D 41 running west for 7½ km to little **Contis-plage** where minor rivers link up to produce the 'courant' of Contis.

Back on the main road and 5 km south of St. Julien, just after passing through the curiously named Lit-et-Mixe, which has a notable romanesque church, go due west on the D 68 for 7 km to another small plage resort called **Cap-de-l'Homy**.

Again on the D 652 south via various small hamlets to Vielle-St.-Girons, which has a romanesque church. The D 42 leads due west over the Grand Tuc (a huge sand dune) to **St. Girons Plage**. Although small it offers all the beach facilities needed.

Back on the D 652 towards Léon passing the lake of that name on the west side, from which the famous Courant d'Huchet hurtles out to sea. There is a hamlet on the beach called Huchet, reached by the D 328, but it is not a recognised Plage.

Léon has the remains of a pagan temple and several old traditional peasant houses of the Landes style, half timbered and with daubed mud walls. Rowing boats can be hired to explore the inland waterways, Tel. 58.48.75.39, May–September. The vegetation is quite remarkable – hibiscus, tamarisk, and all kinds of water flora and fauna; many species of mushrooms, eels and game birds.

East of Léon 14 km on the D 142 is Castets, which makes a short cut onwards by the D 947 a further 18 km to Dax.

But continue on the D 652 southwest from Léon to Moliets-et-Maa, from where one can hire a boat to make the descent on the courant d'Huchet. The D 117 west for 3 km takes one to another small plage of the same name. There are two inland lakes, the Moliets and the Laprade. Four kilometres down the D 652 is **Messanges** which was once a port and a hostellerie for the Compostella pilgrims. The plage is 2 km west on the D 82 near the lake of Moysan. Four kilometres south on the D 652 to **Vieu-Boucau-les-Bains**, also known as Vieux-Boucau Port d'Albret. The Canal de Moisan comes in from the northeast, but the port is fed by the large inland lake of Soustons. The modern arena holds up to 4000 spectators for the corridas and Courses Landaises. The Course à la cocarde is an amateur comic-opera fight played strictly for laughs! The Pelota fronton is one of the most attractive in the Landes, where the game is played every week. Grand Chistera is the same game played with a wicker basket that fits one's hand, allowing a fast, slung scooped shot. Their spectacular fireworks display is on the lake, always on the 15th August. The large marine lake of 125 acres is now a modern inland sailing centre. The three beaches, Vieux Boucau on the north side, and Dune Littorale and Plage de Soustons, are large, clean and beautiful.

Soustons is 10½ km inland and was occupied by the Romans and then the English, each for three centuries. Some of the old fifteenth century farms are still called 'les maisons des Anglais', 'le quartier sterling', 'le Tuc des Anglais'. There are arenas for Courses Landaises, pelota, 'echassiers danseurs' (old time shepherds and shepherdesses dancing on the stilts which enabled them to keep an eye on their straying flocks), regattas on the lake, rugby. Ask also here for the vin de sable, a drinkable wine grown locally on very sandy soil.

The Côte d'Argent route continues 2½ km southeast of Vieux-Boucau by the D 79 17 km into Hossegor. Just 2 km to the west are small plages called des Casernes, Seignosse, Le Penon, where the world (i.e. European) surfing championship is held each year, and Les Estagnots.

Hossegor is built around a long narrow lake of that name, with the inland town called Soorts-Hossegor, where many famous artists have lived (Maurice Ravel, Gabriel d'Annunzio etc.). The museum here is noted for its collection of vintage cars. Courses Landaises, pelota, golf, tennis, fishing, riding plus the verdant flowers, trees and shrubs make this a fashionable resort. The Casino is on the Avenue de Gaujacq, Tel. 58.43.50.10, overlooking the canal d'Hossegor.

Hossegor blends into **Cap-Breton** on the south side. It was once a port competitive to Bayonne under the Romans, and the English, until the River Adour changed its direction southward. Cap-Breton is just as sophisticated as Hossegor and also boasts a marina and casino, Tel. 58.72.13.75. In mid-June is the famous 'Fête de la Mer'.

South on the D 652 towards Labenne one finds the D 126 west for 4 km to the small Labenne-Ocean plage, and south of that another called Ondres-Plage reached by the D 26 from the N 10. These are the last two in the series of plages which form the Côte d'Argent.

A typical midsummer calendar of events on the Côte d'Argent.

18 June	**Hossegor**	Cesta punta/Pelota tournament
19 June	**Soustons**	Songs and ballads evening
20 June	**Hossegor**	Bicycle race
20 June	**Soustons**	Gala tauromachique — bull fighting evening, music, dancing
21 June	**Cap Breton**	Fête de la Mer
21 June	**Hossegor**	Musical fête and Pelota tournament
21 June	**Seignosse–le–Penon**	Musical fête
21 June	**Soustons**	Musical fête
21 June	**Vieux Boucau**	Village fair and 'fête champetre'
23 June	**Seignosse–le–Penon**	Courses Landaises
23 June	**Vieux Boucau**	Folklore of the Landes: Courses Landaises
24 June	**Hossegor**	Musical gala evening: Courses Landaises
24 June	**Mimizan**	Ball of Saint Jean
25 June	**Hossegor**	Pelota tournament
25 June	**Seignosse–le–Penon**	Folklore of the Landes
26 June	**Cap Breton**	Courses Landaises
26 June	**Seignosse**	Pelota basque tournament
26 June	**Vieux Boucau**	Course Landaise
27 June	**Cap Breton**	Painting exhibition
27 June	**Hossegor**	Vintage car exhibition & procession
27 June	**Léon**	School fête
27 June	**Mimizan**	Obstacle Races

This is just part of the events of the summer season June–September. The French like their 'animations' and there is always some social activity in the resort-towns.

Where to stay

	Hotels	Tourist Office Tel. No.
Biscarosse	11 (200 beds)	58.78.20.96
Capbreton	19 (420 beds)	58.72.12.11
Hossegor	20 (363 beds)	58.43.72.35
Léon	2 (28 beds)	58.48.76.03
Mimizan	12 (206 beds)	58.08.11.20
Contis	3 (42 beds)	58.42.89.80
St. Girons	1 (14 beds)	—
Vieux Boucau	6 (188 beds)	58.48.13.47

Each plage has camping sites shown in a following chapter.

There is a surfing course available VVF 'Les Tuquets', 40510 Seignosse, Tel. 58.43.30.18. The best months are May, June and September. Surf-casting courses are available at Gîtes et Soleil, Route du Puntaou, 40550 Léon, Tel. 58.48.74.78. The Surf-casting Club at Marenne will also give one instructions.

Trekland, M. J.M. Lasserre, Villa Potana, 40180 Narosse, Tel. 58.73.50.24, offers one week hiking tours from Biscarosse to Cap Breton averaging 18–20 km per day, through wood, across lakes, down rivers, boat down the Courants, sleeping rough. It sounds enormous fun. June to September for Francs 1850 inclusive of everything including food, insurance and return bus to Biscarosse.

Tourist Offices: Other towns mentioned include Labenne, Tel. 58.45.40.99, Lit-en-Mixe, Tel. 58.42.83.10, Moliets, Tel. 58.48.50.80, Parentis, Tel. 58.78.43.60, Seignosse le Penon, Tel. 58.72.85.62, and Soustons, Tel. 58.41.52.62. All tourist offices will have advice on camping, hiking, canoeing, cycling, horse riding and other activities.

Villages de Vacances at Cap Breton, Tel. 58.72.11.49; at Seignosse, Tel. 58.43.30.18; at Vieux-Boucau, Tel. 58.48.23.94; at Soustons, Tel. 58.48.00.03.

So spare a thought for the two French engineer-planners who created the forests and the silver beaches of the Côte d'Argent. M. Nicolas Brémontier in 1788 stabilised the encroaching dunes by forming a 12 metre high wooden barrier, 70 metres above high tide level, anchored in place by shrubs. The safety zone in the interior was planted with special resistant young pine trees. About 30 years later M. Chambrelent drained the area allowing forestation and crop-bearing fertile land to develop. Between them the annual erosion of 18 cubic metres per metre length was totally halted by the new sand dune barriers.

CHAPTER FOURTEEN:
A BREATH OF GASCONY AIR

One of the main reasons why France still remains such a beautiful, relatively unspoilt country is that in 1970 the government of the day took a decision to protect by law vast tracts of the countryside against the ravages of man.

Nearly 20 years later there are no less than 21 Parcs Naturels Regionaux, with 4 more about to be added. Almost 5% of the land-mass of France, rather over 2½ million hectares (6¼ million acres) has been designated a protected area. Just under a million people live in these natural parks and many millions of tourists visit them each year.

The objectives are laid down by law. The development of agriculture, of local artisans' work, of appropriate business and industry, provided the environmental quality of the region is completely protected. The life of the local population must not be sacrificed to tourism (bouleverser la vie).

Parc Naturel Régional des Landes de Gascogne

The Parc Naturel Régional des Landes de Gascogne (Michelin Map 78) was one of the founder-members of 1970 and covers an area of just under 500,000 acres shared almost equally with the northern department of the Gironde. A population of a little under 30,000 lives in this huge area. The 11 communes in the Landes are Argelouse (F–3), Belhade (F–2), Callen (G–3), Commensacq (E–4), Luxey (G–4), Moustey (F–3), Pissos (E–3), Sabres (F–5), Saugnac-et-Muret (E–2), Sore (G–3) and Trensacq (F–4). The park area in the Landes is square in shape, roughly 30 km on each side. The SNCF railway line from Bordeaux southwards passes along the

171

western edge of the park stopping at Labouheyre. The river Leyre flows into the Bassin d'Arcachon and its tributaries, the Grande Leyre and the Petite Leyre, both commence north-west of Mont de Marsan. The rivers are bordered by alders, oak and chestnut trees. The main roads are the N 10 from Bordeaux which splits at Le Muret (E–2) with the N 134 south-east to Mont de Marsan and the N 10 continuing southwest to Bayonne. Other main roads bisecting the Parc are the D 651 on the east side running north and south to Mont de Marsan, and two lateral roads, the D 43 and D 626 running west and east.

In the last 15 years the 20 churches on the Pilgrims Way to St. Jacques de Compostella have been restored. Over 7000 ethnological objects have been documented and photographed. The railway track of 18 km has been restored as well as the vintage rolling stock. Parts of the rivers have been restocked with trout and pike and the wildlife of the area protected – migrating birds, wild boar, foxes, pheasants, roe-deer and squirrels.

Until the nineteenth century the northern region of the Landes was mostly sandy moors, only fit for sheep grazing. The shepherds used stilts to survey their flocks. The moving sand blown in from the Bay of Biscay shores prevented agri-cultural activities and crop growing. The sea dunes were harnessed by an engineer called M. Brémontier (see the chapter on the Plage-Resorts), shrubs (broom, heather, ferns) grew or were planted, and maritime pines were planted with great success about 150 years ago. The resin was distilled and used for a dozen commercial purposes, but the sheep dis-appeared. However with the progress of petro-chemical research plus the price competition of cheaper resins from Greece and Portugal, the resin business in the Landes is in decline. New cornfields and fruit trees have been planted as well as strawberry and asparagus patches. Wood is still an important commodity used for structural lumber, panelling and wooden crates. Most of the local houses of any age are made of wood and 'torchis' (a form of daub and wattle).

The gastronomy of the northern Landes includes pigeon (palombes), deer, river-fish, foie gras, confit (preserved meat), asparagus, and is usually served in the restaurants mentioned in this chapter.

The Administration HQ of the Parc Naturel is at 15, Place Jean-Jaurès, 4000 Mont de Marsan, Tel. 58.06.24.25.

The Syndicat d'Initiative/Tourisme is at Pissos, Tel. 58.07.70.23.

The eleven communes

Argelouse (F–3) is a tiny hamlet of 37 inhabitants – the least populated in the département. The name derives from the 'argile' clay of the region. The fifteenth century rustic church overlooks the Petite Leyre river. The Fountain of Sainte Marguerite was a pilgrimage point for nursing mothers who wished to retain their milk.

Belhade (F–2) pop. 126, is also on the same river tributary further north. It was the earliest Barony of the Landes, and the Château Rochefort-Lavie and eleventh century romanesque church are worth a visit. The Fountain of Sainte Anne was a pilgrimage point for young mothers who wished to be able to breast-feed their babies. In 1943 the pine forests here were devastated by fire.

Callen (G–3) pop. 129, is on the eastern side of the Parc and has several old Landaise-style farmhouses. The Fountain of Devotion here is named after St. Eutrope, and a fête is held on 30th April each year.

Commensacq (E–4) pop. 33. Once there was an Order of Malta here. The eleventh century romanesque church of St. Martin with notable frescoes overlooks the valley of the Grande Leyre river. The Fountain of Devotion is to the patron saint of Gascony, Ste. Quittérie. The river-harbour of Mexico is here for canoes and kayaks.

Luxey (G–4) pop. 721, was occupied by the Romans and there are traces still visible. The Ecomuseum 'La Gemme' (resin products) is here. There are many lagoons amongst the woods. The village is also on the Petite Leyre river; there are several traditional rural houses.

Moustey (F–3) pop. 568, is near the apex where its two tributaries join up with the river Leyre. The rivalry of the two families of Pelay and de Couyes produced two interesting 'gothic flamboyant' fifteenth century churches: St. Martin and Notre Dame, which are side by side. A treasure trove of 800 Roman coins was discovered at Moustey, which has two Fountains of Devotion, to Sainte Ruffine and St. Yves at Biganon.

Pissos (E–3) pop. 809, was ravaged in 1250 AD by Simon of Leicester, son of Simon de Montfort. There are three notable windmills, the romanesque twelfth century church of Richet, and the Maison des Artisans to look at, since Pissos is one of the main tourist and commercial centres of the Parc Naturel. It is on the N 134 where it crosses the Grande Leyre.

Sabres (F–5) pop. 1105, is at the junction of the N 134, D 44 and D 626 and is the southernmost village in the Parc Naturel. Besides a very interesting eleventh century romanesque church, Sabres has the Ecomusée de la Grande Lande de Marqueze. This is the top-ranking environmental museum in the whole of France. (See separate mention.) Access to Marqueze is only by special toy train 6 km northwest. Essential to visit!

Saugnac-et-Muret (E–2) pop. 655, was a resting place for the pilgrims to St. Jacques de Compostella, where the modern roads of the N 10 and N 134 join. There is a twelfth century chapel of Muret, a seventeenth century church and a Fountain of devotion to St. Eutrope. A special workshop has been set up here to provide environmental lessons, with practical work on local flora and fauna.

Sore (G–3) pop. 918, is on the Petite Leyre between Luxey and Argelouse, and was originally inhabited by a Greek colony. The main town gates are called 'Porte des Anglais', and there are several other early middle age sites, including dovecots, windmills, and a twelfth century church. A gastronomic centre since pheasants, geese, ducks and goats are reared here for the table. The Fête of the lilies of the valley is on 1st May.

Trensacq (F–4) pop. 200, is a small hamlet north of Sabres on the N 134 and has several old Landaise farms, a small gothic church and Fountain of Devotion to St. Eutrope. There is a sandy beach on the river Leyre.

Places to stay and eat

		Tel. no.
Belhade (F–2)	Le Chêne Pascal (R)	72.53
Luxey (G–4)	Relais de la Haute-Lande (H-R)	02.30
Moustey (F–3)	La Fringale (R)	77.85
Pissos (E-3)	Du Commerce (H-R)	70.16
	L'Oasis (H)	70.54
	Chez Elise Daugnague (R)	77.25
Sabres (F–5)	Auberge des Pins (H-R)	50.47
	Le Relais (H-R)	50.05
Sáugnac-et-Muret(E–2)	Le Grandgousier (H-R)	72.19
	Le Caravanier (H)	72.14
Sore (G–3)	Le Caravanier (H)	72.14
	Hotel du Commerce (H-R)	60.05
	J. Reale (H)	63.11
	J. Andreys (R)	62.36
	Des Chasseurs (R)	62.36
Trensacq (F–4)	Au bon Coin (R)	06.55

R = Restaurant, H = Hotel.   prefix 58.07.

Luglon (F–5) has the Chez Laurence (R), 58.07.53.08, and Solférino (E–5) has the Auberge du Vieux Logis (H–R), 58.07.21.01. Both villages are just outside the Parc on the south side.

Chambres d'Hôtes (bed & breakfast)

There are four in the Parc – Moustey (M. de Croix, 58.07.71.42), Pissos (Madame Brot, 58.07.70.50), Sabres (M. Tucoo-Chala, 58.07.52.00), and another in Belhade.

Camp sites

Pissos municipal site (58.07.70.45), Sabres municipal site (58.07.52.51) also at the farm of M. Elie Dupin (58.07.52.63).

Saugnac-et-Muret, Sore and Trensace also have sites known as 'aire naturelle'. The rates are usually Francs 10-13 per head per day.

Gîtes forestiers

Sore has 7 gîtes – Telephone Mairie 58.07.60.06, and Pissos has 20 gîtes, Telephone Mairie 58.07.70.23.

Note that camping in the wilds is strictly forbidden because of the risk of fire and damage to the pine forests.

Ateliers–gîtes

These are working study studio/workshops which accept up to 30 students of ecology of all ages who are genuinely interested in undertaking a sensible and genuine course. The subjects covered, which include working visits, are – flora, fauna, demography, effects of the sun (including sun-dried pottery), the history of the Landes (including migration), local architecture, the water-ways of the Landes, the economy (including saw-mills, agriculture) and many others. The Maison Marginier 40410 Pissos, Tel. 58.07.73.36, the Atelier-Gîte de Saugnac 40410 Pissos, Tel. 58.07.73.01, and the Atelier-Gîte de Pratiques Informatiques 40410 Pissos, Tel. 58.07.73.01, which is at Saugnac et Muret, are the three gîtes. The 1987 Pension complète costs (lodging, breakfast and two meals) Francs 105/110 per head for students, and Francs 125/135 for non-scholars. Other activities include orienteering, archery, bicycling, pinasse (boating) and horse-riding.

Village de vacances

A new holiday village for youngsters has been created at the Domaine de Peyricat in Sabres, Tel. 58.07.51.88.

The ecomusée de la Grande Lande

Each year over 100,000 visitors, including 15,000 students, come to Marquèze from Sabres or Labouheyre only by train. There are nine vintage trains each way every day in the season. The line was first used in 1889; no cars are permitted in the area. The cost of a return rail ticket and visit to the Ecomusée is about Francs 27 for an adult, Francs 11 for a child.

The object of the Ecology Museum is to restore to the area of Marquèze the exact ambience, customs and way of life as it was a hundred years ago at the end of the nineteenth century. The family of Bonnat lived here for generations – certainly in 1824. Near the small station is an old barn which is now a modern museum with audio-visual montages illustrating the traditional cultures.

The 'maison de Maître de Marquèze' is a large one-floor house with a huge roof (an 'airial') totally restored with eight rooms furnished appropriately. Nearby is the 'Maison des Brassiers' for the farm workers, a thatched 'borde', another barn, a bakehouse, not only for baking bread, cakes, roasting the meats, but also for drying out the linen. The 'Poulailler' was a roofed chicken house on four legs to protect the chickens from marauding foxes and to provide droppings for manure. The garden grows vegetables for use in soups and also a range of medicinal plants (artemesia, lilies, borage etc.). A small 'vin de sable' vineyard grows vines called 'Baco' white and red, and 'Noah'. One can see various types of pine including a pine-seeding plot. There is an old working mill 'maison du meunier', a hand-mill, sheep folds, wells, an apiary, an aviary and experimental maize fields and fruit orchards.

Atelier de produits resineux

Luxey is a village 22 km east north east from Marquèze, reached by the D 315 from Sabres. Behind the church is a resin workshop and distillery which was in working order from 1859 to 1954. The address is J & C Vidal, Luxey 40430, Sore, Tel. 58.08.01.39. In the three buildings one can see how the processes and techniques were deployed to produce a whole range of end products – paint, inks, chewing gum, sticky paper, soaps, adhesives and compounds derived from colophane, the clear distilled product. From the turpentine essence came synthetic rubber, many perfumery, pharma-

177

ceutical products, varnishes, polishes and combustibles. The guided visit lasts an hour. The Atelier is open on weekends, 31 March to 27 October, and daily from 1 June to 15 September. A visit costs Francs 11 for an adult and Francs 7 for a child.

The million hectares of Gascon/Landes forests provided a huge reservoir of raw material. The 'Espace Pin des Landes' next to the 'Atelier' shows the modern usages for this timber and the pine oils.

Atelier de pratiques informatiques

The Atelier–Gîte de Saugnac, 40401 Pissos, Tel. 58.07.73.01, is most unusual. There are a whole range of computer-based classes. There are language courses, computer, wordprocessor classes, basic accountancy. The afternoons are allocated to canoeing, horseriding, bicycling, archery, pottery, orienteering, etc. A week's study course, usually for a group of 15 people, costs Francs 300 plus full pension of Francs 110 a day lodging and all meals. An admirable and practical range of courses for intelligent young people who want an active exploration in the Parc Naturel in the afternoon. Saugnac is on the River Leyre and easy to reach by the N 10 on the northern border of Landes and Gironde.

Activities

- **Bicycling**

   There is a 330 km circuit of the Parc and full details of the route and appropriate stops can be obtained from the Atelier-Gîte de Saugnac, 40410 Pissos, Tel. 58.07.73.01.

- **Canoe-kayak**

   The Grande Leyre offers excellent facilities starting at Mexico, the base at Commensacq, Tel. 58.07.05.15, Gîte open May–September inclusive. The first lap northwards is 4.5 km to La Pouloye, Tel. 58.07.06.51, Gîte open July and August, then 6 km to Contegrit, 10 km to La Forge, 2.5 km to Bern and 2 km to Testarouman, Tel. 58.07.70.58, Gîte open mid-June to mid-September. Next 5 km to Richet,

4 km to Moustey and 6 km to Saugnac, Tel. 58.07.73.01, Atelier-Gîte open all the year. From here you can canoe to the Arcachon Basin 45 km due north and the ornithological park of Le Teich, with several Gîtes on the way in the Gironde.

- **Nature studies**
  Trees/flora to be found include cork-oaks, furze, gorse whins, bracken, yellow iris, royal water-ferns, mushrooms. Birds include all kinds of duck, swans, waders, grey-lag geese etc.

- **Train journeys**
  A small train rotates between the small Gare de Sabres and Marquèze 5 km northwest to see the famous Ecomusée (June to mid-September). A steam train operates on Sundays and holidays. The autorail continues to Labou-heyre and the coastal resort of Mimizan.

- **Fishing**
  The two rivers Leyre are in the first category (the best). The fish include eel, pike, plaice, trout, perch and roach. A carte de pêche (fishing permit) is needed. Beats are at Belhade (Madame Poupard), Commensacq (the Mairie), Luxey (M. Villenave), Moustey (ask at the tabac), Pissos (M. Dupuch), Sabres (the Mairie), Sore (the iron-monger, M. Duprat). The Association of the Valleys of the Leyre is at the Mairie of Pissos (M. Chouet-Moustey).

- **Maison des artisans**
  From May to mid-September this is open on the Route de Sore, Pissos, Tel. 58.07.70.66. Local artisans make and sell leather goods, shoes (sabots), baskets, honey, pottery, paintings and handicrafts.

- **Orienteering courses**
  Available at Le Graoux-Saugnac.

- **Museums**
  Besides the Ecomusée, Moustey has one open in summer.

179

- **Riding**
  Facilities at Belhad-Centre Equestre, Tel. 58.07.77.19/ 58.07.75.10 (16 horses and ponies).

- **Tennis**
  Municipal courts in Sabres, Sore, Pissos and Saugnac – open in July–August only.

- **Fairs and markets**
  Pissos Fair is over Easter weekend and also the weekend before the 15th August. Luxey has a market day, the second Thursday in each month. Sabres has a market every Thursday. Sore is the same as Luxey.

- **Running marathon**
  Every year in the Grande Lande on the 14th July (Bastille Day). There are also stilt races, a Landes tradition.

The health spas of Gascony

The Anglo Saxons have many different characteristics from our Latin cousins on the other side of 'La Manche'. We have our quota of hypochondriacs who anxiously await the latest twinge and ache. To the French their annual 'cure' is part of their life and needs no comment. Year after year they go back to their favourite Thermal Spa for a two week course of mud baths, daily imbibing of quantities of spa waters and often more rigorous treatments. A friend of mine, now a farmer in the Lot region, near Cahors, fought at Dien-Bien-Phu as a sergeant-major in the 'Paras'. He is literally built like a tank without a pound of excess weight. Each year he and his wife separately (one has to mind the farm when the other is away) attend the same spa for a health regime. This is at some considerable cost since a clutch of 'médécins' are in attendance! They are two amongst hundreds of thousands who visit the 60 or so spa towns in France. I have visited Vichy out of season (sad, almost mournful and deserted) and Dax in season (crammed with thousands of surprisingly active 'curistes').

Gascony has nine Spa towns – six in the Landes and three in the Gers. Those in the Landes are sited on or near the River

Adour or a tributary of it. Those in the Gers are usually near a river. Some of the smaller ones have a season, usually March to November. All of them have a wide range of quality hotels and Michelin-graded restaurants to aid the 'curistes' in their recovery!

'Hot' dog cure

Legend has it that a Roman legionnaire, about to embark on yet another campaign, rather callously threw his elderly dog, stiff jointed and crippled with rheumatism, into the River Adour in order to drown it. Back from subduing the enemies of Rome, his Legion marched into Dax, only to be greeted by the hound renovated by the healing muddy river waters! As a result the Roman garrison encircled the hot spring – La Fontaine Chaude or Source 'La Nèhe' and built the Imperial Thermal baths, with magnificent spa installations plus temples and monuments. Part of the original hot water spring can still be seen in the centre of Dax.

Before the Roman legionnaire's 'hot' dog there is evidence of hot water springs in this region when it was occupied by the pre-Roman tribe called the Tarbelles. Then the spring waters were called Aquae Tarbellicae.

The facts are that *each day* nearly 2½ million litres of water of a temperature of 64° 'springs' up to the benefit of many thousands of French 'curistes' in Dax. Originally at the time of the land faults which convulsed the present Iberian-French borders of the Pyrénées, a subterannean spring was also created running 2000 metres, two kilometres, below ground level. Flowing at speed underground it gathered beneficial minerals en route.

In the basin of the 'Fontaine Chaude', after periods of intense sun, one can see a collection of algae identical to those found in the mud of the river Adour which now produces a natural medicament called 'le Péloïde de Dax'.

The Thermal Zone extends under the bed of the river Adour for 1200 metres in length and a hundred metres in width. The dolomitic underground rocks give the waters their chemical composition. In Dax, which is the second largest Thermal zone

181

in France, drilled bore-holes in selected places pump up rather over 600,000 cubic metres of thermal water of which 400,000 are utilised for therapeutical purposes. Two old springs called 'Le Trou des Pauvres' and 'Les Puits du Roth' near the Stade Municipale have been capped and abandoned.

The composition of the hot spring water per litre includes the following traces: 101 milligrammes of calcium, 31 milligrammes of magnesium, 143 milligrammes of sodium, 183 milligrammes of chlorate, 320 milligrammes of sulphur oxide. As a result the water is hyperthermal, sulphuric calcium magnesiate, sodium chlorate and radioactive. The radioactivity is characterised by the presence of uranium, radium, thorium and potassium. The water is employed in about thirty different ways: as a drink for a diuretic effect, eliminating uric acid; as baths, showers, douches, below water massage, and, mixed with turpentine from the forests of the Landes, it makes a special vapour for inhalation.

In Dax there are no less than 18 thermal establishments supplied from a huge central tank with their own springs and mud baths of which 15 have had hotels built around them. There are also three separate thermal swimming pools. The mud is called La Boue de Dax (Péloïde) and its composition is controlled by the Régie Municipale des Boues de Dax who also supply it.

In 1987 the treatment prices for a course of 18 treatments of baths or applications of mud 'RHNI' was Francs 892. Additional charges per session varied from a Bain Vapeur Francs 12.65 to underwater massage for Francs 50.90. The terms are standard for every curiste but of course the additional treatments can be very expensive, plus hotel and pension for a fortnight. Each spa has its speciality although all offer relief to rheumatic sufferers and osteomalaccia problems; some offer relief to trauma sufferers (traumatologie), phlebitis and for urinary problems.

Fountains of devotion

There are about 50 villages in Gascony which still have, or until recently have had 'Fountains of Devotion' where miraculous cures have occurred over the centuries. In most cases these were due to small springs of 'eau chaude' from one of the tributaries of the River Adour supplying Dax and the other main thermal spas with the water with 'miraculous' properties. Losse (Landes J–5) has the 'sources miraculeuses de St. Georges' at Moncaut for rheumatism sufferers, and Ousse-Suzan (Landes F–7) has three such fountains: Sainte Rose d'Ages, St. Jean (for eczema) and St. Girons (for rheumatism).

The Spa towns of the Landes

	Tel. No.	
Dax (D–9)	58.74.82.33	Open all year
St. Paul-lès-Dax (D–9)	58.91.60.01	Open all year
Eugenie-lès-Bains (H–9)	58.51.19.01	Mar 1–29 Nov
Préchacq-les-Bains (D–8)	58.57.21.21	Mar 28–8 Nov
Saubusse-lès-Bains (C–9)	58.57.31.04	Mar 9–27 Nov
Tercis-lès-Bains (C–9)	58.57.82.08	Open all year
Gamarde-lès-Bains (E–9)		

Spa towns in the Gers

	Tel. No.		
Aurensan (A–7)	62.09.46.06	Seasonal	
Barbotan-lès-Thermes (B–3)	62.69.52.09	Feb 1–22 Dec	
Castera-Verduzan (F–5)	62.68.13.41	May 2–31	Oct

A short profile of each of the spa towns appears in the appropriate regional chapter.

CHAPTER FIFTEEN:
THE LOCAL WINES AND
FOOD OF LANDES

Even before Eleanor of Aquitaine handed over her domaines as dowry to her English husband in 1152, the wines of the Landes were well known. After her marriage the wines of Tursan (vin délimité de qualité supérieure VDQS) were exported to England, and to Cordoba and Seville in Spain. The pilgrims were enthusiastic ambassadors for the Tursan wines. Later in the period fifteenth–eighteenth century they were shipped to Holland and Germany. More recently in 1958 they were awarded the Appellation d'Origine of VDQS.

To the east of the Tursan wine region, divided by the N 134 south from Aire sur l'Adour towards Pau, is the Madiran wine area in the Gers. To the south and southwest of Mont de Marsan, Géaune (H–10) and Mugron (F–8) are the two main centres for wine growing, although there are wine co-operatives at Pouillon (D–10), St. Cricq-Chalosse (F–9), Labatut (D–10) and Bélus (C–10) which produce 'vin de table'.

The cépage or wine varietals for the production of Tursan, the best quality wine, are as follows. The Barroque for the white wines, the Tannat (known locally as Moustron), Cabernets Franc and Sauvignon for the red wines, and Cabernets Sauvignon and Franc for the occasional rosés.

The Tursan dry white wines are described as 'fruités et nerveux' and are ideal with fish and shellfish. One local expert describes them as 'Nez un peu bonbon anglais, fruité et plaisant'. What a nerve! The Tursan red wines have a good fresh ruby colour, with tannin and a 'gout de terroir' (earthy flavour).

The maximum production per hectare (2½ acres) is limited to 45 hectolitres (a hectolitre is about 12 cases): this compares favourably with the Beaujolais area where production is 60 hectolitres per hectare.

The major producer in the Tursan area is the excellent co-op called Les Vignerons du Tursan, 40320 Géaune, Tel. 58.44.51.25. M. Gallond is the Inspecteur des Ventes. The co-op was founded in 1957 and has 325 vigneron members farming 350 hectares (nearly 900 acres) and produces 18,000 hectolitres of which half are white and half red wines. The co-op also produces considerable quantities of 'vin de table', usually sold 'en vrac' i.e. in bulk at Francs 4.90 per litre, whereas the Tursan VDQS in bottle is priced at Francs 13.30 per bottle. Their selection (Black label) costs Francs 16.80 per bottle. It is described as 'attractive, deep-red colour and pleasant nose. A hint of pine is a reminder of the Landes countryside. Interestingly light on the palate with a slight sparkle.'

It is estimated that the co-op control up to 90% of the Tursan wines grown in the 30 little villages including Bats, Payros-Cazautets, Fargues, Eugénie les Bains, Serres Gaston, Vielle-Tursan, Castelnau-Tursan and many others.

Probably the leading independent grower is Gerard Dulucq et Fils at Payros-Cazautets, Tel. 58.44.50.68, a few kilometres due south of Géaune. The family own the Domaine de Perchade-Pourruchot of 14 hectares (35 acres) which produces rather over 800 hectolitres divided equally between white, red and rosé. The wines usually reach 12° or even 13° of alcoholic strength and in some hot years, even 15°. M. Dulucq has introduced his new red wine called Tuc A Houec (Gascon for Colline à Feu/the hillside on fire). The UK Importers, Sookias & Bertaut, The Cottage, Cambalt Road, Putney Hill, London SW15, Tel. 01.788.4193, describe the red as 'full, rounded, plenty of staying power with good body and tannin: the Tannat/Moustron grape giving the body and the tannin and the Cabernets Sauvignon and Franc the additional refinement'. Both wines sell at £3.55, or £42.60 an unmixed case.

The second major wine area in the Landes is further west around Mugron (F–8) on the D 32 17 km west of St. Sever. The wines of Haute Chalosse are rarely known outside France. The Cave Co-operative de la Haute Chalosse,

Avenue René Bats, 40250 Mugron, Tel. 58.97.70.75 (founded in 1962) has no less than 600 small vigneron members farming rather over 200 hectares (500 acres) and producing 15,000 hectolitres of wine of which 55% are white from the Barroque grape, and the balance red from Tannat, Cabernet and Egiodola grapes. The President is M. Lalanne and the Commercial Director is M.J. Lafargue and they are keen to increase their exports of the Vins de Pays des Landes. Their ex-cave prices per litre 'en vrac' (in bulk) vary between Francs 3.90 and Francs 4.80 depending on the alcoholic strengths of 9.5° to 11°. Their Cuvée du Vigneron rouge superieur is Francs 9.90 per bottle, described as 'of a carmine-purple colour, aromatic and fruity "nose" similar to a Beaujolais.'

The wine growing area includes Hagetmau, Amou, Montfort en Chalosse and St. Sever. Like Tursan these 'vins de pays', lacking as yet Appellation Controlée, were known to the Courts of London and Paris and to the Roman Emperor, according to the writers Strabon and Suetonius.

> 'Entre amis, à la noce
> Et quand la chère est bonne,
> Un vin "Haute Chalosse"
> Emplit d'humeur gasconne'

The third small area of wine production is to the west on the Biscay coast, where several small vineyards around Léon (B–7), Soustons and Messanges (B–8) produce 'vin de sable'. The sandy subsoil gives the name to this wine. Levignac (C–6) was, pre-phylloxera, a well-known area and Bélus (C–10) introduced the Baco 22A blanc hybrid vine.

The Fédération des Caves Co-operatives Landaises is at Cité Galliane, Mont de Marsan, Tel. 58.75.15.62. President M. Lasserre.

Gastronomic specialities

The inland lakes of the Landes produce a wide variety of fresh water fish including brochet (pike), perche (perch), sandre (perch-pike), black bass, calico bass, anguilles (eels), gardons (roach), rotengle, brême (bream), vandoise (dace), tanche (tench), carpe (carp) and truite (trout). The French equivalent is shown so that it can be identified on the menu. Salmon trout are caught in the southern rivers 'des Gaves'. On the west sea-coast are to be found lobsters, crab and other shellfish including écrevisses, huîtres (oysters from Hossegor). Aloses (shad) and goujons (gudgeon) are also caught.

The 'soupe paysanne' or 'la garbure' frequently to be found on the menu is cabbage and bacon soup. Try too Capbreton fish soup and fresh crab soup.

The 'jambon des Landes (local ham), galantine de dinde (turkey), la ballotine au foie gras, le foie d'oie, canard au naturel', or 'aux raisins', 'les confits d'oie' are all derived from the traditional force fed geese and ducks.

This is not the place to debate the moral view of force feeding animals (including our own factory farms in the UK), but like it or not the traditional production of foie gras is big business in many parts of south west and southern France. 'Le Gavage', it is called and several 'élevage d'oies' can be visited, for instance the de Vivies family, 40170 Lit et Mixe, Tel. 58.42.84.38. There are a group of 18 producers around Mugron c/o the Mairie, Tel. 58.97.71.26. Aire sur l'Adour is another noted production area: Aux Foies d'Aire, 2 bis, rue de Méricam, 40800, Tel. 58.71.61.55. No less than 3.4 million ducks/geese are raised each year by 5000 producers, of whom 2000 are specialist breeders.

Other canned specialities include cassoulet, coq au vin, civet de lièvre (hare), civet de chevreuil (young goat), daube landaise (meat and vegetable stew), pipérade basque, salmis de palombes (wood-pigeons), tripes landaises, boudin de campagne (black blood pudding) and all kinds of cèpes and mushrooms. Gigot from the Haute Lande and boeuf de Chalosse are well known locally.

Other delicacies to be encountered 'à table' include sanglier (wild boar), moutons de pré-salé (salt-meadow sheep), alouettes (larks), perdreaux (young partridge), bécasses (woodcock) and cailles (quail). Asparagus is particularly good, so too is the local honey (miel d'Acacia) and patisseries (called tourtières and pastis). The wines of Tursan and Chalosse will be served at table – red, white and rosé to go with the 'Royal Landais' cheese.

CHAPTER SIXTEEN:
WHERE TO STAY IN LANDES

Modest hotels and restaurants

The Landes offers a wide range of budget priced hotels and restaurants. There are 13 Logis de France hotels in the Landes, some of which are mentioned in this chapter. Their rooms are usually 'above budget', i.e. between Francs 150–250 per double room, instead of Francs 100. Nevertheless they offer a week 'en demi pension', sharing a double room, breakfast and main meal for Francs 1300 per person per week, equivalent to Francs 180 per day. Less expensive alternatives are campsites, gîtes and villages de vacances.

Mont de Marsan (pop. 30,000) is the préfecture and capital town of the Landes. There are five hotels within budget. The two largest are the Hotel du Sablar, Place Jean-Jaurés, Tel. 58.75.21.11 with 68 beds, and the Hotel Richelieu, 3 Rue Wlerick, Tel. 58.06.10.20 which has 64 rooms. The Sablar is near the station and the bullrings, easy for a quick getaway to the south via the D 933 and N 124. Parking is easy, but there is no restaurant. The Richelieu is run by M. André Pantel and is in a side street at the north of the town near the market, the D 932 to the east, the river Douze and the large Park Jean Ramou. It has a good restaurant with meals from Francs 61. (The 96 Franc menu includes Jambon de Bayonne, fricassée de soles aux cèpes, pintade rotie à l'Armagnac, coeurs de laitues, and dessert – what a temptation!) The Hotel Le Midou only has 10 rooms in the Place Porte-Campet, Tel. 58.75.24.26, with meals from Francs 55. The Midou is a bit noisy being on a corner off the N 134 in the northwest of the town a few yards from the river Douze. These three hotels have management who speak English.

The other hotels are Le Rendez-Vous des Boulistes, the Zanchettin and the Pyrénées: all three have restaurants with reasonable priced menus around Francs 50 per meal.

Part of the charm of Mont de Marsan is the delightful river Midouze which separates in the centre of the town and becomes the Midou and the Douze.

Dax and St. Paul-lès-Dax (Pop. 28,000) have between them, because of their thermal spa reputation, no less than 28 hotels. So unless you are going there to take the cure, try the hotels *without* thermal baths! Preferably make a telephone reservation in advance as Dax seems always very popular.

There are five hotel-restaurants within budget including L'Europe, Le Centre, Ramuntcho, Chez Calcos and another five without restaurant including Hotel Ducourau, de la Source, Au Bon Coin and Bar Desbieys. There are plenty of restaurants, brasseries, créperies and cafeterias including Fin Gourmet, Bois de Boulogne and Relais des Plage (St. Paul-les-Dax).

Biscarosse(pop. 9000) has four component parts – Biscarosse Bourg, Navarosse, Ispe and La Plage. The Bourg is inland but has two lakes on its doorstep, and Navarosse and Ispe are on the minor road linking Bourg Biscarosse to La Plage, both overlooking the huge inland lake of Cazaux and Sanguinet. The Hotel En Chon with 18 rooms, Tel. 58.78.13.52, and Hotel de la Gare, Place de l'Eglise with 7 rooms, Tel. 58.78.10.28, are within budget. The Hotel La Caravelle, Tel. 58.78.02.67, has reasonable en pension terms.

Mimizan (pop. 7700) has three component parts – Mimizan Bourg, the Plage Sud and the Plage Nord. Most resort towns tend to be expensive as they need to earn their keep from the summer season tourists. However the Hotel Bellevue, 34 Avenue Maurice-Martin with 36 rooms, Tel. 58.09.05.23, and the France, 18 Avenue de la Côte d'Argent with 17 rooms, Tel. 58.09.09.01 (open May to end September) are both within budget.

Aire-sur-l'Adour (pop. 7200) has all of its hotels within budget: the Commerce (M. Labadie), Chez Dupouy, Chez

Pierette, Des Platanes (M. R. Debedan), Terminus et Bec Fin and Hotel Chez l'Ahumat, Tel. 58.71.82.61 (M. Labrouche). The recommended hotel is the last, in the Rue des Ecoles with 13 rooms from Francs 62–85, breakfast Francs 13, and prix fixe menus from Francs 37, 51 and 63.50. For the latter, Michel and Colette Labrouche will offer you potage du jour, jambon du pays, salmis de palombe maison (wood pigeon), entrecôte, légumes, choix de desserts. A quite unbelievable menu at this price. Local wine Francs 14.50 the litre or Madiran and Tursan at Francs 30 the bottle.

Madame Lahouze runs the Hotel Dupouy, 22, rue du 13 Juin, Tel. 58.71.71.76, as well as her 'pub Twickenham'!

Morcenx (pop. 6100) has the Hotel du Commerce (M. Albert Adam), 14 Avenue Foch, 8 rooms, Tel. 58.07.80.25, within budget. During the week of the Grand Fêtes in June, M. Adam will offer you a Sardinade evening and another with 'Escargots and Anguillons' (snails and eels).

Soustons (pop. 5100) The Hostellerie du Marensin, Place Sterling, 14 rooms, Tel. 58.48.05.16, offers good value with a prix fixe menu at Francs 38. Closed in November.

Saint Sever (pop. 4700) Both the Hotel de France et des Ambassadeurs in the Place Cap-du-Pouy, 22 rooms, Tel. 58.76.00.01, (closed October) and Hotel du Commerce et Voyageurs, 12 rooms, Tel. 58.76.00.24 (closed November) offer excellent value. The latter is run by Lucien and Marie Galland and they offer prix fixe menus from Francs 38 up to Francs 140.

Hagetmau (pop. 4300) All four hotels here are within budget: Auberge des Lacs d'Halco, de la Cremaillère, Le Jambon and Relais Basque. They all have prix fixe menus at about Francs 50.

Capbreton (pop. 4300) There are six hotels within budget: Le Béarnais, Le Boudigau, Castel, du Goût, Castel Cap and du Parc

Finally take note that in the spa towns and resort-plage towns there are out of season reduced terms. For a stay of three days or more there are Pension or Demi Pension terms.

For instance, for a room (shared), breakfast and a main meal
Demi Pension terms of Francs 100–150 per head are very
reasonable.

Summary

Map Ref.	Town	Hotel (Rooms)	Tel. (Prefix 58)
I–9	Aire s/l'Adour 40800	du Commerce (19)	71.60.06 (closed Jan)
		Chez Dupouy (14) 22 rue du 13 juin	71.71.76
		chez Pierrette (10) 15 rue du 4 Sept.	71.63.01
		Les Platanes (11) Pl. de la Liberté	71.60.36
		Terminus et Bec Fin (13) Pl. Gen. de Gaulle	71.60.09
		Chez l'Ahumat (13) Rue des Ecoles	71.82.61 closed 2 weeks after Easter. 2 weeks beg. Sept
F–10	Amou 40330	Au Feu de Bois Des Voyageurs (14)	16.89.00.86 89.02.31 (closed Feb.)
E–6	Arjuzanx 40116	L'Auberge Landaise (10)	07.80.52
C–2	Biscarosse 40600	En Chon (18) de la Gare (7) Pl. de l'Eglise	78.13.52 78.10.28
G–6	Brocas-les Forges 40420	de la Gare (M.Taris) (6) Recommended	51.40.67
F–7	Campagne 40090	Relais du Marsan (6)	44.79.58
D–9	Candresse 40180	Le Relais de Candresse (8)	74.30.04
A–9	Capbreton 40130	Le Bearnais, r. Dangou (12)	72.13.33
		Le Boudigau, 24 av. (20) G. Pompidou	72.11.01
		Castel Cap, Bd. de la Mer (10)	72.10.06 (closed Easter)
		du Gout, r. de Quebec (25)	72.10.23 (closed Easter)

		du Parc, Av. Gen. Leclerc (21)	72.10.36
C–7	Castets 40260	de la Cote d'Argent (12)	87.40.33
D–9	Dax 40100	Avenue, 19 av. G. Clemenceau (135)	74.42.77 (closed mid-Dec. Jan. Feb.
	Baignots	des Baignots, Alle des (216)	74.44.46 (closed winter)
	Penitents	de la Paix, r. des (63)	90.16.46 (closed Jan.Feb)
		Auberge des Pins (16) Av. Fr. Plante	74.22.46
		Au Fin Gourmet (24)	74.04.26 (closed Jan.Feb)
		Biscai, 154 Av. St. (10) Vincent de Paul	74.18.59
		L'Escale Fleurie (10)	74.25.78
H–9	Eugénie-les Bains 40320	Les Charmilles (14)	51.19.18 (closed winter)
		Auberge les Trois Pins (20)	51.18.86 (closed winter)
K–6	Escalans 40310	les Tilleuls (10) (M. Dardé)	44.31.10 Recommended (closed Jan)
E–9	Gamarde-les Bains	L'Auberge (11)	98.62.27 Logis
H–10	Geaune 40320	de France (M. Sénac) (22)	44.51.18 Recommended
C–8	Herm 40160	de la Paix (M. Junca) (10)	91.52.17 Recommended (closed Jan)
A–9	(Soorts-) Hossegor 40150	des Troènes (18)	43.52.62
		de la Bonbonnière, (13) Av. Touring Club	43.50.21
		Le Neptune, (23)	43.51.09
		du Rond Point, (8) Av. Touring Club	45.53.11
D–10	Labatut 40300	Le Paris Gascogne, (7)	98.18.26 (closed winter)
		Auberge du Bousquet, (4) (Laccarrau)	98.18.24 Recommended

A–10	Labenne 40530	Chez Léonie, (10)	45.41.64
		Le Relais, (12)	45.40.39 (closed winter)
F–6	Labrit/ Garain 40420	Chez Suzon, (6)	51.41.68
E–4	Labouheyre 40420	Brémontier, (9)	07.01.13 (closed winter)
		Hostellerie Landaise, (12)	07.00.46
I–7	Le Frêche 40190	Auberge de Saint Vidou, (4) (Mme Dumon)	45.24.09 Recommended
B–7	Léon 40550	du Commerce, (13)	48.73.04 (closed winter)
		du Lac, (15)	48.73.11 (closed winter)
C–6	Lesperon-le-Souqeut 40260	Le Pignade, (10)	89.61.05
		Darmaillacq, (11)	89.61.45 (closed 2 weeks Sept)
J–5	Losse 40240	Lapeyrade, (7)	93.61.44 (closed mid-winter)
C–9	Mées 40180	Mora, (6)	97.57.72
G–4	Luxey 40430	Relais de la Haute-Lande, (8)	08.02.30 (closed mid-winter)
F–2	Mano 40410	Selons, (7)	07.71.51 No restaurant
C–4	Mimizan-Plage 40200	Bellevue, 34 Av. Maurice, (36)	09.05.23 (closed winter)
C–4	Mimizan-Bourg 40200	Taris, 19 av. de l'Abbeye, (10)	09.02.18
		de France, 18 av. (17)	09.09.01
		Cote d'Argent	(closed winter)
B–7	Moliets-et Maa 40660	des Ecureuils, (10)	48.51.05 No restaurant
E–7	Mont de Marsan 4000	Richelieu, 3 r. Wlerick, (64)	06.10.20 Recommended
		du Sablar, Pl. Jean Jaurès, (68)	75.21.11
		Le Midou, Pl. Porte-Campet, (10)	75.24.26

		Le Rendevous des Boulistes, (9) 75.19.52 (closed winter)
		Zanchettin 1565 Av. Villeneuve, (23) 75.05.49
E–9	Montfort en Chalosse 40380	aux Touzins, Rte. d'Hagetmau, (15) 98.60.22 (closed Jan.Feb)
E–6	Morcenx 40110	Bellevue, 26 r. Carnot, (24) 07.85.07 Logis de France
		du Commerce, 14 av. Foch (8) 07.80.25
D–3	Parentis- en-Born 40160	Cousseau, r. St. Barthelemy (10) 78.42.46 L'Etrier, r. Marechal Foch, (10) 78.42.62 des Pêcheurs, Parentis-Lac, (16) 78.41.05
K–7	Parlebosq 40310	La Mosaique, (11) 44.32.24 (closed winter)
C–10	Peyrehorade 40300	Au Bon Acceuil, RN 117, (10) 73.03.60 Mimi, r. Nautron-Truquez, (16) 73.00.06
E–10	Pomarez 40360	Auberge du Chalet, (12) 89.82.16
C–4	Pontenx- les-Forges 40200	de la Poste, (10) 07.40.26 No restaurant
D–8	Pontonx-s- Adour 40990	des Arènes, Pl. Arènes, (12) 57.21.48 No restaurant
D–10	Pouillon 40350	Le Relais de Pouillon, (13) 98.20.15 (M. Marquier) Pl. de la Mairie Recommended
D–8	Préchacq- les Baines 40180	des Sources, (52) 57.21.21. Logis de France des Thermes, (67) 57.21.21
E–7	Rion-les Landes 40370	Le Relais des Landes, (14) 57.10.20 (closed Dec)
H–6	Roquefort 40120	Le Colombier (Mme. Deyts), (19) 45.50.57 Recommended
F–5	Sabres 40630	L'Auberge des Pins, (14) 07.50.47 Logis de France
C–9	St. Géours- de-Maremme	Auberge du Coq Hardi, (10) 57.34.06
B–7	St. Girons (Vielle) 40560	Campet, (14) 42.93.07 (closed winter) les Ecureuils. (4) 42.94.04

195

C–5	St. Julien-en Borne/Contis 40170	Le Petit Tabarin, (18)	42.85.14 (closed winter)
		Le Pré Fleuri (Rt. Mezos), (10)	42.80.09
I–6	Saint Justin 40240	Le Cadet de Gascogne, (10) Pl. Mairie	44.50.77
		de France, Pl. Tilleuls, (9)	44.82.08
B–10	Sainte Marie de Gosse 40750	les Routiers RN 117, (15)	56.32.02 (closed winter)
C–10	Saint Lon- les-Mines 40300	du Fronton, (11)	57.80.45
D–9	St. Paul-les Dax 40990	Relais des Plages, Rte., (10) Bayonne	91.78.86 (closed mid-Nov. mid-Dec)
G–8	Saint Sever 40500	du Commerce et Voyageur, (11)	76.00.24
		de France & Ambassadeur, (22)	76.00.01 (closed mid- winter)
B–9	Saint Vincent	Cote d'Argent, (23)	77.02.16
	de-Tyrosse 40230	des Touristes, (10)	77.03.28
		Chez Henriette, (7)	77.00.83
D–9	Saint Vincent de Paul/Buglose 40180	des Pélerins, (7)	89.91.49
C–9	Saubusse 40180	Thermal, (70)	57.31.04 Logis de France (closed winter)
		Vieux Castel, (11)	57.31.02 (closed Jan)
B–9	Seignosse	La Soleillade, Rte. Hossegor, (7)	72.80.38 (closed winter)
E–5	Solférino 40210	Auberge des Touristes, (15) Cap de Pin	07.20.52
B–8	Soustons 40140	Hostellerie du Marensin, (14)	48.05.16 (closed Nov)
		Pl. Sterling (14)	
		Les Pins, Rte. Soustons Azur, (12)	48.01.31 (closed mid- winter)
A–10	Tarnos 40220	de la Jetée, (5)	64.65.12 (closed winter)

E–8	Tartas 40400	de la Paix, (10)	73.43.36
C–9	Tercis 40990	Le Parc, Rte. Vimport, (8)	57.80.16 (closed winter)
A–8	Vieux-Boucau 40480	du Centre, R. Cap St. Géorurs, (36)	48.10.33 (closed winter)
		de la Marenne, (38)	48.12.70

Gites de France

Each department of France publishes every year a yellow and green booklet which gives all the names and addresses of the Gîtes de France in that region.

The Landes address is Service de Reservation des Gîtes de France, BP 279, 40005 Mont de Marsan Cedex, Tel. 58.46.10.45.

The regions are as follows: (A) Pays de Born (NW) 20 gîtes; (B) Marensin (West) 58 gîtes; (C) Maremne/Seignanx (SW) 61 gîtes; (D) Pays d'Orthe (South) 28 gîtes; (E) Chalosse (SE) 52 gîtes; (F) Marsan (SE) 34 gîtes; (G) Hagetmau (SE) 7 gîtes; (H) Tursan (East) 26 gîtes; (I) Armagnac (NE) 16 gîtes; (J) Haute Lande (North) 22 gîtes.

In effect one is renting a house, or part of a house or villa. The prices vary considerably in three categories. The most expensive is high season of July/August. The two months June/September are usually about 30–40% cheaper. The third category is 'Hors saison', i.e. the other 8 months of the year when the prices are much lower. Prices vary according to the size of the gîte and the facilities available. A popular resort will obviously be more expensive than in a pleasant sleepy village in the interior.

As a rough guide high season prices per gîte per week range from France 670 – 1600, and out of season from Francs 335 – 1000.

Fermes auberges

These are farms where you live as part of the family as paying guests. The welcome, food and wine will be most agreeable, but your knowledge of the French language will need to be reasonable! Here is a list of eleven Fermes Auberges:

Name	Place.	Map Ref.	Tel No. (58 prefix)
Cabannes	Mugron	F–8	97.74.23
Labrouche	Vielle Tursan	H–9	79.17.37
Lesca	Castets	C–7	89 41 45
Dupouy/Tachon	Maurrin	H–8	45.48.26
Peyres	St.Lon-les-Mines	C–10	57.83.05
Castaignos	Hagetmau	G–9	79.41.45
Laborde	Peyrehorade	D–10	73.07.43
Lalanne	Morganx	G–10	79.20.04
Herrero	Labastide d'Armagnac	I–6	44.80.97
Laborde	Mayliss	F–9	97.72.91
Lacere	Bahus Soubiran	H-9	44.40.64

Gites and relais equestres (strictly for horse/ponylovers)

Berger	St.Justin & Sarbazen	I–6	45.85.38
Castéra	Saubusse	C-9	57.48.12
Daugey	Parentis en Borne	D-3	78.40.71
Laclau	St. Andre-de-Seignanx	B–10	56.13.30
Bergay	St. Lon-les-Mines	C–10	57.83.62
Etrier de Marsan	Mont de Marsan	G–7	75.14.15
Soubestre	Angresse	B–9	43.52.88
Lalanne	Pouillon	D–10	98.21.14
Lalanne	Morgaux	G–10	79.20.04
Lafourcade	Hastingues	C–10	73.07.27
Lesca	Castets	C–7	89.41.45
Centre Equestre de la Petite Leyre, Belhade	Pissos	E–3	07.77.19
Spiteri	Geloux	F–6	75.22.85

Camping-caravan sites

There are no less than 137 of these in the Landes and a full list is given. Rates vary considerably but the following is a rough guide. Three star (***) sites charge Francs 11/12 per adult, Francs 14/21 for 'emplacement' of car and caravan, Francs 9/10 for electricity consumption. For a two star (**) site the rates would be approximately Francs 7, Francs 8/9 and Francs 7/8. Camp sites are usually open from March–November.

Location	Classification	Places
40800 Aire sur Adour..........	** Camping les Ombrages de l'Adour	100
I 9	Tel.58.71.64.70	
40300 Amou	** Camping municipal	33
F 10	tel.58.89.00.22	
40200 Aureilhan	**** Camping Eurolac..........................	300
C 4	Tel.58.09.02.87	
	** Camping municipal du Lac	440
	Tel.58.09.10.88	
	** Camping Route des Lacs	100
	Tel.58.09.01.42	
40140 Azur...........................	**** Camping la Paillote	310
B 8	Tel.58.48.12.12	
	*** Camping municipal......................	150
	Tel.58.48.30.72	
40300 Belus	*** Camping l'Escarbillat	111
C 10	Tel.58.57.69.07 ou 58.74.37.56	
40170 Bias	** Camping municipal Tatiou...........	505
C 5	Tel.58.09.4.76	
40600 Biscarrosse...............	**** Camping de Mayotte	480
C2	Tel.58.78.00.00	
	*** Camping de la Rive	340
	Tel.58.78.12.23	
	*** Camping municipal Latécoère.....	160
	Tel.58.78.13.01	
	*** Camping municipal Le Vivier.......	416
	Tel.58.78.25.76	
	** Camping Le Bimbo	115
	Tel.58.78.72.33	
	** Camping Les Ecureuils	150
	Tel.58.78.10.00	
	** Camping municipal Navarrosse....	400
	Tel.58.78.14.32	
	** Camping Lou Galip	200
	Tel.58.78.16.16	
40520 Biscarrosse...............	*** Camping municipal Plage Sud	1,387
B 2 Plage	Tel.58.78.21.24	
	** Camping Maguide	225
	Tel.58.78.01.90 et 58.78.01.99	

40130 Capbreton	*** Camping La Pointe Tel.58.72.14.98	228
A 9	*** Camping La Civelle Tel.58.72.15.11	600
	** Camping Bel Air Tel.58.72.12.04	100
	** Camping Labarthe........................ Tel.58.72.02.34	75
	A ** Camping Le Bourret.................... (Group Camp. Universitaires)	100
	A ** Camping Fierbois (EDF).............. Tel.58.72.11.95	450
	A ** Camping «Maria» (FO).................. Tel.58.72.12.01	35
	A * Camping Le Vallon .... (Aérospatiale) Tel.58.72.12.44	266
40260 Castets....................	*** Camping Le Galan........................ Tel.58.89.43.52	210
C 7		
40300 Cauneille	** Camping Les Sources.................. Tel.58.73.04.40	50
D 10		
40170 Contis Plage.............	*** Camping Lous Serrots................ Tel.58.42.85.82	400
B 5		
40100 Dax..........................	**** Camping les Chênes.................... M.Albaladejo — Bois de Boulogne Tel.58.90.05.53	230
D 9		
40160 Gastes......................	**** Camping La Réserve Tel.58.78.45.96	375
C 3	** Camping Les Prés Verts Tel.58.78.46.86	100
40320 Geaune.....................	** Camping municipal Tel.58.44.50.27	50
H 9		
40270 Grenade sur	** Camping municipal Tel.58.45.91.14	70
H 8 Adour		
40700 Hagetmau.................	**** Camping municipal .... Tel.58.79.33.14 poste 427	24
G 9		
40150 Hossegor	**** Camping du Lac........................... Tel.58.43.53.14	250
A 9	*** Camping «Le Rey» Tel.58.43.52.00	600
	*** Camping municipal de La Forêt ... Tel.58.43.75.92	71
40530 Labenne	**** Camping de La Côte d'Argent Tel.59.45.42.02	89
A 10		

200

	**** Camping Le Boudigau.................	320
	Tel.59.45.42.07 ou 59.45.30.34	
	*** Camping de La Mer	300
	Tel.59.45.42.09	
	** Camping Marina..........................	66
	Tel.59.52.42.41	
	** Camping Océanic	100
	** Camping La Savane (LFE)	287
	Tel.59.45.41.13	
	A ** Camping R.A.T.P	200
	Tel.59.45.43.95	
40250 Laurède	** Camping municipal «Vieux Port»..	33
E 8	Tel.58.97.71.93	
40550 Leon.......................	**** Camping «Lou Puntaou».............	720
B 7	Tel.58.48.74.05 et 58.48.74.30	
40260 Lesperon	** Camping «Lou Payou»	50
C 6	Tel.58.89.60.78	
40170 Lit et Mixe	**** Camping L'Univers.....................	300
B 6	Tel.58.42.83.37	
	** Camping municipal de La Plage...	330
	Cap de L'Homy	
	Tel.58.42.83.47	
	** Camping Le Satellite	16
	Tel.58.42.74.12	
40380 Louer......................	** Camping municipal de Laubanère	30
E 8	Tel.58.57.21.26	
40660 Messanges	**** Camping Le Vieux Port...............	1,000
A 8	Tel.58.48.22.00	
	*** Camping Moïsan...........................	220
	Tel.58.48.11.19	
	** Camping d'Albret	290
	Tel.58.48.12.28	
	** Camping d'Albret Plage...............	310
	Tel.58.48.03.67	
	** Camping Lou Pignada	150
	Tel.58.48.11.17	
40170 Mézos	**** Camping Sen Yan	160
C 5	Tel.58.42.60.05	
40200 Mimizan	**** Camping Marina..........................	630
B 4	Tel.58.09.12.66 ou 59.24.37.37	
	*** Camping de La Plage	787
	Tel.58.09.00.32	

	** Camping du Lac Tel.58.09.01.21	250
	** Camping La Lande Tel.58.82.46.62	100
	A ** Village Toile (EDF)......................	110
40660 Moliets et .... A 7 MAA	*** Camping Les Cigales Tel.58.48.51.18	630
	*** Camping Saint-Martin Tel.58.48.52.30	660
	A****Camping M.G.E.T...................... Tel.58.48.52.49	190
40000 Mont de .... G 7 Marsan	** Camping municipal Tel.58.75.04.73	100
40110 Morcenx .... E 6	*** Camping Le Clavé Tel.58.07.83.11	50
40250 Mugron.................... F 8	** Camping La Saucille..................... Tel.58.97.98.50 et Mairie 58.97.71.26	75
40440 Ondres..................... A 10	*** Camping Lou Pignada Tel.59.45.30.65	135
	** Camping Le Coy	130
	** Camping municipal Tel.59.45.31.40	90
	A ** Camping Le Lac (SNECMA)........ Tel.59.45.30.62.	100
	A ** Village Toile E.D.F.......................	200
40110 Onesse-Laharie........ D 5	*** Camping Bienvenu Tel.58.07.30.49	100
40160 Parentis-en.............. D 3 Born	*** Camping l'Arbre d'Or................... Tel.58.78.41.56 et 58.78.41.30	200
	*** Camping municipal Pipiou........... Tel.58.78.57.25	127
	** Camping municipal...................... Tel.58.78.42.27	130
	** Camping Lahitte Tel.57.78.47.17	135
40300 Peyrehorade............ C 10	** Camping Les Gaves...................... (en amont du pont) Tel.58.73.60.20 ou 58.73.00.52	33
	** Camping Les Gaves.................... (en aval du pont) Tel.58.73.60.20 ou 58.73.00.52	33

40410 Pissos....................... E 3	** Camping municipal Tel.58.07.70.45	50
40200 Pontenx-les.............. C 4 Forges	** Camping municipal Guilleman...... Tel.58.07.40.48	100
40350 Pouillon .... D 10	** Camping municipal Tel.58.98.21.62	20
40630 Sabres .... F 5	** Camping Les Cigales Tel.58.07.52.51	33
40390 Saint-André .... B 10 de-Seignanx	*** Camping Le Ruisseau Tel.59.56.15.31	60
40200 Ste.-Eulalie .... C 3 en-Born	*** Camping Les Bruyères................ Tel.58.82.45.36	90
	** Camping de L'Etang.................... Tel.58.09.08.61	150
	** Camping de Labadan Tel.58.09.20.98	240
40230 St.-Geours .... B 9 de-Maremne	** Camping Le Coumé Tel.58.57.31.51	100
40170 St.-Julien .... B 5 en-Born	*** Camping mun. de La Lette Fleurie Tel.Mairie 58.42.74.09	345
	** Camping du Grand Pont.............. Tel.58.42.80.18	75
	** Camping du Vieux Moulin Tel.58.42.80.12	150
40240 St.-Justin.................. I-6	** Camping Le Pin........................... Tel.58.44.88.91	50
40550 St.-Michel .... B 7 Escalus	** Camping «Fontaine St. Antoine» .. Tel.58.48.78.50	233
40200 St.-Paul..................... C 4 en-Born	** Camping municipal .... «Lou Talucat» Tel.58.07.44.16	150
40990 St.-Paul..................... D 9 lès-Dax	*** Camping Les Thermes de Christus Tel.58.91.65.34	199
	*** Camping L'Etang d'Ardy.............. Tel.58.97.57.74	50
40500 St.-Sever.................. G 8	** Camping Rives de l'Adour Tel.58.76.04.60	100
40230 St.-Vincent.............. B 9 de-Tyrosse	*** Camping de Saubis .... Tel.58.77.04.90 Téléx 570454	90
40460 Sanguinet .... D 1	**** Camping Lou Broustaric.............. Tel.58.78.62.62	555

	** Camping du Lac Tel.58.78.61.94	233
	** Camping Le Caton Tel.58.78.60.79	66
	** Camping Langeot......................... Tel.58.78.60.44	199
	** Camping La Mole Tel.58.78.60.44	50
	** Camping Les Grands Pins............ Tel.58.78.61.74	74
	A ** Camping Les Dunes .... (Dassault)	100
	A ** Camping G.C.U	100
40230 Saubion .... B 9	** Camping «La Pomme de Pin» Tel.58.77.00.71	150
40410 Saugnac- .... E 2 et-Muret	** Camping Le Muretois Tel.58.07.72.14	33
40510 Seignosse .... A 9	**** Camping Les Chevreuills............ Tel.58.43.32.80	240
	**** Camping «Les Oyats».................. Tel.58.43.37.94	360
	**** Camping VVF de la Forêt............ Tel.58.43.30.20	240
	***Camping municipal du Penon Tel.58.43.30.30	350
	A *** Camping L'Agréou .... (Caisse Notariat) Tel.58.43.32.20	100
	A *** Camping Le Canard Sauvage..... (Total) Tel.58.72.80.61	40
40180 Seyresse- .... C 9 près de Dax	** Camping Le Luy......................... Tel.58.74.35.42	166
40210 Solférino.................. E 5	** Camping Mayique Tel.58.07.20.52	25
40140 Soustons................. B 8	****Camping L'Airial Tel.58.41.12.48	400
40220 Tarnos .... A 10	** Camping Jobel Tel.59.64.04.76	80
40400 Tartas...................... E 8	** Camping municipal Tel.58.73.41.06	83
40230 Tosse .... B 9	A ** Camping Sparben (LFE) Tel.58.77.06.77	100
40560 Vielle-St.- .... B 7 Girons	**** Camping Le Col Vert.................. Tel.58.42.94.06	500

	**** Camping Eurosol..........................	672
	M. Albaladejo — Tel.58.42.90.14	
	** Camping mun. Les Tourterelles ...	450
	Tel.58.42.93.12	
	** Camping Pro-Nature Arnaoutchot	450
	Tel.58.48.52.87	
40240 Vielle-.......................	* Camping La Launette..................	25
16 Soubiran	Tel.58.45.64.74	
40480 Vieux-.......................	*** Camping municipal «Les Sablères».	414
A 8 Boucau	Tel.58.48.12.29	
	** Camping «Les Chenes»................	350
	Tel.58.48.21.21	
40190 Villeneuve-	** Camping L'Oasis	16
17 de-Marsan	Tel.58.45.36.23	
40160 Ychoux	** Camping du Lac des Forges.........	45
D3	Tel.58.82.35.57	
	Mairie 58.82.36.01	

Caravan only camps

40200 Aureilhan	2* Catégorie «Eurolac».................	175
C4	Tel.58.09.02.87	
40260 Lesperon	1* Catégorie Parc de Couchoy.....	71
C6	Tel.58.89.60.52 ou 58.89.60.15	

Holiday camps

40600 Biscarrosse	Le Bosquet G.C............................	80
C 2	Tel.58.78.02.91 dont	4 HLL
	Le Caravosse G.C........................	62
	Tel.58.78.14.75 dont	34 HLL
	Navarosse Est G.C.	30
	Tel.58.78.10.64	

Notes

A = Camping Secteur Associatif
G.C. = Grand Confort
H.L.L. = Habitations Légères de Loisirs
● = Camp de Tourisme

Nudist camp

The only one in the Landes is Camping Arnaoutchot, 40560
Vielle-St. Girons, Tel. 58.48.52.87.

205

Regional tourist offices

Haute Chalosse, Mairie 40250 Mugron, Tel. 58.97.96.90.
Pays d'Orthe & Pouillon, Mairie 40300 Saint Lon, Tel. 58.57.89.36.
Tursan, Mairie 40320 Géaune, Tel. 58.44.40.99.
Armagnac, Mairie 40190 Villeneuve-de-Marsan, Tel. 58.45.22.68.

Les station vertes

The French Government reserves the accolade 'village fleuri' for a few selected villages or towns which are set in a pretty, floral atmosphere with parks and a 'green' pastoral image. In the Landes these are to be found at Hagetmau, Pouillon, Saint Sever, Morcenx, Amou, Aire-sur-l'Adour, Géaune and Pontex-les-Forges.

The cultural centres

The Tourist Committee for the whole of Aquitaine, the five departments in the south west of France, have selected three towns in the Landes – Dax, Hossegor and Mont de Marsan – as cultural centres. 'Culture' is a rag-bag word, but includes in this instance history, thermal springs, fêtes (including corridas, Courses Landaises), the flora and fauna of the pine forests, the ocean, golf tournaments, and gastronomy!

Villages de vacances/maisons familiales de vacances

These are official holiday villages open to everyone to come and also those only for families with young children. In the first category are Capbreton, Seignosse-le-Penon, Seignosse, Biscarosse, Lit et Mixe, Vieux Boucau, Port d'Albret, Sabres, Moliets and Léon. In the second category are Mimizan, Seignosse and Hossegor.

Local guides

Ask for the blue guide 'Tourisme en Espace Rural' which shows a programme of events in the rural areas, and the pink guide 'oisirs et Animation à la Carte' which gives a daily programme of events in the towns, spas and seaside resorts.

CHAPTER SEVENTEEN:
THIS SPORTING LIFE

The southwest of France has always had a strong affinity with their Hispanic neighbours less than a hundred miles to the south. The Basques straddle the frontier of the Pyrénées and their traditions of pelota and bull-fighting are equally as strong on the French side as on the Spanish. In the tenth century the Spanish kingdom of Navarre was invited to send armies to protect the Vascon-Gascons against the ravages of the Norsemen. The early Dukes of Gascony were the younger sons of the royal family of Navarre.

Bull and cow fights

This history of bull and cow fighting in southwest France is said to go back to the Roman era, and the whole style of the 'Courses Landaises' is strongly reminiscent of the Cretan era much earlier than the Roman occupation.

Every summer from the 1st May until early October there is a full programme of Corridas (Spanish and Portuguese) and Courses Landaises (specialised cow-fighting in the Gers and Landes).

For 'aficionados' the Federation Francaise Course Landaise, 1600 Avenue Kennedy, Saint-Pierre-du-Mont BP21, 40001 Mont de Marsan, Tel. 58.46.50.89, publish an annual calendar of events. The office in Dax is at 7 Rue des Archers 40104, Tel. 58.74.70.10. There is also an office in Nogaro 32110, Tel. 62.09.13.30. The Arenas are to be found in the Landes at over 60 towns and villages, Dax, Mont de Marsan, Pomarez, Aire sur Adour and Saint-Sever being the most important.

Arenas in the Gers are fewer – rather over twenty – but

those in Eauze, Le Houga and Vic-Fezensac are noteworthy. The 1987 'Championnat de France' was held in Nogaro on the 4th October. This was the 32nd championship and the 29th presentation of the sought-after 'Corne d'Or' (The Golden Horn).

In the Middle Ages the Courses and Corridas took place in the central square of the village in front of the church. Pope Pious V published a Bull (sic) in 1567 – 'un interdit general sur les combats de taureaux et de bêtes féroces'. The bullfighters (even from horseback) would be refused the Last Rites if they 'succombent dans ces combats'. Gilles Boutaul, Bishop of Aire sur Adour in 1649 tried to enforce the Church's position, but encountered such serious resistance that he was forced to depart for northern Evreux in Normandy where bull-fighting was unknown. In the same year King Louis XIV in his letters Patent fulminated 'L'Opiniâtreté des Gascons à se livrer encore à ces jeux détestables, coutumes qui provoquent accidents et désordres et gênent l'exercice du culte.' Nevertheless bull and cow fighting persisted – clandestinely at night or in the early morning in a rebellious atmosphere!

Napoleon Bonapart was called upon to ban the Courses, and said of the Gascons 'Qu'importe qu'ils se fassent tuer, pourvu qu'ils s'amusent...' (It does not matter if they are killed, so long as they are amused...) But from 1802 the Courses Landaises were organised officially with bureaucratic laws emanating from the Préfecture. The safety of the spectators and the solid structure of the arenas were the main requirements. Only in 1850 were the arenas strengthened and graded tiers of wooden seats and benches installed within a stone-walled amphitheatre. In that year were formed the first 'ganaderias' or specialist breeding farms – M. Duporté at Betbezer and M. Branenx at St. Justin, who both purchased their breeding cows from Spain. In 1860 M. Druillet installed a 'ganaderia' at Gabarrel, and his Courses Landaises cows under Joseph Barrière, 'Chatelain de Buros', dominated the scene from 1895–1933. Now there are a dozen, including three near Dax and three in Aire sur Adour.

Style of fighting

The three ways of fighting are quite different. In the Spanish Corridas there is a sporting chance that everyone will be killed: the bulls and horses (usually poor old nags) inevitably, and the fighters on foot frequently.

The Portuguese style is different again. I have seen scores of bull fights in Portugal and can vouch for their elegance and skill. The bull is never killed in the ring. The brilliant horse-riders put their short wooden banderillas into the bull's neck whilst both are moving at high speed – quite extraordinary equestrianism. If the bull touches the horse, the rider is booed out of the ring. The Portuguese Forcados are a team of eight or ten young men, usually dressed in elaborate silk costumes of red, green and white, whose task it is, barehanded, to halt a bull charging across the ring. The leader of the Forcados has to *throw* himself between the bull's horns whilst the rugby scrum supports him.

The Courses Landaises are quite unlike the Hispanic combats. There are no bulls but a relatively dangerous breed of longhorned cows trained to charge. Admittedly the bull's horns are muffled and blunted. Admittedly the 'Cordier' has a long cord around the cow's shoulders and endeavours to keep the charging cow's head, horns and shoulders in a straight line so that the dangerous ballet can commence. There are no weapons deployed at all – no banderillas, no lances and no swords. The 'game' is to provoke the young cow (if they are very young and ignorant they do not have a cord attached to them since they are 'ignorantes du jeu' and have learned no wily methods of attack!)

The Quadrilla, a team of four, take it in turn to provoke the cow, dance with it, and if in danger, the other members will distract the beast – one hopes! The Ecarteurs – literally the evaders, tumblers, or bull-dancers, as the Cretans would have called them – are adroit, nimble, brave young men, who, without capes to confuse the animal, pirouette and pivot as close to the cow's dangerous horns as possible. Fatalities are rare, but have occurred regularly since 1888.

There are plenty of subtle plays such as a feint or a double feint to confuse the oncoming beast. Yet another alternative is

209

to stand immobile, arms crossed, waiting for the charge, and then bend the body out of danger at the last moment.

The Sauteurs, as the name implies, are the leapers, divers, or jumpers, who will run, jump and plunge over the cow's horns and body exactly like a racing dive in a swimming pool. This is a most exciting and exhilarating manoeuvre. An alternative and even more daring one is to perform a single or even double somersault in the air over the beast! Permutations exist, such as the feet and hands being tied together beforehand. The 'saut d'ange' (angel), 'le saut perilleux', 'le saut perilleux vrillé' are the technical terms.

The official description of Courses Landaises is 'l'opposition de l'adresse intelligente de l'homme à la force agressive de la bête sauvage.' The cows are sisters to the strain of fighting bulls and of course not only are not killed, but participate for many years in the ring.

The experts

The leading Ganaderias are: André Larrouture of 64990 Mouguerre; Joseph Labat of Buglose, 40180 Dax; Jean-Charles Pussacq of 40360 Pomarez; Marcel Lines of Aire-sur-Adour; Francis Dargelos of 32800 Eauze. Other noted breeders include M. Paul Deyris, M. Bertrand Latapy and M. Michel Darritchon. The Ganaderias also act as local promoters providing training courses, portable arenas, and galas Comico Taurin (a comedy of errors).

M. Robert Castagnon, 29 Avenue des Pyrénées, 32110 Nogaro, is the expert on Courses Landaises and has published illustrated books and a quarterly revue 'La Talenquère'.

There is a jury who mark each action with points of one to five for various degrees of excellence since there are many competitions and Tournament Cups – Challenge Armagnac, Challenge Landes-Bearn, Trophée Vache sans Corde, Concours Landais, Trophy Raoul Pabon etc.

Seven days of spectacle

The major towns such as Dax, Mont de Marsan, Eauze and

Nogaro will devote a week to bull and cow fighting 'spectacles'. Eauze is the first week in July; Dax and Nogaro usually clash in the middle of August; Saint Sever has their Fête des Toros at the end of June; Aire sur Adour has their week towards the end of June.

During the week there will be a procession (défilé) through the streets, often including the young cows. A cockade is attached to the bull/cow's horns to be snatched, if possible, by running youths, but it is not as dangerous as the bull-running in some Spanish towns. There will be a Toro de Fuego (fireworks display), a bal disco every night, perhaps a Fiesta Mexicaine – these are the social frivolities lasting until well after midnight. The noise is indescribable since the Bandas play paso doblas incessantly with maximum decibel count. The serious part of the week will include, for instance at Dax, four corridas de Toros (Spanish), one corrida Portugaise, one Concours Landais and two Novilladas non piquée (young bulls fought without bandillas/darts). There may well be a horse race and a Course de Levriers (greyhounds). The placards will specify 'Sans Mise à Mort' or 'Mis à Mort' so that the spectator is warned in advance of the amount of gore to be encountered! One sobriquet is 'mano à mano'! On a lighter note, you may be lucky enough to encounter the 'Majorettes et Twirling du Gers'.

There are 38 Clubs Taurins in both départements, mainly composed of amateur écarteurs and their helpers and admirers. There is an 'Ecole du Toro' in Dax and another in Mont de Marsan.

An arena can accept up to 3000 spectators and seats range in price from Francs 85–200 (soleil) to Francs 120–225 (ombre et soleil) to Francs 150–260 (ombre). There are usually up to eleven concentric rows or 'rangs' of benches with those in the sun being slightly cheaper. The Novilladas, with young bulls/cows and less experienced fighters/dancers, are half the price of their elders and betters. The Spanish toreros command a premium price, followed by the Portuguese equipes, and the local heroes perform at relatively modest prices.

211

Pelota

Pelota or cesta punta is the name given to the elegant Spanish game for two or four players, each equipped with a long basket-shaped glove, with which a hard ball can be caught and slung or hurled back against a stone wall about 30 metres away. It is almost a blend of our modern raquets and fives – the speed of the former and the cupped gloves of the latter. The original game was played in Spanish villages up against the flat side of a church, much to the annoyance of the priests. The court is called a 'fronton' and there are a score or more of these purpose-built courts in Gascony.

The game is very old indeed. Our King Henry VII in 1528 presented one hundred guineas to a famous pelota player at his court. Originally the game was played with a bare hand with the wooden ball bound and covered with cotton. Then a smaller harder ball appeared, needing a gloved hand. One variation occasionally seen is a wooden non-stringed bat. To lengthen the hand and thus reinforce the strength of the throw, a basket glove was devised called a 'chistera'. The male players are always dressed in white long flannels. Occasionally the court can be L shaped but never with more than two walls.

At Aire sur Adour their week of Fêtes includes an evening of Pelote Basque, featuring not only the Champions of France, but also participants for the Championship of the World.

It is a fast, strenuous and entertaining game and if you have an opportunity do not miss watching Pelota. Some Landais villages make a speciality of the game: Dax will have seven tournaments during June and July as will Seignosse-Bourg and Vieux Boucau. Hossegor hosts the championship with 'main nue'. Other villages with tournaments include Tarnos, Moliets, Ste. Marie de Gosse, Angresse, Labouheyre, Parentis, Mimizan, Mont de Marsan and Vieille Saint-Girons. In the Gers, Nogaro and Ayquetinte have regular 'tournois'. The usual time for start of play is 17.30 hours, but consult the Syndicat d'Initiative for day and exact time.

Le Rugby

The Anglo-Saxon readers of this book may not appreciate the

212

fact that the United Kingdom has devised and originated many fine competitive sports only to find in the twentieth century that other nations have now developed greater, sometimes far greater, skills. One can think of course of cricket, where the West Indies, Australia and other countries beat our national elevens. Even more so in the case of association football and now alas at rugby football, where the French 'équipes' are invincible in Paris or elsewhere in France. Moreover, their brilliant aggressive attacking moves and dynamic tackling make their Gallic style irresistibly fascinating to watch.

It was in 1830 that rugby football was introduced into France, partly through English Army officers and Marine Officers from the Navy in the French ports of the Channel and Atlantic – such as Le Havre, Nantes, La Rochelle and Bordeaux. The game was later played in Paris but inevitably by the English gentlemen and occasional 'milord' visiting or studying in the metropolis. At that early stage in its development it was considered a game for gentlemen emanating from the Public Schools of the mid-nineteenth century. After all it was at Rugby School in 1823 that William Webb Ellis picked the round ball up and ran with it like the wind!

The Le Havre Athletic Club in 1872 boasted 'des maillots bleu, ciel et bleu', blue jerseys because all the members were either Oxford or Cambridge graduates or Marine officers. Five years later in Paris the only club (boasting two fifteens) was the English (Merchant) Taylors Club 'negociants anglais en tissus'. Shortly after the French took up this strange new game and adopted a 'system de jeu avec 8 avants (forwards) and 4 trois-quarts'. Very quickly they made their policy clear which a hundred years later still holds good – 'la mobilité prime sur la puissance, la ruse prime sur la force'. Outgunned then and sometimes now by the sheer weight of the Anglo-Saxon packs, they realised that speed and cunning was their best chance, plus 'l'adresse de leurs arrières' i.e. ferocious and deadly tackling by their backs! Before the turn of the century the first rugby club formed in Bordeaux, Le Bordeaux Athletic Club, was still 100% British in membership! As late as 1899 the side was trained by a Scotsman and contained three British players called Cartwright, Campbell and Harding and a

213

Marine officer from Wales called Billy Morgan.

However the popularity of the game increased such that the first international match between France and England was played in 1906, but the results for many years were very one-sided, although the Parisian clubs of Racing and Stade Francais were formed before 1885.

In 1880 the Stade Rochelais team in La Rochelle contained five English players and in 1911 a Welshman who lived in Gascony, called Owen Roe, and two Englishmen called Tom Potter and a Mr. Crockwell, were the stalwarts in the Aviron-Bayonne team.

At the turn of the century the South West of France took to the game with a vengeance. It was called rather rudely 'un sport de paysans d'Occitanie'. The Gascon teams of Auch, Dax and Mont de Marsan were formed in the period 1897/1904/1908 along with forty others in the South, South West and South East of France including Mimizan (Landes), Toulouse, Tarbes, Bayonne, Bagneres, and a dozen in the Basque area.

By 1925 there were no less than 880 rugby societies/clubs, and by 1979 1680 clubs in France with 176,111 licenciés/members. These were heavily concentrated in the South West – Armagnac/Bigorre 63 clubs with 5930 members, Bearn (just south of Gers) 53 clubs and 5300 members, the Cote Basque 55 clubs and nearly 10,000 members. Specifically there are now 37 clubs in the Gers with 3400 members, and as many as 71 clubs with 6500 members in the Landes.

Being a very competitive sport, competitions and leagues were quickly formed. Initially the Palmares du Championnat de France de Rugby was won in the period 1882–1898 by the Parisian clubs since they had no real competition (other than from British residents in the south). In 1899 power was wrested from Paris by the Stade Bordelais and in 1909 the final was fought between *two* provincial sides. Since then the 'équipes' of Bayonne, Toulouse and Perpignan have been consistently amongst the winners of the Coupe de France and the Championnat de France.

It is appropriate to record that William Webb Ellis died in Menton on 24 June 1872. He would have been proud of his 'handiwork'!

Some of the heroes in the folklore of Le Rugby of the South West include the brothers, Guy and Andre Boniface, Benoit Dauga, Jean Dauger, Jean-Pierre Rives, Roger Martine, Pierre Albaladejo and the Lamberabo brothers.

As I write this, I read in 'La Dépêche du Midi' that little Peyrehorade (Landes) drew 6 points to 6 points with mighty Maçon (Burgundy) in the National Cup quarter-finals and won after 110 minutes 'qualifié au bénéfice des penalties', to play even larger Vichy in the semi-final. In the modest Third Division quarter-finals, Eauze (Gers) thrashed Capbreton (Landes) by 22 points to 13 at Hagetmau thanks to the brilliant Christopher Meillon who kicked 14 points. But alas poor Labastide-Armagnac were hammered into the ground to the tune of 29 points to nil, so humiliating that the report of the game was not published!

The English are responsible for many unusual exports. It is clear that the evolution of rugby union – a game played by fifteen players a side – has transformed the morale of the French Republic. That strange game played in the north of England, mainly in Yorkshire and Lancashire, with 13 players a side, has also caught on in France. Yes, the professionally-paid rugby league has also developed strongly in France, predictably mainly in the South and South West. After eight years of negotiation 'les treizistes francais', under the direction of M. Bernard Garel 'maître ouvrier de l'ecole de rugby', invited the British clubs of Halifax and Castelford to play in Albi for the title of 'superchampion'. And the reason for this unusual request was to restore the morale of the French 'treizistes' who have not been playing particularly well recently! A view of the War of the Roses being replayed ('les dirigeants d'outre Manche') would boost morale and give plenty of encouragement and worthwhile updating in techniques by the équipes of Perfidious Albion!

CHAPTER EIGHTEEN: TRAVEL TIPS

Travel to Gascony

The majority of travellers will arrive by car either from Bordeaux (N 10), Agen (N21 or D 931) or from the east, Toulouse (N 124) or Montauban (D 928). All the roads are well surfaced and well signed, and driving on the minor roads is a delight.

Train services for Bordeaux, Agen, Montauban and Toulouse connect with Auch, Lectoure, Condom, Mont de Marsan and Dax, but travel west-east is difficult. The Auch railway station telephone number is 62.05.60.95.

Package holidays

Slipaway Holidays 90 Newland Road, Worthing, W. Sussex BN11 1LB, Tel. 0273–834534.

French Leave Holidays 21 Fleet Street, London EC4Y 1AA, Tel. 01–583–8383.

Eurocamp Travel Ltd., Edmundson House, Tatton Street, Knutsford, Cheshire WA16 6BG, Tel. 9565–3844 or 01–935–0628. Brochure Region 4.

Canvas Holidays offer campsite holidays in the Landes de Gascogne at Léon.

Meon Travel offer villas in the Landes.

Beach Villas, 8 Market Passage, Cambridge CB2 3QR offer flats and villas in Mimizan.

Starvillas 25/27 High Street, Chesterton, Cambridge CB4 1ND offer flats and villas in Hossegor.

Vacances France 14 Bowthorpe Road, Wisbech, Cambs. PE13 3HJ offer flats and villas in Hossegor, St. Girons and Mimizan.

David Walker Travel, 10b Littlegate Street, Oxford OX1 1QT offer a wine tour to Gascony.

Sports and Rugby event holidays are offered by CIE Tours International, by French Leave, by Sports Tours and Gullivers Travels.

The Conseil General des Landes, Tourist Office in Mont de Marsan offer a range of 'Classes Culture', archaeological at Hastingues, ethnological at Sabres, archivists at Arthez d'Armagnac, theatre at Mont de Marsan, architecture at Ondres, music at Saint Sever, environment at Ondres.

Walking holidays

The Grandes Randonées, 2000 km of them, are signed and marked up cross country walks which thread their way across the Gers and the Landes, in particular the G.R. 653, G.R. 652 and the G.R. 65. The first two are the old pilgrim routes to Compostella. For information write to Delegation des Sentiers de Grandes Randonnées, 32700 Lectoure, Tel. 62.68.76.98 or to Federation Départemental de la Randonnée Pedestre, Mison de l'Agriculture, Cité Galliane, 40000 Mont de Marsan, Tel. 58.75.15.62.

Riding holidays

Association Départementale de Tourisme Equestre, Chambre d'Agriculture des Landes, 40000 Mont de Marsan, Tel. 58.75.15.62 and S.L.A. Découverte de la Gascogne, Maison de l'Agriculture BP99, 32000 Auch, Tel. 62.63.16.55.

Cycling holidays

Comité Départemental de Cyclotourisme, M. Cassiau, 281 Chemin du Barade, 40000 Mont de Marsan, Tel.

58.46.57.93, will advise you of the 24 regional circuits in the Landes. The Comité Départemental de Cyclotourisme du Gers is run by M. Jacques Aylies, Rte de Jégun, 32190 Vic-Fezensac, Tel. 62.06.51.97.

Canoë-kayaks

In Gers there are clubs at Préchac-sur-Adour, Tel. 62.69.43.43; at Auch, Tel. 62.05.26.42; L'Isle Jourdain, Tel. 62.07.26.90 and Samatan, Tel. 62.62.55.40.

The Comité des Landes de Canoë-Kayak are at 8 Rue Guibert, 40500 Saint Sever, Tel. 58.76.00.51; at Brocas, Tel. 58.41.40.68; at Roquefort, Tel. 58.45.66.45; at Mont de Marsan, Tel. 58.75.75.74; at Aire sur l'Adour, Tel. 58.71.67.88 and Grenade sur l'Adour, Tel. 58.45.18.71.

Mosaics

The number of Gallo-Roman villas discovered in Gascony has sparked off a great deal of interest in the technique of producing, painting and assembling mosaics. Madame Daniele Justes, Fontaine d'Yon, 40380 Gamarde-les-Bains, Tel. 58.98.55.31 runs weekly courses four times a year at an all-in cost including food and lodging of rather less than Francs 2000. The courses are small with eight places. Gamarde-les-Bains (Landes E–9) is in the Haute Chalosse 15 km east of Dax.

Swimming

In the Landes, with its long coastline and plage-towns, there is no shortage of swimming opportunities. The Gers, being inland, has solved the problem since 26 towns have municipal outdoor pools.

Fishing

In the Gers there are 1000 km of classified rivers. No less than 43 communes have fishing clubs on 18 different rivers. A permit is needed, obtainable for a small fee. (1) Fédération

Dept. de Pêche et de Pisciculteur du Gers, 75 Bd. Sadi-Camot, Auch, Tel. 62.05.15.95, (2) Fédération Dept. de Pêche, Place Aristide Briand, 40400 Tartas, Tel. 58.73.43.79 and (3) for sea fishing write to M. Rousse, Fédération Nationale de Pêche en Mer. S.I. Biscarosse, Tel. 58.78.20.96.

Traditional Gascon music and dance

The Centre Lapios, St. Vital, 33830 Belin-Beliet (in the Gironde), Tel. 56.88.10.08, offers a wide range of two day courses. The Centre Animation du Graux, 33830 Belin-Beliet, Tel. 56.88.04.62, offers environmental courses. Belin-Beliet is 10 km north of the Landes border on the N 10 on the river Eyre.

Le Folklore Landais

The retention of the old customs, songs, dress and artisan skills is taken seriously by the 'Amicale des Groupes Folkloriques Landais', Tel. 58.72.18.94. The local groups are as follows:

Aurice	Pastous et Pastourettes
Biscarosse	Louis Esqui Rous
Capbreton	Groupe Basco-Landais
Dax	Lous Gouyats de l'Adou
Eugénie-les-Bains	Lous las Aygues
Hossegor	Lous Paloumayres
Labouheyre	Bouheyrins et Bouheyrines
Mont de Marsan	Groupe Folklorique Essor
Mont de Marsan	Groupe Folklorique Elan
Mont de Marasn	Lous Tchancayres
Morcenx	Lous Cigalouns de Mourseuns
Paris	Les Echassiers de l'Amicale des Landes
Pouillon	Gainuts de Pouillon
St. Julien en Born	Lous Becuts de Countis
St. Justin	Lous Tchinques-Tchanques
Seignosse	Lous Pastous
Soustons	Lous Cadetouns de Soustens

A Festival Folklorique is held in mid July for three days each year at Morcenx. Artisanal exhibitions are held at Habas,

Sabres, Poyanne and Pissos. An exhibition of local costumes is held at La Bastide d'Armagnac (May–October p.m.) and traditional Landaise pottery and ceramics at the Museum de la Chalosse at Montfort-en-Chalosse. Historical evenings are held in Saint Sever during the summer. Most towns in the Gers have their local Groupe Folklorique. For instance, in Samatan on 20th June they celebrate le Feu de la St. Jean.

Music

Each year there is a two week Festival of Music at Auch in the first half of June. Contact M. Claude Desbons, S.I., 1 rue Dessoles BP 83, 32003 Auch, Tel. 62.05.22.89. The Abbey of Flaran stages five concerts each year, contact Mme. R. Lassus, Centre Culturel Dept., 32310 Valence-sur-Baise, Tel. 62.28.50.19. The annual Jazz week in Marciac takes place in mid-August. Contact M.J.L. Guilhaumon, Mairie de Marciac 32230, Tel. 62.09.38.03.

Two day gastronomic and cultural tour

The Tourist Office, 22 rue Victor Hugo, 40012 Mont de Marsan, Tel. 58.46.40.40, offer two guided two day/two night tours. The first is to Dax and Chalosse, and the second to the Armagnac country. They are called 'Patrimoine et Gastronomie en Chalosse et Armagnac'. The first cost Francs 978 and the second Francs 1430 per person. Other regional inclusive tours are offered by VVF Seignosse 'Les Tuquets', 40150 Seignosse, Tel. 58.43.30.18, 'Découverte du Pays Landais'.

Main tourist offices

Auch Office de Tourisme BP 83, 32003 Auch, Tel. 62.05.22.89. The main tourist office is the oldest and prettiest house in the town, in the Place Cathedral. For the Dept. of the Gers consult Service Loisirs-Acceuil, Rte. des Tarbes, 32003 Auch, Tel. 62.63.16.55.

Mont de Marsan Comité Départemental du Tourisme, 22 rue Victor Hugo BP 407, 40012 Mont de Marsan, Tel. 58.46.40.40.

Dax S.I. Place Thiers, 40100 Dax, Tel. 58.74.82.33.

In the Landes there are 55 towns with Tourist Offices or Syndicats d'Initiative and the Gers a total of 31, of whom four offer regional tours (Lectoure, Samatan, Termes d'Armagnac and Marciac).

World championships

To end on a thoroughly frivolous note, the Gers stages a series of world championships.

1. Vitesse d'Escargot (snail race), the Monday after the 2nd weekend in August is held at Lagardere (E–4).
2. Des Leveurs de Bottes (boot throwing), the first Sunday in August at Tournan (H–9).
3. Des Tuteurs de Grillons (trained crickets) at Lavardens (F–5) in mid-summer.
4. Des Puiseurs de Puits (drawing up water from a well) at Pavie (G–7) on the last Sunday in June.
5. Du plus gros mangeur de melons at Lectoure (G–3) in mid-August.
6. Le Houga (A–5) stages in August three even more peculiar championships. Des Roucoulayres (human warblers), des Mangeurs de Demoiselles (theoretical?) and des Joueurs de Quilles à l'escabeilhe (skittles on stilts).

The reader will appreciate that in the mid-summer silly season when every town and village in Gascony has a fête, some original 'concours' are composed, probably after a good lunch of garbure, cèpes, a salmi of palombes, and croustade washed down with a fine Madiran, and ending with a superb Armagnac brandy.

BIBLIOGRAPHY
and Suggested Reading

Pays d'Armagnac	Paulette Aragon-Launet
English Gascony (1399–1453)	M.G.A. Vale
Histoires de Gascogne	Charles Samaran, J.J. Monlezun, P. Courtenault, M. Bordes, Loubens, Puech, J.F. Blade
Les Emigrés Gascons (1453–1485)	A. Peyregne
Roles Gascons	Yves Renouard, C. Bemont, T. Carte
Gascon Calendars	G.P. Cuttino
La Fidelité des Gascons aux Anglais	E. Troplong
Châteaux Gascons	Ph. Lauzun
Le Prince Noir en Aquitaine	J. Moissant
Les Anglais en Guyenne	B. Brissaud
Voyage de Froissart en Gascogne (1388)	Jean Froissare
Le Gers	Comité Départemental du Tourisme
Guide de l'Art et de la Nature, Landes, Gers	Michel de la Torre
Syndicats d'Initiatives in Gers and Landes	